UNEASY ALLIANCES

PRINCETON STUDIES IN AMERICAN POLITICS:
HISTORICAL, INTERNATIONAL, AND
COMPARATIVE PERSPECTIVES

SERIES EDITORS

IRA KATZNELSON, MARTIN SHEFTER, THEDA SKOCPOL, EDS.

A list of titles

in this series appears

at the back of

the book

UNEASY ALLIANCES

RACE AND PARTY COMPETITION
IN AMERICA

Paul Frymer

PRINCETON UNIVERSITY PRESS   PRINCETON, NEW JERSEY

Library of Congress Cataloging-in-Publication Data

Frymer, Paul, 1968–
Uneasy alliances : race and party competition in America / Paul
Frymer.
p.   cm.— (Princeton studies in American politics)
Revision of the author's thesis (Ph. D.) — Yale University, 1995.
Includes bibliographical references and index.
ISBN 0-691-05795-8 (cloth : alk. paper). — ISBN 0-691-00464-1
(pbk. : alk. paper)
1. United States — Race relations — Political aspects.   2. Racism —
Political aspects — United States.   3. United States — Politics and
government — 1865–1900.   4. United States — Politics and
government — 20th century.   5. Political parties — United States —
History.   6. Afro-Americans — Civil rights — History.   I. Title.
II. Series.
E185.615.F79   1999
324'.086'930973 — dc21   98-38411

This book has been composed in Sabon

The paper used in this publication meets the minimum requirements of
ANSI/NISO Z39.48-1992 (R1997) (*Permanence of Paper*)

http://pup.princeton.edu

Printed in the United States of America

1   3   5   7   9   10   8   6   4   2

(Pbk.)
1   3   5   7   9   10   8   6   4   2

To My Parents
Barbara and Murry Frymer

Contents

Illustrations

FIGURES

TABLES

Acknowledgments

FALU BAKRANIA, Tom Kim, and Corey Robin have all immeasurably influenced the way that I think about politics and political science. They have also read numerous chapters of the book and have offered a great many critical suggestions on both specifics and the broader scope of the manuscript. Jon Oberlander has been a constant friend, supporter, adviser, and constructive critic of the project. Among my graduate student colleagues at Yale, Gordon Lafer was enormously helpful with many of the ideas structuring chapter 5. Terri Bimes, Jon Cowden, Heather Elliott, David Hughes, Phil Klinkner, Kristin Madsen, Jon Mermin, Cass Moseley, Rachel Roth, Eric Schickler, and Eve Weinbaum all offered advice and friendship during the course of graduate school and afterward. GESO, the graduate student labor union at Yale, not only helped make it possible for me to survive graduate school, but also taught me the possibilities of "organizing" for political battles.

This book is a major revision of my doctoral dissertation. I am deeply indebted to the chair of the dissertation committee, David Mayhew, as well as to my other committee members, Steve Skowronek and Cathy Cohen. Also at Yale, courses and discussions with Vicky Hattam, Adolph Reed, Jim Scott, and Rogers Smith influenced the project in a number of significant ways. At the University of California at Los Angeles, Scott James and Pam Singh have been supportive and intellectually engaging during our frequent dinner conversations about this project and about the broader ideas intrinsic to the American political development literature. Shana Bass and Adam Simon read and improved various chapters and provided helpful suggestions throughout. Joel Aberbach, Kathy Bawn, Jim Desveaux, Kevin Finney, Frank Gilliam, Neal Jesse, David Karol, Mike Thies, Brian Walker, and John Zaller read specific chapters and offered notable advice for various aspects of the project. Adam Simon and Jessica Villardi were extremely helpful with the maps and computer graphics. Linda Choi and Michael Hockman provided more than a year of helpful research assistance. Also providing research assistance for shorter periods of time were Bobby Amirian, Michelle Gu, Amy Hu, An Lee, and Daryl Singhi. Jim Bondurant, Jose Cue, Kathy Escobedo, Cora Gamulo, Nancy Gusten, Tarry Kang, and Ashley Wilson all made it much easier to complete the project at UCLA. Outside of UCLA, both David Plotke and Rick Valelly generously read and offered very helpful and constructive comments on the manuscript. I worked with John Skrentny for an awfully long time on an article about

Richard Nixon and the process of electoral capture, and I benefited greatly from our daily E-mail correspondence and from the writing of roughly a half-dozen "final" versions of the paper. Sean Clegg gave me a lot of insight into the consulting community; so did Marshall Ganz during the course of a long and enjoyable interview in Cambridge. In a talk at Stanford University, Barry Weingast offered a number of sharp but helpful criticisms that made me think more carefully about some of the dynamics of electoral capture. At Princeton University Press, Malcolm Litchfield has been extremely supportive of the project and has pushed me to make the book a great deal better than when it initially arrived on his desk. Cindy Crumrine did an excellent job of copyediting. The anonymous reviewers at Princeton University Press were also immensely helpful in improving the manuscript.

I'd also like to thank the various housemates and friends who have put up with me while I sat around working, thinking, pacing, and procrastinating in New Haven, Cambridge, San Francisco, Los Angeles, and even while on vacation: particularly Corey, Julie, and Pete, who lived with me during the course of writing this project, as well as (not including those already mentioned above) Aaron, Ben, Carrie, Chris, Chris, Dave, David, David, Doug, Gregg, Inna, Jim, Joe, Joe, Kathe, Kerry, Kristi, Linda, Maureen, Mike, Nick, Pete, Randy, and Willy.

My family has always been supportive of the project, from Ben and Carrie to my cousins, aunts, uncles, and Grandma Sylvia, to my favorite cat, Hershey. I dedicate this book to my parents, Barbara and Murry Frymer. From the most literal to the most figurative, this book would not have happened without their help and love.

UNEASY ALLIANCES

CHAPTER 1

Introduction

In November 1992, Democratic party leaders did not merely celebrate the first victory by their presidential nominee in sixteen years. They celebrated the revitalization of their party in national electoral politics. Unlike in previous campaigns, which had been marked by division and disorganization, the party's leadership could claim this time that they were an important factor in Bill Clinton's successful run for the executive office. In fewer than four years as party chairman, Ron Brown transformed the Democratic National Committee into an effective campaign organization. The DNC provided financial, media, and consulting resources to the party's national candidates, enabling them to compete more effectively against their Republican opponents.[1] Brown also maintained a degree of solidarity between the party's various ideological factions not seen in nearly three decades. He successfully exhorted Jesse Jackson, Mario Cuomo, and Paul Tsongas to unite behind Clinton once it became apparent that the Arkansas governor was both the front-runner and the most threatening opponent to Republican incumbent George Bush.

Perhaps most important, Brown took an active role in formulating the party's new ideological and policy agenda.[2] Responding to critics who deemed the pre-1992 Democratic party out of touch with significant portions of the national electorate, Brown worked closely with Clinton and the Democratic Leadership Council, an organization composed of moderate and conservative party officials. Together they pushed an agenda that would bring ideologically moderate voters back into the party.[3] Brown and Clinton emphasized throughout the cam-

[1] See Anthony Corrado, "The Politics of Cohesion: The Role of the National Party Committees in the 1992 Election," and Paul S. Herrnson, "Party Strategy and Campaign Activities in the 1992 Congressional Elections," in Daniel M. Shea and John C. Green, eds., *The State of the Parties: The Changing Role of Contemporary American Parties* (Lanham, Md.: Rowman and Littlefield, 1994); and Philip A. Klinkner, *The Losing Parties: Out-Party National Committees, 1956–1993* (New Haven, Conn.: Yale University Press, 1994), 189–91.

[2] Corrado, "Politics of Cohesion," 64–69; Klinkner, *Losing Parties*, chapters 8–9.

[3] For just a few examples of this criticism, see Thomas Byrne Edsall and Mary D. Edsall, *Chain Reaction: The Impact of Race, Rights, and Taxes on American Politics* (New York: W. W. Norton, 1991); Peter Brown, *Minority Party* (Washington, D.C.: Reg-

paign that this was a "new" Democratic party with a revised message, better equipped to handle the politics and problems of the 1990s. Voters and political elites alike were impressed by the changes. One of the many prominent critics of the pre-1992 Democratic party, *Washington Post* writer Thomas Edsall, commented shortly after the election that "the rhetoric and strategy of the Clinton campaign restored the Democratic party's biracial coalition and made the party competitive again in the nation's suburbs."[4] Another critic, political pollster Stan Greenberg, claimed that the party's moderate ideological mandate "allowed for a Democratic party that could once again represent people in the broadest sense."[5] Even the prominent third-party candidate, Ross Perot, attributed his initial resignation from the presidential campaign to Clinton and the Democrats' recommitment to the moderate voter.

Yet while Democratic leaders were celebrating their party's revival, many African American Democrats were less enthusiastic. They expressed ambivalence about the party's general neglect of their interests during the campaign.[6] Intrinsic to the revamped message formulated by Brown and articulated by Clinton was a distancing from the Democrats' previous efforts to implement the civil rights goals of the 1960s. Party leaders believed that the Democrats' identification with policies explicitly designed to integrate blacks more completely into the nation's social, economic, and political institutions damaged their party's appeal among key groups of white voters. According to this line of argument, the active promotion of African American concerns made it difficult for the party to maintain the support it once had received from the successful New Deal coalition of southern, working-, and middle-class whites.

In order to increase the Democrats' standing among white voters and to revive the decaying New Deal coalition, Clinton called for extensive welfare reform, as well as cutbacks on "excessive" unemployment benefits and other areas of government spending widely perceived as benefit-

---

nery Gateway, 1991); Stanley Greenberg, "Reconstructing the Democratic Vision," *American Prospect* (Spring 1990): 82–89; and Richard M. Scammon and Ben J. Wattenberg, *The Real Majority* (New York: Coward-McCann, 1970).

[4] Thomas Byrne Edsall, "Now What? Cracks in the Clinton Coalition: How Urban Conflicts Undermine the Democrats," *Washington Post* (November 8, 1992), C1.

[5] Stanley B. Greenberg, *Middle Class Dreams: The Politics and Power of the New American Majority* (New York: Times Books, 1995), 277.

[6] See Gwen Ifill, "Clinton Waves at Blacks as He Rushes By," *New York Times* (September 20, 1992), D1; Michael C. Dawson, "Demonization and Silence: Preliminary Thoughts on the 1992 Presidential Election, The New Consensus on Race, and African American Public Opinion" (paper presented at the Symposium on Race and American Political Culture, 1993); Adolph Reed, Jr., "Old-Time New Democrats," *Progressive* (April 1993); 16–17; and Kimberle Crenshaw, "Running from Race," *Tikkun* 7 (September–October 1992).

ing "undeserving" African American citizens. The Democratic party platform reflected this new message. For the first time in almost three decades, it contained no mention of redressing racial injustice. Clinton's own policy platform, spelled out in a book (entitled *Putting People First*) cowritten with vice-presidential candidate Al Gore, had only one reference to race, and this was to oppose the use of racial quotas as a remedy for employment and education inequality.[7] A chapter entitled "Cities" did not mention the problems of inner cities or the continuing existence of de facto racial segregation, while the chapter on civil rights devoted more space to people with physical disabilities than to African Americans.[8]

On the campaign trail, Clinton also distanced himself from representatives of the party's African American constituency. In perhaps the defining moment of his campaign, Clinton seized upon the Los Angeles riots as an opportunity to articulate his differences with Jesse Jackson and the Rainbow Coalition and to attack an obscure rap music artist, Sister Soulja, for allegedly advocating black-on-white violence. According to public opinion polls, whites not only were aware of Clinton's speech — twice as many knew about the Sister Soulja incident as knew about Clinton's economic plan — but they approved of it by a three-to-one margin. Blacks, meanwhile, disapproved of Clinton's comments by nearly the same margin.[9] Earlier in the campaign, in an effort to dispel the beliefs of many voters that the party had grown too permissive toward criminals, Clinton traveled to his home state of Arkansas to watch a mentally impaired black man convicted of murder die in the electric chair. Shortly after the Democratic convention, meanwhile, he and Al Gore toured "America" by bus, which ultimately translated into their wearing plaid shirts, chewing on straw, visiting predominantly rural communities, and speaking to primarily white faces.[10]

The actions of Clinton and the national party leadership — troubling to many African Americans but deemed necessary by many party elites — reveal a great deal about the relationship between national electoral incentives, competitive parties, and black representation.[11] The actions

[7] Bill Clinton and Al Gore, *Putting People First* (New York: Times Books, 1992).

[8] See Andrew Hacker, "The Blacks and Clinton," *New York Review of Books* (January 28, 1993), 12–15.

[9] Thomas B. Edsall, "Black Leaders View Clinton Strategy with Mix of Pragmatism, Optimism," *Washington Post* (October 28, 1992), A16.

[10] See Gwen Ifill, "The 1992 Campaign: The Democrats; Tour Touches Small-Town America," *New York Times* (July 21, 1992), A15.

[11] What, if anything, constitutes itself as an African American political interest is a quite complex and difficult question (at least in the post–civil rights era). It is one I deal with in

taken by Democratic leaders in 1992 mark merely another chapter in a long-running saga — the efforts of national party leaders to downplay the interests of their black constituents in order to broaden the party's electoral base and increase its chances in presidential campaigns. At most moments in American history, the desire of political parties to elect candidates to national office has meant marginalization for African Americans. Why this is so often the case and what impact it has had and continues to have on race relations in the United States are the subjects of this book.

In the process of examining these questions, I hope to reformulate some of the ways we think about our national parties as political institutions. Most broadly, I challenge the common belief that a competitive two-party system produces a more democratic and inclusive society. Scholars argue that competition between two parties forces at least one party to reach out to those groups not represented by the other party. As a result of this competition, parties will mobilize these groups to participate in electoral politics; educate these groups about important policy issues; educate and persuade other party members to support the interests of these marginalized groups; and, finally, place the interests of these groups on the political agenda and represent them in the legislative arena. I will argue that while parties often do perform these positive democratic functions, there is nothing that *necessitates* their doing so. In fact, there are politically compelling reasons for parties *not* to behave in this manner, especially with regard to African Americans. In their efforts to win elections, party leaders often resist mobilizing and incorporating blacks into the political system, and at times will go so far as to deny completely black Americans their democratic rights.

Insofar as our party system provides incentives for leaders to marginalize black political interests, the United States is unusual. Unlike those in other democratic societies, our party system exacerbates rather than diminishes the marginalized position of a historically disadvantaged minority group. The United States is not the only democratic nation with sharp racial divisions, nor are we the only democratic nation with cleavages between a large majority and small minority. We are, however, one of the few democratic nations where party leaders have an incentive to appeal almost exclusively to the majority group. This type

---

greater detail in chapter 6. For additional discussion, see Carol M. Swain, *Black Faces, Black Interests* (Cambridge: Harvard University Press, 1994), chapter 1; Lani Guinier, "The Representation of Minority Interests," in Paul E. Peterson, ed., *Classifying by Race* (Princeton: Princeton University Press, 1995), 24–25, and in particular n. 12; and Iris Marion Young, *Justice and the Politics of Difference* (Princeton: Princeton University Press, 1990), 42–48.

of majority rule is undemocratic, as the minority group is frequently denied effective access to power and is excluded from involvement in a great deal of substantive decision making.[12]

Equally troubling, the founders of our modern party system understood and, in some ways, even *intended* for party competition to have this negative impact on African American political interests. More than 150 years ago, party leaders conceived of a party system that would avoid, or at least minimize, racial and sectional conflict. As we will see in chapter 2, the Democratic party was founded to a significant degree with this in mind. In the mid-1820s, northern and southern elites agreed to put existing differences on the slave issue aside for the sake of combining forces to elect candidates to national office. They formed the Democratic party, a powerful electoral agency that influenced any potential opposition to follow a similar strategy in order to compete effectively for national office. Both the Democratic and Whig parties in the period prior to the Civil War derived a great deal of legitimacy and strength from their ability to keep slavery off the political agenda. The leaders of the two-party system not only structured electoral competition around the average voter. Over the long run, they structured competition around the white voter.

Although two-party competition broke down in the 1850s and 1860s, it reemerged little more than a decade later when the Republicans and Democrats resumed "normal" electoral competition. The competitive two-party system still provides incentives for party leaders to deemphasize black interests in order to create broad-based electoral coalitions. The party system helps us avoid potentially devastating conflicts — not by appeasing both sides of the racial divide, but by appealing to racially moderate to conservative whites and suppressing the open expression of black political interests.

ELECTORAL CAPTURE

This apparent contradiction, that the success of broad-based parties rests on the marginalization of black interests, demands an explanation.

[12] This is an argument made by Lani Guinier, *The Tyranny of the Majority* (New York: Free Press, 1994); and Ronald Walters, *Black Presidential Politics in America* (Albany: State University of New York Press, 1988). It is also made by a number of comparative scholars: see Arend Lijphart, *Power-Sharing in South Africa* (Berkeley, Calif.: Institute of International Studies, 1985); Pierre L. van den Berghe, "Introduction," in *The Liberal Dilemma in South Africa* (London: Croom Helm, 1979); and Donald L. Horowitz, "Ethnic Conflict Management for Policymakers," in Joseph V. Montville, ed., *Conflict and Peacemaking in Multiethnic Societies* (Lexington, Mass.: Lexington Books, 1990).

I begin by examining the impact of electoral incentives on party leaders, which reveals two important features of our party system, features generally overlooked by scholars. First, it highlights the tendency of our political parties to "capture" specific minority interests, and in particular African American interests. Hypothetically, "electoral capture" refers to any politically relevant group that votes overwhelmingly for one of the major political parties and subsequently finds the primary opposition party making little or no effort to appeal to its interests or attract its votes. Simply voting for one party, however, is not sufficient for a group's interests to become captured. A group, for instance, may be loyal to a particular party because it finds its interests well represented by that party or because of historical or organizational reasons. In turn, the opposing party's leaders may wish to appeal to the group's vote, but over time stop doing so because they find a significant portion of this vote unattainable. In this instance, the group has *chosen* to align itself with one party.

By electoral capture, I mean those circumstances when the group has no choice but to remain in the party. The opposing party does not want the group's vote, so the group cannot threaten its own party's leaders with defection. The party leadership, then, can take the group for granted because it recognizes that, short of abstention or an independent (and usually electorally suicidal) third party, the group has nowhere else to go. Placed in this position by the party system, a captured group will often find its interests neglected by their own party leaders. These leaders, in turn, offer attention and benefits to groups of "swing" voters who are allegedly capable of determining election results.

Why would the opposing party not want a group's vote, allowing the other major party to take the group's vote for granted? There are a number of potential reasons. Leaders of both parties will consider the size of the group in relation to the overall electorate; how much power the group's leaders wield in the party organization as well as in local and state politics; whether the group can offer financial support to party candidates; and whether the group's votes are concentrated within strategic electoral locations. Moreover, if party leaders see the group's primary political interests as ideologically opposed to those of a large segment of the public, they are likely to ignore the group as they compete for those voters ideologically closer to the majority of the nation's voters.

While all of these factors are important, none of them is as powerful as the party leaders' belief that appeals to the group will *disrupt* the party's electoral coalition. To form an electoral majority, a party must avoid appealing to groups that alienate its base or diminish its ability to reach out to median "swing" voters. Party leaders have an incentive not to appeal to a group if they believe that such appeals will lead larger numbers of voters to defect to the opposition. Support from the group might alter entirely the makeup of both parties' coalitions. In such situations, party leaders will find it in their interests to ignore the group and make it more or less invisible in electoral battles. If one party perceives a group as a danger to the party's electoral majority, the group cannot threaten to leave the party. Faced with this situation, the captured group is likely to find its support taken for granted and its interests neglected by the other party's leaders as well. Even if the group remains loyal to one party, and even if its numbers can provide the difference in either local or national elections, its own party's leaders will find it in their strategic interest to keep the group more or less invisible in national political discourse.

African American political leaders have experienced great frustration and difficulty in attempting to move their group from this captured position. In part, this is a function of black voters fitting the profile of electoral capture mentioned above: they have remained loyal to one political party and have chosen not to reward the efforts made by the opposition for their vote; they are ideologically to the left of center on a number of important economic and social issues, and on some of these issues they are quite far to the left; and as a group, they are financially disadvantaged and unable to make large contributions to national campaigns. Aside from these factors, the historical legacy of slavery, legal discrimination, and racism has left large numbers of African Americans in need of policies and programs not easily provided by a government that favors an incrementalist approach to politics.

I argue in this book that all of these factors lend themselves to the capture of black interests, but that none of these factors alone is in itself sufficient or primary. For instance, while ideologically liberal on a number of issues, black voters are also ideologically moderate to conservative on a number of other issues — issues that ought to allow for opposition party appeals. There are a number of issues in the post–civil rights era that make black voters ripe for appeals from the Republican party, particularly regarding "family values," religion, and abortion rights.[13] Groups with similar ideological agendas have been courted by parties at precisely those moments that blacks were ignored.[14] Moreover, while financially underrepresented in political action committee (PAC) spend-

[13] Pat Robertson in the 1988 Republican primaries is one example of a national party candidate to make appeals to black voters on religious grounds. For examples of the ideological heterogeneity among African American voters, see Katherine Tate, *From Protest to Politics: The New Black Voters in American Elections* (Cambridge: Harvard University Press, 1993), chap. 2; and Michael C. Dawson, *Behind the Mule: Race and Class in African American Politics* (Princeton: Princeton University Press, 1994).

[14] See Paul Frymer and John David Skrentny, "Coalition-Building and the Politics of Electoral Capture during the Nixon Administration: African Americans, Labor, Latinos," *Studies in American Political Development* (Spring 1998).

ing, black votes have often been crucial in national elections.[15] In all three Democratic party presidential victories since the 1965 Voting Rights Act, the party would have lost the election without the numerical support of black voters. Despite the efforts of black political leaders to point this out, Democratic party leaders have refused to credit the pivotal role of black voters. Finally, even when black leaders and voters have expressed interest in defecting to the opposition party or to a third party, the opposition's party leaders have generally been reluctant to make even the most general of political appeals to blacks.

I argue that the primary reason for African American electoral capture is the worry of national party leaders that public appeals to black voters will produce national electoral defeats. The perception among party leaders that important blocs of white voters oppose the political goals of African Americans influences party leaders in ways simply not comparable to the perceptions about other potentially captured groups. Disagreements over race do more than limit the ability of white and black Americans — who might otherwise have similar economic or social interests — to join in a coalition. Precisely because racism is so divisive and repelling, African Americans are in the unique position of not being able to join in the give-and-take of normal coalition politics. Party leaders recognize this divisive quality and are reluctant to reach out to black voters, since doing so often results in a larger loss of white voters from their existing electoral coalition. They fear making appeals to black voters because they fear that the salience of blacks will overwhelm an electoral coalition of white voters united by largely economic concerns. Thus, party leaders have incentives to ignore black voters, and as such are willing to lose the black vote. Given this situation, black leaders cannot represent their voters as a "swing vote," even in close national elections and even if their numbers can influence state or local elections. Party leaders not only believe that appealing to black votes may actually decrease the party's total vote, but that it also will alter entirely the makeup of both parties' coalitions.

PARTIES AS INSTITUTIONS

I have been focusing on how electoral incentives often lead political leaders to distance their parties from African American citizens. I believe that these incentives have been operative throughout most of American history, that party leaders have been cognizant of these incentives, and that the incentives have had detrimental effects for blacks.

---

[15] See Walters, *Black Presidential Politics*.

That being said, how can we understand why our national parties have at times taken it upon themselves to join, if not lead, the fight for civil rights? It is a question that I will explore throughout the book, particularly in chapters 2–4 and 6. I will provide a number of explanations. Sometimes (although quite rarely as we will see) party leaders do not perceive public appeals to black voters as electorally disruptive. Sometimes party leaders are motivated by ideological principle instead of electoral incentives. It is important to remember that many people have influence within parties. Some of them are electorally minded but others are more ideological. Even party leaders who are more concerned about elections may very well have different understandings of what course of action is optimal.

It is important to remember as well that parties are not composed of only leaders and constituents, but of rules and procedures. These rules allow some voices in the party more power than others. Party rules sometimes limit the ability of leaders to make decisions. These rules may reflect the interests of its core constituents more than the interests of its electorally minded leadership. If the party's rules favor its African American members, then the perceptions among party leaders about the relationship between black voters and the party's electoral opportunities are less relevant than whether the leaders have the organizational power to do anything about those perceptions. Particularly since the early 1970s when voters in national party primaries began to influence greatly the nomination of each party's presidential candidate, party leaders have often been unable to marginalize certain constituencies. If Jesse Jackson, for instance, wants to run for president as a Democrat, Democratic party leaders are only so powerful in stopping him. If he can win party primaries, party leaders are even less powerful. If the procedures that govern primaries are beneficial to Jackson's success, then party leaders are even further marginalized.

In the following chapters, I will explore how party organizations and rules matter. More importantly, however, I will explore how long-term electoral incentives continue to dominate strategic considerations and party organizational rules. For a party to be successful, its leaders must be able to make the decisions they perceive are necessary to win elections. Party rules sometimes do not allow leaders this flexibility. If the party consistently loses national elections, its leaders will take measures to restore their upper hand in party affairs. The consistent electoral defeats of the party usually provide the justification and opportunity for these leaders to regain control of the party apparatus and change the rules to give them more power. Thus, the necessity to follow structural incentives has immense implications for the groups involved. Electoral incentives will promote some interests over others regardless of party rules and, as such, will shape the interests and agendas of those people the parties represent and those people they choose to exclude.

Parties matter in a second way: they have a tremendous impact on existing social hierarchies. Parties need to be understood as more than umbrella organizations that unite various factions into a single force. They are organizations that shape how people think and act politically.[16] When parties choose to mobilize or exclude groups, they influence the actions of those groups in politics and society. Examining this important but often neglected role of the party helps us better understand the impact of the two-party system on both white and black political representation. How does the two-party system shape the ability of blacks to secure government access? Does electoral competition encourage party leaders to ignore or minimize black concerns? Does this in turn shape the efforts of party leaders to mobilize other political groups? Finally, does this lead to an alternative understanding of how parties could fulfill the role ascribed to them by scholars — namely, as a vital agency for incorporating all groups into the political system?

POLITICAL SCHOLARS AND THE CHAMPIONING OF PARTIES

Most American political scientists place parties at the center of democratic political life, arguing that they are the most effective institutions for promoting equality for the powerless and the disadvantaged. A long line of thinkers have maintained that parties are essential to both the creation and the furthering of democratic values.[17] More than five de-

---

[16] This view of political parties is influenced by a number of sources, most directly from the "new institutionalism." See James G. March and Johan P. Olsen, "The New Institutionalism: Organizational Factors in Political Life," *American Political Science Review* 78 (1984); 734–49; Theda Skocpol, "Bringing the State Back In: Strategies of Analysis in Current Research," in Peter Evans, Dietrich Rueschemeyer, and Theda Skocpol, eds., *Bringing the State Back In* (New York: Cambridge University Press, 1985), chap. 1; Stephen Skowronek, *Building a New American State: The Expansion of National Administrative Capacities, 1877–1920* (New York: Cambridge University Press, 1982); and Martin Shefter, *Political Parties and the State: The American Historical Experience* (Princeton: Princeton University Press, 1994). I have also been influenced by the work of comparative party scholars and a number of the tenets of the "power" debates of the 1960s. Among comparativists, see Giovanni Sartori, *Parties and Party Systems* (Cambridge: Cambridge University Press, 1976); and Donald L. Horowitz, *Ethnic Groups in Conflict* (Berkeley: University of California Press, 1985). On the power debates, see E. E. Schattschneider, *The Semi-Sovereign People* (New York: Holt, Rinehart, and Winston, 1960); and Peter Bachrach and Morton S. Baratz, "The Two Faces of Power," *American Political Science Review* 56 (1962); 947–55.

[17] In fact, one needs to go back to the turn of the century to find major challenges to the norms of the scholarly debate. See Moshei Ostrogorski, *Democracy and the Party System*

cades ago, E. E. Schattschneider claimed that parties "created democracy" and that "modern democracy is unthinkable save in terms of the parties."[18] Today, few scholars state their support as bluntly as Schattschneider did, but their assumptions reinforce his views, as is evidenced by most introductory American government textbooks.[19]

Political parties are said to offer the best hope for the powerless and disadvantaged because, unlike interest groups and individuals who use their wealth and inside information to advance their cause, parties "enable the many to pool their resources to offset the advantages of the few."[20] Unlike uncompetitive single-party systems, which deny voters a choice and allow the "haves" to obstruct electoral accountability, two-party competition provides the necessary organization and the ability to mobilize the public around programs more beneficial to the "have-nots."[21] "Party organization is generally an essential ingredient for effective electoral competition by groups lacking substantial economic or institutional resources. Party building has typically been the strategy pursued by groups that must organize the collective energies of large numbers of individuals to counter their opponents' superior material means or institutional standing."[22]

To gain electoral office, scholars argue, parties must appeal to and include all potential voters and groups into the political system. The logic of party competition assures that "no group has reason to feel that the rest of society is a kind of giant conspiracy to keep it out of its legitimate 'place in the sun.' No group feels that it may at any moment have to drop everything else and defend itself against onslaught by some other group."[23] According to Judson James, "It is in [the party's] interest to involve previously uncommitted groups in politics. To gain and retain this support, political parties have strong motivation to be re-

---

in the United States (New York: Macmillan, 1910); and Herbert Croly, *Progressive Democracy* (New York: Macmillan, 1915).

[18] E. E. Schattschneider, *Party Government* (Westport, Conn.: Greenwood Press, 1942), 1.

[19] See John Kenneth White, "E. E. Schattschneider and the Responsible Party Model," *PS* 25 (June 1992): 167–71. Among textbooks, see Theodore J. Lowi and Benjamin Ginsberg, *American Government* (New York: W. W. Norton, 1996); Edward S. Greenberg and Benjamin I. Page, *The Struggle for Democracy* (New York: HarperCollins, 1995), 268.

[20] Robert A. Dahl, *Pluralist Democracy in the United States* (Chicago: Rand McNally, 1967), 245.

[21] V. O. Key, Jr., *Southern Politics in State and Nation* (New York: Knopf, 1950), chap. 14. See also Walter Dean Burnham, *Critical Elections and the Mainsprings of American Politics* (New York: Norton, 1970), 132–33.

[22] Lowi and Ginsberg, *American Government*, 479.

[23] Austin Ranney and Willmoore Kendall, *Democracy and the American Party System* (New York: Harcourt Brace, 1956), 508.

sponsive to the concerns of these recruited supporters."[24] William Keefe maintains that parties "are remarkably hospitable to all points of view and to all manners of interests and people," while Frank Sorauf agrees that "neither party ignores or writes off the political interests and aspirations of any major group."[25] For Edward Greenberg and Benjamin Page, parties "are important for achieving popular sovereignty because in an effort to win majorities, and thus win elections, they attempt to include as many groups as possible. Parties are by nature inclusive."[26] For Martin Shefter, as long as parties are in competition with each other, "the losers in [the] conflict, in an effort to reverse the outcome, undertake to mobilize popular support for their cause, thereby threatening to swamp their opponents at the polls or to make it difficult for them to govern in the face of popular turbulence. To meet this threat politicians on the other side seek to establish a mass base for themselves."[27]

These theoretical claims regarding the democratizing capabilities of U.S. parties are for the most part rooted in historical examples. The Democratic party of Andrew Jackson and Martin Van Buren in the 1820s and 1830s broke the power of politically dominant notables and elites, expanded the suffrage to all white males, and increased voter participation.[28] Parties continued to encourage participation throughout the mid-nineteenth century, both at the national level and in cities where budding party machines integrated millions of immigrants.[29] The Republican party during Reconstruction won the passage of critical amendments legalizing voting rights and citizenship for African Americans.[30] The Democratic party in the twentieth century furthered this tradition, providing the legislative vehicle to bring about the Civil Rights

[24] Judson L. James, *American Political Parties in Transition* (New York: Harper and Row, 1974), 4.

[25] William J. Keefe, *Parties, Politics, and Public Policy in America* (New York: Holt, Rinehart and Winston, 1972), 10; Frank J. Sorauf, *Political Parties in the American System* (Boston: Little, Brown, 1964).

[26] Greenberg and Page, *Struggle for Democracy*, 268.

[27] See Shefter, *Political Parties and the State*, 7.

[28] See ibid., chap. 3; and Richard P. McCormick, "Political Development and the Second Party System," in William Nisbet Chambers and Walter Dean Burnham, eds., *The American Party Systems* (New York: Oxford University Press, 1975), 90–116.

[29] On the ways in which nineteenth-century mass-based parties enhanced democratic behavior, see Joel H. Silbey, *The American Political Nation, 1838–1893* (Stanford, Calif.: Stanford University Press, 1991). On benefits provided by the urban machine, see Robert A. Dahl, *Who Governs?* (New Haven: Yale University Press, 1961), 32–62; and Steven P. Erie, *Rainbow's End* (Berkeley: University of California Press, 1988), chaps. 1–3.

[30] See Eric Foner, *Reconstruction: America's Unfinished Revolution, 1863–1877* (New York: Harper and Row, 1988); and Morton Keller, *Affairs of State* (Cambridge: Harvard University Press, 1977).

Act of 1964 and the Voting Rights Act of 1965 in what many have called the "second Reconstruction."

African American political interests have clearly benefited from this party activity. Republicans during the first Reconstruction and the Democrats during the second helped mobilize black voters and integrate black concerns into party platforms and into national legislation.[31] It is important to recognize, however, that these two examples are quite exceptional, and they occurred during periods notable for the *absence* of a strong, competitive two-party system. The Republicans of the first Reconstruction, already a politically powerful organization in their own right, faced a Democratic party severely weakened by its association with the Confederacy and the disenfranchisement of many southern whites. The Democrats of the second Reconstruction passed important civil rights legislation after the Republican party had ceased to be competitive in national and congressional elections. As two-party competition was revived, the dominant party deemphasized issues important to their black constituents. Party leaders perceived that racial advocacy was diminishing their electoral base, weakening their internal organizational structure, and hurting their electoral chances.

ELECTORAL STRATEGY AND THE INCENTIVES OF PARTY LEADERS TO DOWNPLAY AFRICAN-AMERICAN POLITICAL ISSUES

Scholars by no means deny that the party system has at times failed to integrate black political interests. They argue, however, that it is the absence of two-party competition that should be held responsible. According to this line of argument, when one of the parties fails to be competitive, the incentive for the dominant party to reach out and incorporate groups outside the political process disappears, and these groups are neglected and demobilized. As an example, scholars argue that blacks and many poor whites were disenfranchised in the South at the turn of the century largely because the Republican party failed to compete in the region.[32] In the early-twentieth century, according to this argument, newly arriving blacks and immigrants in the north failed to

---

[31] See Richard M. Valelly, "Party, Coercion, and Inclusion: The Two Reconstructions of the South's Electoral Politics," *Politics and Society* 21 (1993): 37–67.

[32] See Key, *Southern Politics*; Shefter, *Political Parties and the State*; Richard M. Valelly, "National Parties and Racial Disenfranchisement," in Paul E. Peterson, ed., *Classifying by Race* (Princeton: Princeton University Press, 1995); and Walter Dean Burnham, "The System of 1896: An Analysis," in Paul Kleppner, ed., *The Evolution of American Electoral Systems* (Westport, Conn.: Greenwood Press, 1981).

be incorporated into urban politics because of entrenched one-party machines.[33] Many party scholars, meanwhile, point to the cessation of party competition between social classes as the main culprit for the decline in working-class participation in national elections.[34]

Since party competition is seen as inherently positive, efforts to improve the functioning of the two-party system have focused exclusively on reforming the internal institutions (i.e., party organizations) and not the electoral structures (i.e., winner-take-all, single-member districts). During the 1950s and 1960s, when an internally divided Democratic party was resisting a civil rights agenda, scholars argued that the party was incapable of promoting civil rights for two reasons. First, they maintained that the South was characterized more by factional conflict than by a competitive two-party system and, as a result, the Democratic party there was dominated by white segregationist interests. Second, they claimed that the national Democratic party leadership was not internally strong enough to discipline its southern white-supremacist wing, either in presidential politics or in Congress.[35] As a result, many of these scholars promoted reforms to create more internally "responsible" party organizations. Greater internal discipline and party leadership would supposedly translate into responsible parties offering a progressive civil rights platform and increased levels of legislative cohesion.[36]

Given that these reforms were proposed during a period of public support for the broad goals of the civil rights movement, it made sense that more responsible, majority-based parties would empower those favoring racial equality over the minority of racist southern Democrats. Responsible party scholars cannot be faulted for failing to recognize at the time how short-lived this majority would prove. By the late 1960s, the public mood toward civil rights changed dramatically, and as a result, the incentive for responsible parties to be inclusive instead of exclusive lessened considerably. In general, no matter how internally disciplined, party leaders have little incentive to promote the goals of a group whose interests are divisive as well as unpopular with the majority. Nonetheless, party scholars have continued to focus primarily on the need for institutional reform rather than on the negative consequences of electoral competition.

This focus on institutional reform is perhaps most notable in the

---

[33] Erie, *Rainbow's End.*

[34] Burnham, "System of 1896."

[35] Key, *Southern Politics*; Schattschneider, *Party Government*, 122; and James MacGregor Burns, *The Deadlock of Democracy* (Englewood Cliffs, N.J.: Prentice-Hall, 1963).

[36] See the American Political Science Association Committee on Political Parties, "Toward a More Responsible Two-Party System," *American Political Science Review* 44 (1950), supplement.

scholarly reaction to the Democratic party's reforms, established in the early 1970s to include more African Americans and other historically underrepresented groups into the party's nomination procedure. Scholars have argued that opening up the nomination process to more groups has taken away the party leadership's ability to select viable candidates and bring together broad groups of people into a common coalition.[37] By opening the party's nomination process to groups advancing goals that conflicted with those of mainstream voters, party leaders could no longer serve "as neutral agents which mobilize majorities for whatever candidates and programs seem best suited to capturing public fancy."[38] More recently, scholars have attacked court-ordered racial redistricting on many of the same grounds. Drawing congressional district lines in order to maximize the number of districts with majorities of African American voters may lead to an increased number of black representatives in the House of Representatives, but scholars argue that this has decreased the overall numbers of Democrats in the House.[39]

Party scholars correctly show how both of these reforms have hurt the Democrats' ability to elect candidates to national office (and I will deal more extensively with both of these reforms later in the book). Yet what the failure of these reforms illustrates is not the need for counteracting reforms to strengthen party leadership and two-party competition, but the limits of using the majority-based party as a vehicle for more effective black representation. Scholars have ignored a number of factors that hamper the ability of majority-based parties, responsible or otherwise, effectively to represent African American political interests.

As these scholars have argued, the primary motivation of competitive party leaders is the election of their candidates to political office.[40] A number of consequences follow from this, some of which have been discussed by scholars, but others of which have been generally overlooked. Political scientists have understood that in a two-party system, ideologies are developed by each party to attract the greatest number of votes. Parties do not seek election to promote policies; they promote policies to win elections. Assuming that the American population is dis-

[37] See Nelson W. Polsby, *The Consequences of Party Reform* (New York: Oxford University Press, 1983); and Byron E. Shafer, *Quiet Revolution: The Struggle for the Democratic Party and the Shaping of Post Reform Politics* (New York: Russell Sage Foundation, 1983). For a dissenting view, see Denise L. Baer and David A. Bositis, *Elite Cadres and Party Coalitions* (New York: Greenwood Press, 1988).

[38] James Q. Wilson, *The Amateur Democrat* (Chicago: University of Chicago Press, 1962), 18.

[39] See Swain, *Black Faces, Black Interests*.

[40] See Anthony Downs, *An Economic Theory of Democracy* (New York: Harper, 1957); and Joseph A. Schlesinger, *Political Parties and the Winning of Office* (Chicago: University of Chicago Press, 1991).

tributed ideologically on a linear continuum (i.e., in the shape of a bell curve), the appeals by parties to gain the support of the median voter will necessarily concentrate on those ideologically in the middle.

This model of party competition posits that groups lined up at the margins of the distribution (i.e., at the tails of the bell curve) will find their interests neglected by parties spending most of their time and effort appealing to ideologically moderate voters. Extreme liberals and conservatives at opposing ends of the bell curve, then, are constantly frustrated by the two-party process. They believe there is little difference between one moderate party and another. According to political scientists, however, parties are ultimately responsive to these groups' interests because electoral competition provides the opposition party with an incentive to make appeals to all potentially susceptible voters. Put simply, at least one political party will reach out and incorporate those who can be added against an opposition's coalition.[41] Anthony Downs, for instance, believes that the current out-of-power party can follow a "coalition of minorities" strategy in order to defeat the majority party.[42] Even though "the effect of the two-party system" is to produce "moderate parties," Schattschneider still argues that "the hospitality of the parties to all interests is one of their most pronounced characteristics."[43] Moreover, even if these marginalized groups are unable to elect representatives of their own, their presence at least ought to push the median voter closer to their interests, moving the position of national party appeals closer to their interests as well.[44]

Parties, however, clearly do not target all groups who can potentially add to their coalition. Groups that do not participate in electoral campaigns often find their positions no longer considered in party appeals. Faced with limited resources, party leaders have incentives to target those who are most likely to respond without much prodding: that is, those already participating in the political system.[45] Swing voters, moreover, almost always will be at the center of two electorally competitive parties vying for the deciding votes of a close contest.[46] When faced with

[41] Key, *Southern Politics*.

[42] Downs, *Economic Theory of Democracy*, 55–60. Also see Key, *Southern Politics*.

[43] Schattschneider, *Party Government*, 88 and 85.

[44] Kenneth Benoit and Kenneth A. Shepsle, "Electoral Systems and Minority Representation," in Paul E. Peterson, *Classifying by Race* (Princeton: Princeton University Press, 1995).

[45] See Steven J. Rosenstone and John Mark Hansen, *Mobilization, Participation, and Democracy in America* (New York: Macmillan, 1993).

[46] See Earl Black and Merle Black, *Politics and Society in the South* (Cambridge: Harvard University Press, 1987); and Scott James, "A Theory of Presidential Commitment and Opportunism: Swing States, Pivotal Groups, and Civil Rights under Truman and Clinton" (paper presented at the American Political Science Association, Chicago, Ill., 1995).

issues of race, however, parties so alter their behavior that they cannot carry out the roles ascribed to them by scholars. While on some issue dimensions the United States population is normally distributed on a left-right continuum, this is not the case on racially specific issues: blacks tend to be skewed strongly to one side, while the majority of whites are skewed, often equally strongly, to the other.[47] Scholars who confront this problem in other racially and ethnically divided nations have shown that the two-party majoritarian-based systems are rarely an adequate solution. They fail to represent the groups that find it difficult to enter majority-based coalitions.[48] Downs, in fact, recognized that the two-party system does not offer much to any minority group in permanent opposition to the dominant majority: "Fear of this is precisely what caused many European aristocrats to fight the introduction of universal suffrage."[49]

Fear of majority tyranny also led James Madison and the other architects of the U.S. Constitution to devise a governing system embedded with checks and balances intended to slow down and, if necessary, block altogether the power of the majority public to threaten minority rights and interests. The potential for majority tyranny, Madison believed, necessitated safeguards to protect "one part of the society against the injustice of the other part."[50] Not coincidentally, few people in the 1990s support Madison's minority-empowered system as strongly as do some African American politicians and analysts. For instance, in 1993 Lani Guinier's nomination to head the Department of Justice, Civil Rights Division was derailed after a great deal of public controversy over her proposals to ensure that majority rule did not become majority tyranny.[51] Likewise, members of the Congressional Black Caucus have defended racially drawn congressional district lines, arguing that they secure blacks greater representation within the Democratic party's House delegation. Again, not surprisingly, the larger part of the Democratic party (and for that matter, most party scholars) has argued that such districts are damaging to broader — that is, majoritarian — party interests.[52] When the Democrats lost the House in the 1994 mid-

---

[47] For recent public opinion data on these differences, see Tate, *From Protest to Politics*. For long-term trends see Howard Schuman, Charlotte Steeh, and Lawrence Bobo, *Racial Attitudes in America* (Cambridge: Harvard University Press, 1985).

[48] See Arend Lijphart, *Democracy in Plural Societies* (New Haven: Yale University Press, 1977); Benoit and Shepsle, "Electoral Systems and Minority Representation"; and Bernard Grofman and Arend Lijphart, eds., *Electoral Laws and Their Political Consequences* (New York: Agathon Press, 1986).

[49] Downs, *Economic Theory of Democracy*, 121.

[50] James Madison, *Federalist 10*.

[51] Guinier, *Tyranny of the Majority*.

[52] Most notably, see Swain, *Black Faces, Black Interests*.

term elections to the Republicans, redistricting was invoked prominently as a factor.

In many ways, the failure of party scholars to confront the consequences of two-party competition for African Americans is a direct result of their neglecting to recognize the existence of a long-term, white-
based majority interest in the United States.[53] Party theorists champion
the concept of a majority interest only because they believe an individual who is in the minority on one issue will be in the majority on another issue. Yet, when it comes to race issues, black Americans continue
to be in the minority and white Americans are in the majority. Unable
to form coalitions with other groups facing similar socioeconomic concerns, or even to become junior partners of the majority interest, blacks
often lack the substantive power to persuade party leaders to take their
interests seriously. Moreover, racial cleavage makes party elites hesitant
about attracting African Americans to an existing party coalition. They
fear that mobilizing black votes will lead to a decrease in the overall
votes of the coalition. If voter hostility to black political interests is
great, then the threat of defections among the party's current supporters
will likely diminish the party's efforts to appeal to black voters.[54] As
long as political party leaders believe that racial appeals to whites are a
successful method for gaining votes and attaining office, it will remain
in their interests to continue such efforts, and it will remain in the interests of the other party to try to take race issues off the agenda entirely.

PARTY INSTITUTIONS AND REFORM
OF THE ELECTORAL STRUCTURE

Existing party theory, then, promises more than it can deliver. This failure poses a problem not just for theory but for politics. As multiple
chapters of this book will show, the impact of the two-party system on
African American political representation and empowerment can be
profoundly negative. To achieve majorities, party leaders are induced by
the electoral system to ignore and demobilize those who hurt their campaign opportunities. Parties, then, are not just umbrella organizations
that take voters and, more broadly, society's hierarchies as they see
them. They also shape people's ideas about politics, their level of involvement, and the kind of policies that are pursued in government.
Even when parties simply gather up groups of already existing political
interests, they nonetheless communicate a message and shape the politi-

---

[53] For further discussion on this, see Walters, *Black Presidential Politics*, chap. 1.

[54] See Stephen Elkin, "Political Structure, Political Organization, and Race," *Politics and Society* 8 (1978).

cal identity and behavior of these voters. If parties attempt to moderate their platform in order to be more electorally competitive, they communicate to voters a moderate position. They will mobilize moderate voters, educate moderate voters, and pursue policy agendas with moderate voters in mind. This does not offer a great deal of hope to those outside the middle, let alone those groups historically disadvantaged and in dire need of substantive representation. These voters are neglected during campaigns, left uninformed on issues, and often excluded from policy debates.[55]

I do not wish to argue, however, that parties cannot establish themselves as democratizing agents. If we change the electoral incentive structure, parties will be in a position to establish themselves as democratizing agents. Scholars of party organizations outside the United States have long recognized the importance of parties as more than pluralist vote-gathering institutions. Parties "forge collective identities, instill commitments, define the interests on behalf of which collective actions become possible, offer choices to individuals, and deny them."[56] They "create opinion as much as they represent it; they form it by propaganda; they impose a prefabricated mould upon it."[57] And while American parties may not "penetrate" their society and influence individual preferences in precisely the same ways many international parties do, they already exert some influence in these arenas and have the potential to apply even more.[58] Research has shown that party elites influence public opinion on foreign policy matters, health policy, and civil rights issues. The actions of party leaders during the 1950s and 1960s helped change citizens' attitudes toward civil rights.[59] If we understand that political institutions do not merely aggregate opinion, but influence

[55] It is not the case that only voters on the extremes drop out or are removed by party electoral competition. Moderates can also be demobilized via negative advertising, the absence of face-to-face contact, and the like. In fact, parties may recognize that it is in their interests to induce swing voters not to vote. This is logical since the goal of party actors is not vote maximizing, but simply winning. For one account of the demobilization of moderate voters by national party campaigns, see Stephen Ansolabehere and Shanto Iyengar, *Going Negative: How Attack Ads Shrink and Polarize the Electorate* (New York: Free Press, 1995).

[56] Adam Przeworski, *Capitalism and Social Democracy* (Cambridge: Cambridge University Press, 1985), 101.

[57] Maurice Duverger, *Political Parties* (London: Metheun, 1951), 422.

[58] See Alan Ware, *Citizens, Parties, and the State* (Princeton: Princeton University Press, 1988), chap. 7.

[59] See Edward G. Carmines and James A. Stimson, *Issue Evolution: Race and the Transformation of American Politics* (Princeton: Princeton University Press, 1989); Elisabeth R. Gerber and John E. Jackson, "Endogenous Preferences and the Study of Institutions," *American Political Science Review* 87 (1993): 639–56; and John R. Zaller, *The Nature and Origins of Mass Opinion* (New York: Cambridge University Press, 1992).

the development of political preferences and roles, we better can explore how elite actors shape the political agenda, the scope of alternatives, and the degree of information available in public discourse.[60]

Currently, our national parties do not understand themselves as having this role. Party leaders and scholars accept the Downsian notion that voters have fixed preferences. Campaigns, meanwhile, are dominated by polling organizations and consultant groups that treat the process as they would a commercial advertising effort. Consultants are paid by individual politicians and national parties alike to find what the market will bear. They then figure out the best way to appeal to public preferences, no matter how ambiguous; by tailoring the candidate's policies to fit these allegedly static positions. As Gary Mauser has written, "Because individuals are to be left fundamentally intact, marketing necessarily limits its purview to making only relative changes. It cannot, nor does it attempt to, change any individual's basic goals, values, needs, or interests."[61] Among the consequences associated with this form of campaigning is increasing public alienation and confusion, and decreasing levels of voter turnout.[62]

For African Americans, this reliance on market indicators is further complicated since even the most charitable public opinion polls show that while white Americans support the broad ideals of racial equality, they are less supportive of specific government measures to redress racial inequality, and strongly opposed to measures requiring any form of economic, social, or political redistribution.[63] In the effort to follow market indicators, both of the national parties' campaign and policy activities have tended to reflect this public ambivalence. The parties more often reinforce racism rather than confront and educate citizens about it.[64] Yet if parties are to promote the interests of blacks or any other group disadvantaged by socioeconomic hierarchies, both the "pushing" and educating functions are essential—one or the other is insufficient.

What is needed, then, are institutions that mobilize those not currently incorporated into the decision-making process and that, as a re-

---

[60] See, for example, March and Olsen, "The New Institutionalism."

[61] Gary A. Mauser, "Marketing and Political Campaigning: Strategies and Limits," in Michael Margolis and Gary A. Mauser, eds., *Manipulating Public Opinion* (Pacific Grove, Calif.: Brooks/Cole, 1989), 23.

[62] Ansolabehere and Iyengar, *Going Negative.*

[63] See for instance, Schuman, Steeh, and Bobo, *Racial Attitudes in America*; and Donald R. Kinder and Tali Mendelberg, "Cracks in American Apartheid: The Political Impact of Prejudice among Desegregated Whites," *Journal of Politics* 57 (1995): 402–24.

[64] For some examples of this see Alan Ware, *The Logic of Party Democracy* (London: Macmillan, 1979), 140–52.

sult, exert pressure on their behalf. Efforts to create more effective pressure organizations within the existing party system have failed, however, because of the nation's electoral structures and its incentives. Given that the modern-day party system was designed to keep potentially divisive black interests off the table, electoral reforms are imperative. With reforms, parties — no longer forced to pursue the median voter — will have more freedom to ignore majority-based strategies. They will have incentives to mobilize and educate their specific constituencies, and in the process will have far less of an incentive to appeal solely to white voters to win elections. Without these reforms, there are two likely alternatives: either a social movement will have to generate external pressure or large numbers of African Americans will withdraw from the political system entirely. Given the political difficulties of the first[65] and the moral implications of the second, reforming the electoral structure is all the more vital if we wish to bring about a more inclusive democratic polity.

WHAT FOLLOWS

Before I discuss what follows this chapter, let me point out what is *not* covered in this book. First, the focus of my discussion is national party politics and party leaders seeking to win national political offices. With the exception of chapter 6, the emphasis is exclusively on presidential politics. Clearly, this is not the whole story of African American involvement with the two major political parties or with other minor parties.[66] African Americans have achieved a number of dramatic victories in local political campaigns and are effectively represented by many local politicians. Many scholars have analyzed the relationship between black voters and local politicians.[67] I do not address this area in detail

[65] See for instance, Doug McAdam, *Political Process and the Development of Black Insurgency, 1930–1970* (Chicago: University of Chicago Press, 1982); and Aldon D. Morris and Carol McClurg Mueller, *Frontiers in Social Movement Theory* (New Haven: Yale University Press, 1992).

[66] On black third parties, for instance, see Hanes Walton, *Black Political Parties: An Historical and Political Analysis* (New York: Free Press, 1972).

[67] On local congressmembers, see Swain, *Black Faces, Black Interests.* Most of the discussion has centered around urban politics. See Raphael J. Sonenshein, *Politics in Black and White: Race and Power in Los Angeles* (Princeton: Princeton University Press, 1993); Rufus P. Browning, Dale Rogers Marshall, and David Tabb, *Protest Is Not Enough: The Struggle of Blacks and Hispanics for Equality in City Politics* (Berkeley: University of California Press, 1984); Paul Kleppner, *Chicago Divided: The Making of a Black Mayor* (DeKalb: Northern Illinois University Press, 1985); Dianne M. Pinderhughes, *Race and Ethnicity in Chicago Politics: A Reexamination of Pluralist Theory* (Urbana: University of Illinois Press, 1987); Manning Marable, *Black American Politics: From the Washington Marches to Jesse Jackson* (New York: Verso, 1985), chap. 4; and Charles H. Levine, *Racial Conflict and the American Mayor* (Lexington, Mass.: Lexington Books, 1974).

because it would entail a discussion of different electoral structures, different constituencies, and, hence, party leaders responding to a different set of electoral incentives. Clearly, if the majority of a constituency is African American, the median voter will not be opposed to African American interests. I do not diminish the importance of local politics. The fact that black political leaders see opportunities at the local level that they do not see at the national level leads them to focus much of their time and energy increasing their representation at the local level. This, in turn, potentially leads to a deemphasis on joining and participating in national party coalitions.

Second, I will not discuss, except in passing, the issue of descriptive representation — the representation of black interests by elected officials who are black.[68] This is perhaps surprising because the issue has been at the center of not only recent scholarly debate, but of congressional and courtroom debate as well.[69] Again, I do not believe this issue is unimportant. However, the primary focus of the book is on substantive representation. To the degree that descriptive and substantive representation overlap, I will deal with the distinction. I simply am not making the argument that descriptive representation is the only measure of black political representation.

Third, and perhaps most surprisingly, I will not deal extensively with the question of whether racism exists in the United States. This seems quite odd given that the book assumes the median, or "swing," voter in most national elections is generally racist or at least opposed to many specific policy goals of black voters. At certain moments in history — the late 1850s or early 1960s, for example — the median voter might have supported civil rights and federal programs promoting racial equality. One might argue that since the 1960s, racism has largely diminished as an important political force and has been replaced instead by economic, ideological, or social interests. Doesn't this matter for whether black voters are represented in politics? Doesn't it directly matter for whether the two-party system is able to represent their interests? Certainly, it does in a number of ways, and I will attempt to deal with this reality

---

[68] For initial discussion of the distinction between substantive and descriptive representation, see Hanna Fenichel Pitkin, *The Concept of Representation* (Berkeley: University of California Press, 1967); and Anne Phillips, *Engendering Democracy* (University Park: Pennsylvania State University Press, 1991).

[69] See Guinier, *Tyranny of the Majority*; Swain, *Black Faces, Black Interests*; Luis R. Fraga, "Latino Political Incorporation and the Voting Rights Act," in Bernard Grofman and Chandler Davidson, eds., *Controversies in Minority Voting* (Washington, D.C.: Brookings Institution, 1992); and Kenny J. Whitby and Franklin D. Gilliam, Jr., "Representation in Congress: Line Drawing and Minorities," in Herbert Weisberg and Samuel C. Patterson, eds., *Great Theater: American Congress in the 1990s* (Cambridge: Cambridge University Press, 1997).

when it is historically appropriate. But for the purposes of understanding party politics, the opinions of voters are less important than the perception among party leaders that race does matter and that the median voter does not support black interests. This perception, whether it is based in reality or not, has been fairly continuous throughout American history, and it continues to have huge consequences not only for black representation but for white voter opinion as well. It is this perception of party leaders that I analyze throughout the book. Whether it is correct is the subject of another book.[70]

In the chapters that follow, I examine the issues addressed in this introduction. Chapter 2 provides the theoretical foundation for the study. In this chapter, I lay out in detail how party leaders following electoral incentives will often capture African American interests, and I analyze the implications of this for black political representation. A series of spatial models, backed up by historical example, will help illustrate how party theorists from Schattschneider to Downs have ignored what happens when party elites are confronted by a majority of whites voting along racially specific lines. I will argue that as black voters are captured they become more or less "invisible" to party leaders. As a result, and contrary to the beliefs of those who argue that the mere presence of liberal African Americans is sufficient for pushing parties closer to their interests (and thereby for representing their interests), rational party actors will try to move their organization farther to the right on the political spectrum. In fact, depending on specific circumstances, parties may be influenced to move farther to the right on the ideological spectrum than they otherwise would were they absent entirely from the electoral process.

In chapters 3 and 4, I explore two different historical periods, the Republican-dominated party system of the late-nineteenth and early-twentieth centuries and the post–civil rights era of the 1960s–90s, in order to illuminate how electoral laws led to the capturing of African American interests. While at the end of both of these periods blacks found their interests captured, their status throughout was not static. How black interests have made momentary gains necessitates a discus-

---

[70] It is also the subject of an enormous literature. For the argument that party leaders are correct to see race as a divisive force, Donald R. Kinder and Lynn M. Sanders, *Divided by Color* (Chicago: University of Chicago Press, 1996); David O. Sears, "Symbolic Racism," in Phylis Katz and Dalmas A. Taylor, eds., *Eliminating Racism: Profiles in Controversy* (New York: Plenum, 1988); Lawrence Bobo, "Group Conflict, Prejudice, and the Paradox of Contemporary Racial Attitudes," in Katz and Taylor, *Eliminating Racism*; and Keith Reeves, *Voting Hopes or Fears? White Voters, Black Candidates, and Racial Politics in America* (New York: Oxford University Press, 1997). The most prominent counterargument comes from Paul M. Sniderman and Thomas Piazza, *The Scar of Race*, (Cambridge: Harvard University Press, 1993).

sion of both party and nonparty factors. What enabled party elites to promote (albeit briefly) civil rights while following electoral incentives? What factors led to the recapturing of blacks shortly thereafter? What role did organizational reforms play in these momentary successes? In the long run, did these organizational reforms maintain a significant degree of black political representation in national politics?

Once I lay out the theoretical and historical dimensions of the captured minority group in the competitive two-party system, I turn to its consequences for party behavior. Chapters 5 and 6 examine some of the implications of captured status in the post–civil rights era. With the passage of the Voting Rights Act in 1965 and the subsequent enfranchisement of hundreds of thousands of black voters, the post-1960s is a period when the African American electorate is at its largest and most formidable. This has been a historic time period for the representation of black interests in the party system. Blacks have elected a substantial number of representatives to both national and local offices, achieved a number of notable legislative victories, and have witnessed the first significant presidential campaign by an African American politician. Nonetheless, a number of features of electoral capture continue to exist and have political consequence, serving to marginalize African American interests in varying ways.

These two chapters are organized around the functions widely associated with political parties, and in particular with vigorous party competition. Chapter 5 focuses on the mobilization of voters as well as on the efforts of parties to educate voters in order to win elections. Chapter 6 looks at the Democratic party's legislation on behalf of African Americans. On the one hand, both chapters show the enormous potential that parties have to incorporate blacks more completely into the democratic process. On the other hand, both show how electoral structures inhibit this potential and lead to negative consequences.

Finally, in chapter 7, I attempt to apply the concept of the captured group to other political interests in society. Are African Americans exceptional in their captured status, or are their experiences relevant to those of other marginalized political groups? I compare the position of blacks in recent presidential campaigns with two other potentially captured groups: gay and lesbian voters in the Democratic party and evangelical Christians in the Republican party. Since these two groups have differed in their ability to influence their own party's political agenda, what explains the success of some groups to avoid the marginalization of their potentially captured status? What lessons can other group leaders learn from their strategies? Finally, what possibilities exist for changing the real culprit for captured interests—the majority-based electoral system? What alternatives are most viable?

CHAPTER 2

Competitive Parties and the "Invisibility" of Captured Groups

> I am an invisible man. No, I am not a spook like those who haunted Edgar Allan Poe; nor am I one of your Hollywood-movie ectoplasms. I am a man of substance, of flesh and bone, fiber and liquids — and I might even be said to possess a mind. I am invisible, understand, simply because people refuse to see me. Like the bodiless heads you see sometimes in circus sideshows, it is as though I have been surrounded by mirrors of hard, distorting glass. When they approach me they see only my surroundings, themselves, or figments of their imagination — indeed, everything and anything except me.
>
> (Ralph Ellison, *Invisible Man*)

PARTY SCHOLARS contend that two-party competition ensures the representation of a wide variety of groups, both the "advantaged" and "disadvantaged," in national politics. Not only does competition between the parties provide voters with the opportunity to alter the power balance, but the opposition party ought to have an incentive to incorporate groups that find themselves excluded or disaffected from the party in power. Competitive parties, under specific conditions, have incentives to treat some groups as "invisible." In particular, national party leaders have often followed perceived electoral incentives to "capture" and ignore African American voters, even when such votes had the clear, short-term potential of proving the difference between victory and defeat in a given election. In this chapter, I explore this phenomenon further, and attempt to provide a more formal theoretical argument for the behavior of our national parties.

In doing so, I am claiming that race belongs at the center of our understanding of national party politics, even in periods of "normal" party competition, and even in periods when racial issues appear absent from the political agenda. This claim challenges the assumptions of most party scholars. To be sure, numerous scholars have focused on the impact of racial cleavage on African American representation in national electoral politics.[1] Others have argued that race *at times* can affect the behavior of national party leaders. Keith Poole and Howard Rosenthal, for instance, argue that racial issues dominated the legislative process at two distinct moments of American history (the period prior to the Civil War and the period surrounding the civil rights movement).[2] Edward Carmines and James Stimson have contended that racial conflict "emerged" on the political agenda in the 1960s, pushing party leaders to respond in new and consequential ways.[3] Few studies, however, have incorporated the role of racial cleavage into a broader theoretical understanding of normal competitive party politics. Instead, it is seen as an irrational and exceptional feature of American politics. As Dianne Pinderhughes suggests, "When political institutions handle racial issues, conventional rules go awry, individuals react irrationally, and constitutional rules are violated."[4]

By prematurely accepting the conclusion that racial divisions create theoretically intractable problems for the science of politics, party scholars have missed the degree to which the conventional rules are themselves based on these divisions. Even when race is not "present" in the party system, its underlying presence has great consequences for both party leaders and the way black interests are represented. Party leaders work actively and almost constantly to deny the salience of black interests. The failure to address seriously the consequences of white racism on party behavior has led, in turn, to a relative ignorance of how electoral institutions have legitimated, empowered, and ultimately perpetuated ideologies and policies of racial inequality. Instead of giving rise to a truly nonracial politics and nonracist ideologies, the two-party system legitimates an agenda reflecting the preferences of white voters, and it structures black interests outside party competition.

Racial cleavage is not only a constant influence on the behavior of

[1] For just a few examples, see Ronald W. Walters, *Black Presidential Politics in America: A Strategic Approach* (Albany: State University of New York Press, 1988); Patricia Gurin, Shirley Hatchett, and James S. Jackson, *Hope and Independence: Blacks' Response to Electoral and Party Politics* (New York: Russell Sage Foundation, 1989); Katherine Tate, *From Protest to Politics: The New Black Voters in American Elections* (Cambridge: Harvard University Press, 1993); Hanes Walton, Jr., *Black Political Parties* (New York: Free Press, 1972); Lani Guinier, *The Tyranny of the Majority* (New York: Free Press, 1994); and Robert Huckfeldt and Carol Kohfeld, *Race and the Decline of Class in American Politics* (Urbana: University of Illinois Press, 1989).

[2] Keith T. Poole and Howard Rosenthal, "Patterns in Congressional Voting," *American Journal of Political Science* 35 (February 1991).

[3] Edward G. Carmines and James A. Stimson, *Issue Evolution: Race and the Transformation of American Politics* (Princeton: Princeton University Press, 1989).

[4] Dianne M. Pinderhughes, *Race and Ethnicity in Chicago Politics* (Urbana: University of Illinois Press, 1987), 261.

competitive party leaders. This cleavage was a central factor in the initial design and development of the nation's two-party system, as I will show in this chapter. The two-party system arose at a historical juncture when the political exigencies of slavery placed a premium on the ability of the major parties to bring together broad coalitions that could bury the tensions surrounding the "peculiar institution." Political elites at the time understood that parties could effectively develop, and in fact had a great incentive to develop, majority coalitions that would ignore the problem of slavery. The two-party system would thus exclude the interests of African Americans. I am not contending that the two-party system was designed solely to deal with racial cleavage. Historians have examined a number of factors in the development of the two-party system, including the preexisting constitutional design, preexisting economic and ethnic cleavages, collective action problems, the desire to limit presidential power, in addition to the problem of racial cleavage.[5] Yet while party scholars have incorporated most of these explanations into a larger theoretical understanding of two-party behavior, they have neglected the long-standing salience of racial conflict. As a result, scholars have formulated an understanding of the modern two-party system that is at odds with its initial purpose and development, as well as with its current behavior.

This chapter begins with a discussion of the conditions under which two-party competition is expected both to function and to provide representation to a wide variety of groups. I then examine the initial development of the two-party system and find that many of the expected conditions — in particular, a bell-curve-shaped ideological distribution of voters — were notably absent at this time. Party leaders in the 1830s did compete around a normal left-right ideological distribution, but they

[5] See John Ashworth, *Slavery, Capitalism, and Politics in the Antebellum Republic, Vol. 1, Commerce and Compromise, 1820–1850* (New York: Cambridge University Press, 1995); Richard Hofstadter, *The Idea of a Party System: The Rise of Legitimate Opposition in the United States, 1780–1840* (Berkeley: University of California Press, 1969); Richard P. McCormick, *The Second Party System: Party Formation in the Jacksonian Era* (Chapel Hill: University of North Carolina Press, 1966); Robert V. Remini, *Martin Van Buren and the Making of the Democratic Party* (New York: Columbia University Press, 1951); James W. Ceaser, *Presidential Selection: Theory and Development* (Princeton: Princeton University Press, 1979), chap. 3; John H. Aldrich, *Why Parties? The Origin and Transformation of Party Politics in America* (Chicago: University of Chicago Press, 1995), chaps. 2–5; Fred S. Rolater, "The American Indian and the Origin of the Second American Party System," *Wisconsin Magazine of History* 76 (1993): 180–203; Douglas W. Jaenecke, "The Jacksonian Integration of Parties into the Constitutional System," *Political Science Quarterly* 101 (1986): 85–107; and Michael Wallace, "Changing Concepts of Party in the United States: New York, 1815–1828," *American Historical Review* 74 (1968), 453–91.

recognized that they were actively denying a second and potentially disruptive ideological dimension, that of race. I argue that the conditions that initially drove the development of the two-party system continue to influence the behavior of party leaders today. In the remaining portion of the chapter, I describe how this behavior by party actors leads to the more-or-less continual capture and invisibility of black voters.

WINNER-TAKE-ALL ELECTORAL SYSTEMS, PARTY INCENTIVES, AND THE CONSEQUENCE FOR BLACK INTERESTS

To provide a theoretical framework for understanding the behavior of competitive parties, I begin with a well-known assumption and an observation. The assumption is that party leaders in the United States are primarily concerned with electing candidates to political office. The observation is that the office of the presidency is a winner-take-all position. When this assumption and observation are taken together, we see that the country's winner-take-all electoral structure encourages party leaders to promote policy positions appealing to a majority of the voters. When the ideological distribution of the electorate is shaped in a normal fashion — that is, in the shape of a bell curve — party leaders will have an incentive to target the moderate voters occupying ideological positions roughly equidistant to the two major parties. The ideological center is where the electoral majority lies. Hoping to maximize their vote share, party leaders have an incentive to "deliberately change their platforms so that they resemble one another."[6] Their goal is both not to alienate important swing voters and to maintain their hold on their electoral base. They will try to "becloud their differences in a fog of ambiguity," remaining as ideologically close to each other as possible (see figure 2.1), and attempting to persuade swing voters that the party is ideologically similar to their beliefs.[7]

As electoral scholars recognize, voters outside the ideological center will often be dissatisfied with the emphasis on moderate policies. As a group, African American voters in the post–civil rights era tend generally to be more liberal than white voters, particularly on those issues most pertinent to the African American political agenda.[8] This provides part of the explanation for why black voters find their interests captured inside one of the two major parties. Nonetheless, theories of party

[6] Anthony Downs, *An Economic Theory of Democracy* (New York: Harper and Row, 1957), 115.

[7] Ibid., 136. Also, see Charles Plott, "A Notion of Equilibrium and Its Possibility under Majority Rule," *American Economic Review* 57 (1966): 787–806.

[8] See Tate, *From Protest to Politics*, chap. 2.

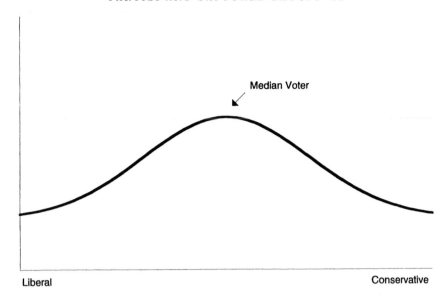

Median Voter

Liberal

Conservative

2.1 Distribution of ideology on nonracial dimensions

competition contend that any group's active participation in the party
and in the electoral system will result in a significant degree of political
representation. Party leaders often lack perfect information about where
the median voter stands. They have a great deal of leeway in determining which message to propose and which groups to appeal to in the
effort to form electoral majorities. Party leaders, moreover, appeal to
those groups that are highly mobilized, regardless of their ideological
proximity to the median voter.[9] Since national electoral battles are
fought not in one winner-take-all election, but in fifty separate winner-
take-all electoral college states, the median voter can vary from state to
state, requiring parties to make specific appeals to various groups that
maintain the balance of power in their respective states.[10] Also, the current out-of-power party can follow a "coalition of minorities" strategy
in order to defeat the majority party.[11] Even if a party cannot gain the
support of a majority on certain issues, it is in its interest to gather

[9] See Steven J. Rosenstone and John Mark Hansen, *Mobilization, Participation, and
Democracy in America* (New York: Macmillan, 1993); Aldrich, *Why Parties?*; and Angelo
Panebianco, *Political Parties: Organization and Power* (Cambridge: Cambridge University
Press, 1988).

[10] See Scott C. James and Brian Lawson, "The Political Economy of Voting Rights Enforcement in America's Gilded Age," *American Political Science Review* (forthcoming).

[11] Downs, *Economic Theory of Democracy*, 55–60.

those who are in the minority on a variety of issues into a majority coalition of disparate groups.

Other scholars have argued, finally, that two-party competition by definition adapts and is receptive to black interests as much as to any other group's interests, merely due to the presence of African Americans in the electoral arena. Parties need not directly appeal to black interests. The existence of blacks in the overall distribution of voters means that the median voter (and the policy agendas of the political parties) will be closer to black interests than it would be were blacks absent from the distribution.[12] For example, take some southern congressional districts where white electoral majorities tend to vote against black electoral minorities. In the post–Voting Rights Act era, the participation of black voters means that elected representatives will respond to black concerns more than elected representatives did prior to the 1965 Voting Rights Act.[13] Even when the candidate representing black interests loses, the winning candidate, driven by the logic of two-party competition in a winner-take-all district, should nonetheless be closer to black interests because of the shift in the position of the median voter. Simply the presence of black voters on one side of the ideological spectrum ought to move the voter median in their direction. Thus, voting in and of itself shapes the ideological distribution and enables some degree of representation (see figure 2.2).

Both of these spatial models, however, conceive of African Americans as merely a subgroup of a larger coalition of ideologically liberal voters to the left of the national median. Race itself is not identified as a significant dimension of electoral politics. The salient axis is a broader left-right spectrum revolving around issues such as government economic intervention and social welfare policies. However, when race is a salient aspect of electoral conflict, national party leaders rarely face a public aligned along a bell curve as in the two spatial models above. Instead, party leaders generally face a distribution that is skewed quite strongly to the right, with the bulk of white voters on the conservative end of the continuum and the bulk of black voters on the liberal end. Given this distribution, a two-party system does not lend itself so easily to the

[12] See Kenneth Benoit and Kenneth A. Shepsle, "Electoral Systems and Minority Representation," in Paul E. Peterson, ed., *Classifying by Race* (Princeton: Princeton University Press, 1995), 54–59.

[13] David W. Rohde, "Something's Happening Here, What It Is Ain't Exactly Clear: Southern Democrats in the House of Representatives," in Morris P. Fiorina and David W. Rohde, eds., *Home Style and Washington Work* (Ann Arbor: University of Michigan Press, 1991). For an excellent account of both the advantages and disadvantages black voters face in the South with their increased enfranchisement, see Earl Black and Merle Black, *Politics and Society in the South* (Cambridge: Harvard University Press, 1987), chap. 6, and particularly pp. 138–151.

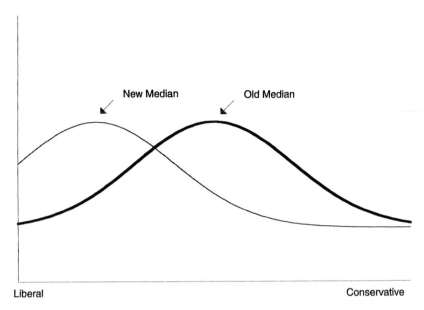

2.2   Putative distribution after African American enfranchisement

inclusion of all groups. Two-party competition either devolves into one-
party domination — a trait not generally associated with a healthy democratic society — or centers entirely around the majority group.

Before I continue to explain how this second dimension influences
party leaders, it is important to examine whether the United States is
indeed divided along racial lines. Is the median voter racist? Particularly
in the post–civil rights era, scholars have debated whether a racial divide still exists, and whether it affects political life.[14] Complicating this
debate is the recognition that racism often has been embedded in non-
race-specific national ideologies and institutions.[15] To understand the

[14] For references to the debate among scholars over the degree of racism in the post-
civil rights era, see chap. 1, n.70.
[15] Refer to chapter 1 for further discussion regarding why I deal only marginally with
this question of whether the median voter is "racist." The literature on racism's complicated nature and its impact for public behavior and institutions prior to the civil rights era
has produced a number of excellent discussions. For just a few examples, see George M.
Frederickson, *The Black Image in the White Mind* (Hanover, N. H.: Wesleyan University
Press, 1971); W. E. B. Du Bois, *Dusk of Dawn: An Essay toward an Autobiography of a
Race Concept* (New York: Harcourt Brace, 1940); Eric Foner, *Free Soil, Free Labor, Free
Men* (New York: Oxford University Press, 1970); Reginald Horsman, *Race and Manifest
Destiny* (Cambridge: Harvard University Press, 1981); and Gunnar Myrdal, *An American
Dilemma* (New York: McGraw Hill, 1964). For a discussion of the post–civil rights era,
see chap. 1, n. 70.

actions of strategic party leaders, however, the answer to this question is less relevant than the question of whether party leaders factor racial cleavage into their strategic equations. And against the view of party scholars who assume that the two-party system has flourished on the premise of ideological consensus[16] — I argue that the answer to this second question is an unequivocal yes. As we will see in the following discussion of Martin Van Buren and the development of the competitive two-party system, and as we will see throughout the chapters of this book, the behavior of party leaders reflects their belief that the nation is divided along racial lines, and that the prominence of racial issues is bound to disadvantage one of the parties in a system of two-party competition. Sometimes, party leaders are clearly right in their perception that the median voter is racist. Other times, it is not so clear. Party leaders are no doubt aided by their own racial attitudes when trying to gauge public attitudes toward blacks. Their own ambivalence about promoting black interests may lead them to exaggerate and be excessively sensitive to white hostility toward those interests. The stakes of a winner-take-all electoral system only heighten this ambivalence, since it is crucial for party leaders to respond to the opinions of the median voter. These concerns lead party leaders to attempt to manipulate the two-party system in a manner that denies the primacy of race, all the while confirming that very primacy.

MARTIN VAN BUREN AND THE DEVELOPMENT OF THE DEMOCRATIC PARTY

Throughout American history, laws and institutions have been developed to avoid potentially divisive national conflicts. For the authors of the Constitution, the debate over slavery was dealt with most notably by the "three-fifths rule," which allowed northerners and southerners to agree on a method to count slaves as three-fifths of a person in the levying of taxes and the apportionment of representatives. The slave issue led to compromises in the Constitution over issues as varied as the slave trade, export taxes, and the makeup up of the two houses of Congress.[17] Yet at the time, leaders such as James Madison were quite fo-

---

[16] See Robert A. Dahl, "The American Oppositions: Affirmation and Denial," in *Political Oppositions in Western Democracies* (New Haven: Yale University Press, 1966); and Louis Hartz, *The Liberal Tradition in America* (New York: Harcourt Brace Jovanovich, 1955).

[17] See Derrick Bell, *And We Are Not Saved* (New York: Basic Books, 1987), chap. 1; Paul Finkelman, *Slavery and the Founders: Race and Liberty in the Age of Jackson* (Armonk, N. Y.: M. E. Sharpe, 1996); and William W. Freehling, *The Road to Disunion*, vol. 1, *Secessionists at Bay, 1776–1854* (New York: Oxford University Press, 1990).

cused on protecting the economic interests of aspiring merchants from those of small yeoman farmers who were skeptical of, if not resistant to, widespread capitalist free-market expansion. Since merchant capitalist interests represented a distinct minority in the new nation, efforts were made by the framers of the Constitution to check the potential tyranny of majoritarian rule. For Madison, majority "factions" represented "violence" and a threat to what he perceived as liberty and the common good. Such a threat could be controlled only through a society with "so many separate descriptions of citizens as will render an unjust combination of a majority of the whole very improbable, if not impractable."[18] Since society itself did not naturally break into a sufficiently large number of combinations to avoid a majority faction, government institutions would have to do it for them. Mass parties representing coherent majorities were not only antithetical to such a government based on divisions and checks and balances; they were something to be feared.

Although rejected by many of the Constitution's authors as tyrannical, mass-based majoritarian parties certainly did not produce the type of "mob rule" or powerful and homogeneous special interests that Madison feared.[19] In fact by 1819, with a legislative battle beginning to brew over the potential admission of Missouri as a state, economic conflict between merchants and agrarians was beginning to be overshadowed by the sectional conflict over slavery. Northerners in Congress that year voted overwhelmingly for the Tallmadge Amendment, which, had it passed, would have prohibited slave expansion into Missouri. Southerners voted 66 to 1 against the amendment. Although Senator Jesse Thomas of Illinois ultimately would put forward a compromise outlawing slavery in the area of Louisiana Purchase north of the 36°30' line, a national cleavage potentially more explosive than the economic division had reemerged very clearly, to the dismay of political leaders across the country. The country remained divided between two distinct groups, but this division was now developing into two large single-interest factions (abolitionists in New England and plantation interests in the Deep South), neither of which necessarily composed a majority, but both of which had substantial power to push their views without regard for the threat of national strife. According to scholars of electoral politics, when an extreme group of voters at either end of the ideological spectrum controls the political agenda, two competing parties are expected to remain "poles apart in ideology."[20] As Downs

[18] James Madison, *The Federalist Papers: A Collection of Essays Written in Support of the Constitution of the United States*, ed. Roy P. Fairfield (Baltimore: Johns Hopkins University Press, 1981), *Federalist 10*; and Hofstadter, *Idea of a Party System*.

[19] See Hofstadter, *Idea of a Party System*.

[20] See Downs, *Economic Theory of Democracy*; and Gary Cox, who points out that if the two major parties stay too close to the center in a bipolar electorate, new parties will

writes, "Whichever party wins will attempt to implement policies radically opposed to the other party's ideology. . . . In such a situation, unless voters can somehow be moved to the center of the scale to eliminate their polar split, democratic government is not going to function at all well."[21]

The controversy surrounding the Missouri Compromise would not appear again until the Gag Rule Controversy of the mid-1830s, and later in the battle over the annexation of Texas and the Wilmot Proviso of the mid-1840s. It did, however, significantly influence the behavior of those most directly responsible for building the second-party system.[22] For Martin Van Buren, a political leader from New York State with presidential aspirations, the "solution" for sectional conflict over slavery was to create an electoral organization that would advocate positions unrelated to slavery. In an attempt to form a new national party that, like Jefferson's, could combine southern slave owners with northern interests indifferent or even opposed to slavery, Van Buren and other Democratic party leaders devised an electoral coalition that muted the tension over slavery by promoting the decentralization of political power.[23] After the Missouri Compromise threatened to break apart the more than three-decade compromise on slave matters, Van Buren and other leaders recognized that unless the issue was deemphasized, the union could break apart as well. The Missouri Compromise and the notion of the "balance rule" for the admission of free and slave states was one method of trying to keep the issue off the agenda because neither side would gain too much power over the other.[24]

Strengthening the influence of national party identity over local preferences also would minimize sectional conflict. Van Buren wrote in

---

enter to compete for the polarized groups' votes. See Cox, "Centripetal and Centrifugal Incentives in Electoral Systems," *American Journal of Political Science* 34 (1990): 903–35.

[21] Downs, *Economic Theory of Democracy*, 118 and 120.

[22] See Ashworth, *Slavery, Capitalism, and Politics*; and Freehling, *The Road to Disunion* pts. 5–7.

[23] See Hofstadter, *Idea of a Party System*, 226–69; Ceaser, *Presidential Selection*, chap. 3; Remini, *Van Buren and the Making of the Democratic Party*, esp. chap. 10; Aldrich, *Why Parties?*, chaps. 4–5; J. David Greenstone, *The Lincoln Persuasion: Remaking American Liberalism* (Princeton: Princeton University Press, 1993), chap. 7; Richard H. Brown, "The Missouri Crisis, Slavery, and the Politics of Jacksonianism," *South Atlantic Quarterly* 65 (1966): 55–72; Wallace, "Changing Concepts"; and Richard Williams Smith, "The Career of Martin Van Buren in Connection with the Slavery Controversy through the Election of 1840" (Ph. D. dissertation, Ohio State University, 1959), chap. 2.

[24] See Barry R. Weingast, "Institutions and Political Commitment: A New Political Economy of the American Civil War" (manuscript, 1991).

1827 that if national party feelings "are suppressed, geographical divisions founded on local interests or, what is more, prejudices between free and slaveholding states will inevitably take their place."[25] There was a precedent. Party attachment during the era of conflict between Federalists and Republicans also had softened sectional prejudices. Only if sectional attachments remained muted would it be possible for the "clamour against Southern Influence and African Slavery" to cease and for the Union survive.[26] Van Buren believed parties would influence what types of issues arose and which issues could be avoided. As James Ceaser writes, Van Buren believed that "party competition would prevent personal factionalism and control popular leadership; discourage sectional divisions and encourage moderate, coalitional majorities; [and] ensure the existence of candidates with broad national support."[27] "Instead of the question being between a northern and Southern man," Van Buren wrote, "it would be whether or not the ties, which have heretofore bound together a great party should be severed."[28] Since the party would be constrained by its attempts to build a national coalition, it could hardly articulate clear policy positions on the issue of slavery.

In 1828, Van Buren successfully gave his support to a unifying candidate (Andrew Jackson) who could win the nation's largest electoral prize, the presidency. Andrew Jackson's presidency would emphasize the Democratic party's commitment to states' rights, Indian removal, and economic issues such as the opposition to the rechartering of the Bank of the United States. Moreover, Jackson's personality would make it easy for the party to avoid taking strong stands on potentially divisive issues: "indeed, Genl. Jackson has been so little in public life, that it will be not a little difficult to contrast his opinions on great questions with those of Mr. Adams."[29] As John Aldrich remarks, Van Buren effectively told various state-level political leaders, "Take our popular leader and no controversial policies. We will provide resources to you, so long as you agree to call yourself Democrats. For your part, you can continue to hold to your current policy positions."[30]

Van Buren and other Democrats further institutionalized this commitment to avoid sectional conflict by adopting a rule that representation at the party's nominating convention would be proportional to each

[25] Remini, *Van Buren and the Making of the Democratic Party*, 132.

[26] As quoted ibid.

[27] Ceaser, *Presidential Selection*, 168. Also see Foner, *Free Soil*, chap. 5.

[28] As quoted in Remini, *The Election of Andrew Jackson* (Philadelphia: Lippincott, 1963), 5. Also see Jaenecke, "Jacksonian Integration"; and Wallace, "Changing Concepts."

[29] Van Buren, as quoted in Remini, *Election of Andrew Jackson*, 6.

[30] Aldrich, *Why Parties?* 124.

state's electoral college votes. The roughly 40 percent representation by southern states was then protected from a majoritarian northern constituency by a second rule that mandated that the party nominee had to win by a two-thirds majority vote. As Aldrich points out, "This two-thirds rule effectively ensured that the South would have to agree to any nominee, made certain that no extremist, whether pro- or antislave, could be nominated, helped produce balanced tickets, and effectively attained and maintained the intersectional alliance in the Jacksonian Democratic party."[31] The party's commitment to maintaining a strong presence in all sections of the nation required that majorities in both the North and the South support the party's platform. In 1832, the two-thirds rule led to Van Buren's nomination as the Democratic presidential candidate over the more vehemently pro-slavery candidate, John Calhoun. In the 1840s and 1850s, it led Democrats at the state and congressional level, such as in New York and Michigan, to push for congressional legislation that avoided strong positions on slavery throughout the controversies over the Texas annexation, the Mexican War, the Wilmot Proviso, and the Kansas-Nebraska Act.[32] It led the first Democratic national chairman, Benjamin Hallett, to demand that the party oppose both the Wilmot Proviso and the Alabama test (which demanded that Democratic candidates endorse slavery).[33]

As president, Van Buren worked to keep his bisectional coalition together. On the one hand, he supported southern Congressman James Polk's reelection to the Speakership of the House, supported the gag rule that prevented discussion of antislavery in congressional debates, and closed southern mail to antislave propaganda. He took federal patronage away from radical Democrats such as William Leggett when they grew too vocal in their opposition to slavery, and he promoted three southern pro-slavery judges to the Supreme Court.[34] On the other hand, he opposed the annexation of Texas as a slave state. This effort to remain neutral on the slave issue in order to boost both his own and his party's electoral opportunities ultimately broke down in the early 1840s. It was in response to electoral pressures in the North against the expansion of slavery into new territories and in an effort to quell the rise of abolitionism in states like New York (a state the Liberty party

[31] Ibid., 132.

[32] See Eric Foner, "The Wilmot Proviso Revisited," *Journal of American History* 56 (1969); and Ronald Formisano, *The Birth of Mass Political Parties: Michigan, 1827–1861* (Princeton: Princeton University Press, 1971), 208–45.

[33] See Jaenicke, "Jacksonian Integration," 100–101.

[34] See Donald B. Cole, *Martin Van Buren and the American Political System* (Princeton: Princeton University Press, 1984), 274, 376.

threatened to take in the 1844 presidential election) that Van Buren opposed the South on Texas annexation and the Mexican War. In 1844, a distrustful southern wing of the party, using the two-thirds rule, helped prevent Van Buren from once again attaining the party nomination for president (the party instead went with a perceived moderate on the slave issue, James Polk). Two years later, Van Buren would support the Wilmot Proviso, which limited the expansion of slavery in the territories, a bill that forced one of the first dramatic splits between northern and southern Democrats in Congress.[35] In 1848, the New York Democratic party divided into a Van Buren wing that was generally antislavery (the Barnburners) and a more conservative wing (the Hunkers). Shortly thereafter, Van Buren would find himself the Free Soil party's candidate for the presidency.

To be sure, avoiding conflict over slavery was not Van Buren's sole goal in creating the Democratic party. In many ways, economic division continued to influence electoral considerations, and would do so until the 1840s.[36] It is also quite likely that given the general framework of the Constitution, with its emphasis on balance and compromise, the United States would have been inclined toward a two-party system regardless. Van Buren did not change electoral laws (although once the two-party system developed, both major parties proceeded to limit competition to only two parties); he merely responded to them in a somewhat unique fashion. This unique strategy was Van Buren's legacy, not only for the slave issue and the representation of future African Americans, but for the tactics and philosophies of future parties. At a tactical level, the cross-sectional coalition of the Democratic party pushed the newly formed Whig party to adapt a similar broad-based, cross-sectional strategy.[37] The Whigs also chose personalities as their presidential candidates (usually war heroes) and avoided controversial issues. The Whigs did not adopt a platform in three of their first four presidential campaigns, and they avoided entirely distinguishing themselves from the Democrats on slave matters. Although the Civil War would destroy the second-party system, the notion that two-party politics could shape and

[35] See Foner, "Wilmot Proviso," 270–77.

[36] See Ashworth for a recent authoritative argument that economic struggle dominated the attention of Van Buren, and most greatly influenced the development of the second-party system.

[37] See Foner, *Politics and Ideology in the Age of the Civil War* (New York: Oxford University Press, 1980), chap. 3; and Aldrich, *Why Parties?* chap. 5. For a specific example of this process in the state of New York, see John Langley Stanley, "Majority Tyranny in Tocqueville's America: The Failure of Negro Suffrage in New York State in 1846" (Ph.D. dissertation, Cornell University, 1966).

protect the nation from potentially divisive conflicts had been strongly ingrained in the minds of the nation's political leaders.[38]

At a philosophical level, the development of the Democratic party instilled in political leaders and scholars the belief that a powerful and effective electoral party needed to be national and broadly based. Not only did the Democratic party continue to struggle with maintaining this bisectional coalition, but the leaders of the Republican party by and large agreed that their success depended on broad coalitional appeals. The notion of a competitive party system grew entrenched in a belief that coalitions were forces of moderation that protected the nation from fragmentation and divisiveness. This notion of the political party persists to this day among party leaders and scholars. Like Van Buren, contemporary theorists and politicians continue to cast parties as strong and competitive only when they diminish the significance of racial issues.[39] When racial conflict does come to the surface, parties are either not responsible or are deemed failures for their inability to prevent conflict.

TWO-DIMENSIONAL POLITICS AND THE CAPTURE
OF BLACK INTERESTS

During the period of second-party system, racial division was kept out of electoral politics because of both institutional arrangements and a general agreement between governing elites. Since then, however, elites have not always maintained such an agreement. As we will see in chapters 3 and 4, conflict over race has at times been initiated by a party actively promoting African American interests. During both the Civil War period of the 1860s and the civil rights era in the 1960s, party activists supporting black representation became vocal leaders in setting the nation's political agenda. Both time periods are remarkable in that overt racial conflict emerged as the dominant dimension of politics, despite the efforts of many party leaders at the time to suppress it. In the mid-1860s, Radical Republicans, buoyed by the Civil War, promoted with vigor and passion the interests of freed slaves in the South. In the mid-1960s, civil rights supporters boldly proclaimed a new era of equality. Both periods are also quite remarkable in that one party dominated the political scene while the other was in radical decline. The Democrats of the 1860s were not only stigmatized for their support of southern

---

[38] See Jaenicke, "Jacksonian Integration."

[39] See Joel H. Silbey, "The Rise and Fall of American Political Parties 1790–1993," in L. Sandy Maisel, ed., *The Parties Respond: Changes in American Parties and Campaigns* (Boulder, Colo.: Westview Press, 1994).

Confederates; they had to cope with the disenfranchisement of their party's southern base. The Republicans of the 1960s were overwhelmed by the assassination of a popular Democratic president and landslide defeats in the 1964 presidential and congressional campaigns.

After both periods saw a return to a competitive two-party system, the majority of whites reacted either negatively or ambivalently to the dramatic gains made by black Americans during these years of reform. The party out of power during the period of one-party domination quickly discovered that it could make serious inroads among white voters by using race-based appeals as a divisive wedge. By appealing to the median white voter along racial lines, they could pry away votes from the party in power. After a time, the party advancing black interests began to realize that substantial numbers of white voters were defecting to the opposition party precisely because of the majority power's promotion of civil rights. Even today, more than three decades after the civil rights movement, the perception by party leaders that racial conflict matters for electoral outcomes continues to affect their actions, and usually manifests itself in ways far less obvious than appealing to white voters via the symbolism of a black rapist, Willy Horton. Behind the decision of party leaders to avoid appeals to black voters are a host of assumptions that party leaders routinely make in order to deal with the uncertainty typically associated with running a campaign.

Party scholars have always recognized that political leaders are seldom certain about which issues will appeal to the broadest electoral majority. Scholars have concluded that this uncertainty leads party leaders to formulate a wide variety of messages and to seek the voters of many potential groups. I believe the opposite is true. Precisely because party leaders operate in an uncertain environment with incomplete and imperfect information they avoid taking risks. They offer only a few messages and appeal to a smaller set of groups. As rational actors operating under conditions of uncertainty, party leaders are much more likely to use a few time-honored, familiar electoral strategies, rather than newer, untested strategies. The familiar strategies reflect both the early days of the two-party system's development as well as the repeated nature of electoral politics and its outcomes. The successes and failures of previous electoral strategies are used to legitimate certain types of party behavior and condemn others. For American party politics, this has meant that party leaders continually focus on primarily white swing voters who party leaders believe are hostile to black interests. Armed with assumptions coming out of the initial design of the two-party system and from repeated electoral strategies, party leaders shy away from more volatile and less certain appeals to black voters in favor of appeals to a hypothetical median white voter.

The iterated nature of electoral politics also means that a highly controversial electoral strategy is likely to have ramifications on future elections. Barry Goldwater's repudiation of the 1964 Civil Rights Act during the 1964 presidential campaign had serious consequences for the African American vote in every subsequent presidential election. The perception by Democratic party leaders that Jesse Jackson's participation in the 1984 and 1988 Democratic nomination was detrimental to their national campaign also had, and continues to have, serious consequences for black voters. Because the high-profile failure of an electoral strategy may lead not simply to a single defeat, but to long-term consequences as well as difficulties for candidates farther down on the ticket, party leaders are more likely to be risk-averse rather than risk-taking. Risk-averse party leaders are more likely to utilize familiar and reliable strategies. Primarily white swing voters are even more likely to be the targets of party appeals.

THE DISTINCTION BETWEEN ELECTORAL INSTITUTIONS AND PARTY ORGANIZATIONS

Not all party leaders, of course, wish only to win campaigns. Some — perhaps most — party leaders are motivated by principles and ideas while recognizing the necessity of winning elections. These party leaders calculate quite differently the degree of racial division in society and within their electoral coalition, and as a result make appeals to blacks with electoral incentives in mind. Mass-based political parties, after all, are diverse organizations with diverse opinions about "the best course of action," even when all of the members involved recognize the incentives of the electoral structure. For those who wish to aggressively promote black interests, institutional arrangements and ideological debate may very well provide short-term advantages that might be parlayed into real policy decisions. Furthermore, even if party leaders believe that an appeal to black voters will hurt the party at the ballot box, they may not have the organizational capacity to implement their beliefs.[40] While party leaders follow prescribed incentives to elect candidates, their organizations are not always equipped to respond in the manner that they

---

[40] This distinction between the incentives provided by electoral structures, and the ability of party organizations to respond to these structural incentives draws on work by Jack Knight, *Institutions and Social Conflict* (New York: Cambridge University Press, 1992); Douglass C. North, *Structure and Change in Economic History* (New York: Norton, 1981); and James G. March and Johan P. Olson, *Rediscovering Institutions: The Organizational Basis of Politics* (New York: Free Press, 1989).

believe is most strategic. Party organizations are shaped by internal battles and historical events, many of which are the result of passionate ideological struggles. At times, these forces can severely inhibit the ability of strategic actors to lead.[41] If strategic party actors, for instance, do not have the capacity to nominate those they deem to be appropriate national candidates, their control over the party's ideological platform and electoral strategy will be greatly restricted.

As an example, take the Democratic party's organizational reforms and counterreforms after the 1968 presidential election. Initially, the party's McGovern-Fraser reforms greatly enhanced the position of black political interests (as well as those of other previously underrepresented groups) in the party's nominating process. The reforms also decreased the ability of party leaders to focus the party's message on the median white voter.[42] In the 1980s, Jesse Jackson took advantage of these rules. Mobilized groups of black voters concentrated in southern and midwestern states elected delegates for Jackson, and he became a prominent player at the party's national conventions. These new rules allowed blacks to play an unprecedented and empowering role in two national campaigns.

Party leaders, however, believed that Jackson's presence made it difficult for candidates Walter Mondale and Michael Dukakis to distance themselves from black voters and appeal to white swing voters. Jackson's message, while successful in mobilizing the African American vote, received only lukewarm support from white Democrats and even less support (in public opinion polls) from independent white voters. Reacting to their fifth defeat in the six presidential elections since the 1965 Voting Rights Act, Democratic leaders instituted counterreforms to strengthen their own power. They wished to shape campaigns that would appeal more to the national median voter. In chapter 4, I will examine how these counterreforms succeeded in giving party leaders more control over the ideological position of their party. For now, it is simply important to recognize that the McGovern-Fraser reforms served their purpose. They incorporated blacks into the Democratic party and its nomination process. Party leaders, in turn, blamed these reforms for limiting their ability to keep black issues off the party's agenda and

---

[41] On this general point about institutional design, see March and Olson, *Rediscovering Institutions*; Stephen Skowronek, *Building a New American State: The Expansion of National Administrative Capacities, 1877–1920* (New York: Cambridge University Press, 1982); and Karen Orren and Stephen Skowronek, "Beyond the Iconography of Order: Notes for a New Institutionalism," in Lawrence Dodd and Calvin Jillson, eds., *The Dynamics of American Politics: Approaches and Perspectives* (Boulder, Colo: Westview Press, 1993).

[42] See chap. 4 for further citations and discussion of the reforms.

eventually mustered the legitimacy and organizational power to do something about it.

The Jackson example is also instructive for illustrating the distinction between organizations and electoral institutions. Party organizations change; our national electoral structure does not. Electoral institutions perpetually create incentives for parties to develop a message that appeals to the majority. This incentive persists in the face of any short-term victories for African Americans, even if those victories are momentarily institutionalized. Fierce party competition encourages those messages that are less "marketable" to be squeezed out by those that resonate with the majority. Just as Max Weber argued that rationality had become an "iron cage," so can the necessity of winning elections become an iron cage.[43] Potential dissent to the party message is weeded out with each electoral defeat. Once politicians decide that changes are necessary, they gather the power and legitimacy to pass the institutional counterreforms that allow the party as a whole to more adequately respond to the electoral demands of the median voter.

ELECTORAL CAPTURE

As a result of these electoral incentives, the party that most represents black interests begins to act in a predictable pattern. As the party begins to lose elections, and as party leaders focus on the party's advocacy of black concerns as the reason for this electoral trouble, the party goes through a period of intense inner turmoil. Many party leaders insist on continuing the struggle for African American concerns. Other leaders, however, argue for downplaying the African American agenda and focusing on the white median voter, the voter that it is necessary to woo in order to succeed electorally. While these leaders may be motivated by ideological agendas of their own, they focus on — and are legitimated by — the strictly strategic considerations of maintaining or gaining office. The process of working out these arguments may take time. The first group of party leaders may hope for a few electoral victories so that they will not have to stop advocating on behalf of African Americans. Yet further defeats mandate changes. Finding encouragement in each electoral defeat, the second group of party leaders grows more vocal, and finds its views assuming greater legitimacy. Supporters of black political interests become deflated. Faced with the argument that their protests are dividing and weakening the party, the group's leaders

[43] Max Weber, *The Protestant Ethic and the Spirit of Capitalism* (New York: Charles Scribner's Sons, 1958). See also Deborah Satz and John Ferejohn, "Rational Choice and Social Theory," *Journal of Philosophy* (February 1994): 71–87.

themselves become divided, and those who refuse to honor the electoral incentives are marginalized.

Throughout this inner-party turmoil, the opposition party recognizes that it can absorb whites turned off by the racial agenda of the other major party without disrupting its own preexisting electoral coalition. The opposition party can exploit racial tension without adjusting its position on the left-right ideological spectrum. By appealing to the racial fears of white voters, the party can reach out to those who lie on the other side of the ideological spectrum in terms of economics without compromising the party's economic platform. In figure 2.3, we see this dynamic at work in multidimensional space. On one axis, we see a normal left-right ideological distribution. On a second axis, we see a skewed distribution on the issue of race. A third axis indicates the density of the vote when the two ideological dimensions intersect. The race axis ensures that a party can appeal to voters who are economically liberal but racially conservative without changing its economic position. As long as the racial appeals are invoked, the debate revolves around the agenda of the white, racially conservative voter, regardless of how voters are situated on alternative issue dimensions.

Notice the impact of this on African American interests. As long as the party championing black interests makes those issues the central part of the campaign, it is more or less doomed to failure. Not only must party leaders distance themselves from black interests; they must find other issues to be viable contenders in electoral politics. If these other issues are not tinged by an association with African Americans, black voters may remain part of the winning electoral coalition if they come to be seen simply as liberal voters similar to other nonblack liberal voters. Nonetheless, party leaders will continue to distance themselves from any black leaders who attempt to raise issues of specific concern to black voters. Meanwhile, if the new issues dominating the political agenda are associated in subtle ways with African Americans (e.g., contemporary welfare politics, crime, or social spending in inner cities), then party leaders will distance themselves from these issues as well, and black voters will be further marginalized.

As long as the party closest to African American voters fears the opposition party will make attacks on racial grounds, it will compensate by distancing itself from black interests, ironically leading to situations where it, and not the opposition party, launches high-profile attacks on black interests. When dealing with African American voters, party leaders must engage in the very unique calculation of weighing the potential advantage of bringing in black voters against the potential loss of white voters. Few other interest groups — whether demographic or occupational — carry such a burden. Modern-day parties can reach out to

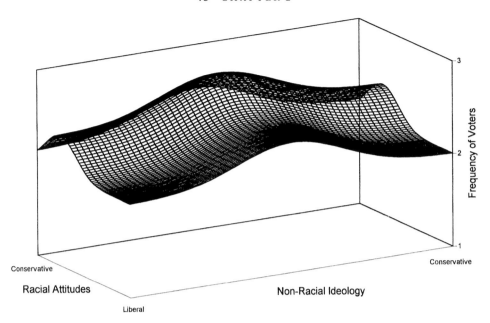

Conservative

Racial Attitudes

Liberal

Non-Racial Ideology

Conservative

Frequency of Voters

2.3   Politics in three dimensions

the farm lobby, for example, with specific policy initiatives that do not disrupt the rest of the party's coalition.[44] The options of black political leaders are thus limited in ways that those of other interest groups are not.

CONCLUSION

We can see, then, that the fear of the disruptive costs of advancing the cause of African Americans precludes party leaders from prominently competing for the African American vote. This dynamic, the fear of disruptiveness, is the most important cause of electoral capture, over-shadowing the other causes discussed in chapter 1. For instance, if black voters were seen as nothing more than an ideologically liberal group, then we should see party leaders appealing to their nonracial concerns. The fact is that we do not, because the fear of disruptiveness keeps

[44] For examples of strategic considerations by President Nixon that show contrasting opinions of blacks with labor and Latinos, see Paul Frymer and John David Skrentny, "Coalition-Building and the Politics of Electoral Capture during the Nixon Administration: African Americans, Labor, Latinos," *Studies in American Political Development* 12 (Spring 1998): 75–105.

party leaders from making such appeals. This fear radically limits the ability of black voters to threaten to defect and vote for the opposing party. Ideally, if black voters threatened to defect from one party to the other major party, the party's leaders would respond, for that would entail a double loss: the defection of black votes from the party along with the corresponding additional votes to the opposition party. As Dianne Pinderhughes argues, if black voters considered candidates from all parties before deciding whom to support, no party would be able to take their vote for granted without delivering substantive policy proposals.[45] Ronald Walters similarly claims that "in circumstances where a social [racial] minority such as Blacks is consistently part of the [objective] losing minority, the political strategies of the minority should become as competitive as possible in order to influence vital decisions affecting their status."[46] He advocates the development of a third party or the utilization of a "Black presidential strategy," where an African American candidate would advocate policy objectives despite the improbability of actually winning the election.

But for this scenario to be realized, the opposition party has to make a public appeal to African American voters. Black leaders and their followers, like any rational voters, will not simply run from one party to another if the second party gives them no added value. Offered a choice between two political parties making similarly vague appeals, a group is likely to maintain its traditional allegiance simply for institutional and historical reasons. Long-standing allegiance to a party inevitably results in the group's leading politicians becoming embedded in the party's organizational structure, particularly at the local levels. The group's political leaders who have been recruited and elected through one political party are unlikely to endorse the opposition party without substantial reason. Moreover, the group's voters undoubtedly develop long-standing ties to their party. While frustrated, and perhaps alienated by their party's reluctance to advance their cause in a public forum, voters are nonetheless likely to continue voting for the party, assuming no fruitful alternative — if for no better reason than historical attachment and habit. For the opposition party, in turn, to shake the negative connotations that the group's voters associate with it requires more than vague and halfhearted appeals.

Note, however, that the same logic that dictates a deemphasis of black interests in one major party also governs the policy of the other. If party leaders believe that white voter hostility to black representation is

---

[45] Dianne Pinderhughes, "Political Choices: A Realignment in Partisanship among Black Voters?" in *The State of Black America* (New York: National Black Urban League, 1984).

[46] Walters, *Black Presidential Politics*, 5.

significant, then their perception will likely stifle any effort to increase the party's black votes. If opposition party leaders believe that appeals to black voters will undermine both their own preexisting coalition and their appeals to white swing voters, they too will refrain from appeals to black voters. Support from black voters is not perceived by strategic actors as merely an addition to a party's existing electoral count, but as an entire alteration of the makeup of both parties' coalitions. As a result, black voters remain captured. The logic of two-party competition and the primacy of white swing voters (who party leaders believe are hostile to specific black interests) make it difficult for black leaders to wield the same type of power that other groups maintain despite similar numbers of voters, similar ideological backgrounds, similar geographical concentrations in key areas, and similar financial resources. Thus, *pace* Pinderhughes and Walters, parties will do little more than make token appeals to black voters and will force black voters to choose between a second and third choice. In this regard, Jesse Jackson's recent efforts to bring black voters out of their captured status in the Democratic party is notable. Prior to the 1992 election, Jackson reached out to both Republican George Bush and independent candidate Ross Perot in order to make the black voter more visible. Neither was willing to entertain his overtures; both parties eventually lost on election day.

If a party's championing of a group's interests were inconsequential, then a good deal of this discussion would be irrelevant. But as we will see in later chapters of this book, political parties privilege interest groups when they make appeals toward them, acting as powerful agents who can translate electoral victory into governing policies. The cycle of two-party competition and occasional one-party domination cannot overcome racial inequality, and in fact perpetuates it and the status quo. As long as the median voter in the United States maintains ambivalent-to-conservative views toward African American political interests, the two-party system will fail to represent all interests democratically. For black interests to be addressed seriously by the party system, either black political leaders must reshape national public opinion or we must devise an electoral system that provides incentives for parties to appeal to black voters and win elections at the same time.

CHAPTER 3

National Party Competition and the Disenfranchisement of Black Voters in the South, 1866–1932

DESPITE the efforts of Martin Van Buren and the other leaders of the second-party system, race emerged as the dominant issue in national party politics by the late 1850s, destroying two-party competition in the process. The rise to power of the Republican party during these years in many ways represented the antithesis of Van Buren's vision of party politics. Unlike the Democrats between the 1820s and the 1850s, the Republicans did not make strong appeals for a cross-sectional alliance, nor did they attempt to minimize or contain the emotions and ideologies surrounding slavery. Although there is still some scholarly debate about the motives of Republican party leaders, it is undeniable that in its first decade in office the party championed the interests of abolitionists and civil rights advocates.[1] For roughly five years at the end of the 1860s, Radical Republicans in Congress dominated the political agenda. They enacted a number of dramatic pieces of civil rights legislation, including the Thirteenth, Fourteenth, and Fifteenth Amendments to the Constitution which abolished slavery, guaranteed equal protection, and gave blacks the vote.[2] Congressional Republicans enforced these amendments by disenfranchising southern whites who threatened Reconstruction efforts and by authorizing federal military troops and "Freedmen's Bureaus" to aid and protect black citizens in the region.[3]

To a significant extent, the Radical Republicans in Congress acted in the absence of two-party competition. The Democratic party in the

[1] For discussion of the motives of Republican party leaders, see Eric Foner, *Free Soil, Free Labor, Free Men: The Ideology of the Republican Party before the Civil War* (New York: Oxford University Press, 1970).

[2] The Fifteenth Amendment deals specifically with African American voting rights. In order to pass the legislation, the amendment needed to be written in a way that appeased western Republican concerns about the potential voting rights of Chinese immigrants.

[3] Two of the best and most thorough summaries of the era of Reconstruction are W. E. B. Du Bois, *Black Reconstruction: An Essay toward a History of the Part Which Black Folk Played in the Attempt to Reconstruct Democracy in America, 1860–1880* (New York: Harcourt, Brace, 1935); and Eric Foner, *Reconstruction: America's Unfinished Revolution, 1863–1877* (New York: Harper and Row, 1988).

North was struggling to overcome the stigma of its association with the southern Confederacy, and much of the party's southern base was either disenfranchised or simply not participating in electoral politics, at either the local or the congressional level. Once the Democrats reemerged as a nationally competitive party, the Radical Republicans' plan to maintain a long-term electoral majority built in part on southern black voters became a point of bitter contention within the party. As other wings of the Republican party's leadership focused on the divisiveness of building an electoral coalition involving blacks, the ability of the Radicals to sustain Reconstruction weakened considerably.

In this chapter, I wish to illustrate how the efforts of party leaders to win electoral majorities in an intensely competitive post-Reconstruction two-party system led to the capture of black voters within the Republican party and to their subsequent political marginalization. Most of this history has been told before: Through the use of extreme violence, intimidation, and fraud, newly organized groups such as the Ku Klux Klan working in conjunction with key members of the Democratic party in the South returned the region to a system of white domination and, later, apartheid. By the mid-1870s, black voting rates had dropped significantly from those of the first days of Reconstruction. By the early-1900s, state conventions across the region had legalized public discrimination and segregation as well as the disenfranchisement of an overwhelming majority of black voters.[4] Two decades later, legal segregation would make its way into the national government and into some areas outside of the South.[5]

In retelling this story, however, I emphasize the symbiotic relationship between white racism and our electoral structures. In particular, I argue that electoral incentives and two-party competition led black Americans in the South, and later in the North, to lose many of their newly established constitutional rights. I will challenge previous party scholars who have claimed that black marginalization was the result of the *absence* of two-party competition in the South. In their view, the precipitating cause of the decline of African American civil and voting rights was the defeat of the Republican party in the South. In his classic work *Southern Politics in State and Nation*, V. O. Key laid out the dominant version of this argument. Of particular importance is the fourteenth chapter of the book, entitled "The Nature and Consequences of One-Party Factionalism."[6] Writing at the end of the 1940s, when racial segregation

---

[4] See J. Morgan Kousser, *The Shaping of Southern Politics: Suffrage Restriction and the Establishment of the One-Party South, 1880–1910* (New Haven: Yale University Press, 1974).

[5] See Desmond King, *Separate and Unequal* (Oxford: Oxford University Press, 1995).

[6] V. O. Key, Jr., *Southern Politics in State and Nation* (New York: Vintage, 1949). For

and the wide-scale disenfranchisement of blacks and many poor whites was firmly entrenched in the South, Key blamed this state of affairs mainly on the absence of party competition in the region. Without two parties, he believed, there was no clear choice for voters, no accountability for the party in office, no need to mobilize voters to attain office, and no desire among voters to participate.

According to Key, in a one-party system there were no battles over policy. Political leaders attracted the attention of voters through demagoguery. These demagogues failed to produce any real political organization, a situation that generated especially adverse consequences for the disadvantaged.

> Over the long run the have-nots lose in disorganized politics. They have no mechanism through which to act and their wishes find expression in fitful rebellions led by transient demagogues who gain their confidence but often have neither the technical competence nor the necessary stable base of political power to effectuate a program.[7]

As long as political leaders remained unchallenged, he argued, no one would speak for African Americans. A two-party system, regardless of its other deficiencies, would produce a second group of politicians who "of necessity must pick up whatever issue is at hand to belabor the 'ins.' "[8]

Many contemporary scholars share Key's assessment of the relationship between a one-party system and southern disenfranchisement. J. Morgan Kousser claims that the end of party competition in the South led to the drastic marginalization of black interests. The Democratic party, he argues, followed their electoral interests to keep blacks disenfranchised, since "the presence of a large potential Negro vote, which was for the most part alienated from the established order, tempted any enemy of those in power to bolt the Democrats."[9] The Republican party, while often under serious attack by white supremacists, nonetheless counteracted Democratic electoral incentives by mobilizing those groups left out of the majority party coalition. Only when the Democratic party made it sufficiently difficult for whites to vote Republican without fear of violent repercussions and when the national Republican

---

discussion specifically of this 14th chapter, see David R. Mayhew, "Why Did V. O. Key Draw Back from His 'Have-Nots' Claim?" in Milton C. Cummings, Jr., ed., *V. O. Key, Jr., and the Study of American Politics* (Washington, D.C.: American Political Science Association, 1988).

[7] Key, *Southern Politics*, 307.

[8] Ibid., 310.

[9] Kousser, *Shaping of Southern Politics*, 18.

party after the electoral realignment of 1896 no longer needed southern votes to win presidential elections and majorities in Congress were the majority of southern blacks disenfranchised. Had a competitive Republican party remained in the South, Kousser argues, interracial democracy would have emerged by necessity. The opposing party in the region would have had a permanent incentive to appeal to any and all groups disgruntled with the dominant group in power.

A third scholar of post-Reconstruction party politics, Richard Valelly, has shifted the attention from Kousser's emphasis on the Democrats to the role of the national Republican party in bringing about southern black disenfranchisement. Similar to Kousser, Valelly maintains that Republicans continued to compete for black votes in the South until the mid-1890s, when party leaders recognized that they could win national elections without southern support or black voters. Only then and only when it became increasingly difficult to attain black votes in the face of violence, intimidation, and fraud did the Republican party "disinvest" from the southern vote, allowing for the final stages of black disenfranchisement at the turn of the century.[10]

Both Key and Kousser make powerful arguments about the Democratic party's ability to demobilize southern voters. Valelly correctly points out that the Republican party had electoral incentives to abandon African American interests in the region. Yet all three accounts ultimately miss a necessary part of the explanation. Blacks were a captured group in the Republican party at that time, and this had serious consequences for the behavior of party leaders. I argue, first, that even during the 1870s and 1880s, when the Republican party believed it needed electoral votes in the South to maintain power nationally, party leaders focused a great deal of their efforts on promoting policies disadvantageous to black interests. These party leaders believed that appealing to blacks through stronger enforcement of voting and civil rights would result in the loss of critical numbers of northern white voters.

This scenario fits with the argument that I make in chapter 2. As long as the status of blacks is the primary issue in a campaign, the party representing African American feels obligated to appeal to racially conservative white voters in order to win elections. In this case, the Republican party was dominated initially by Radicals who believed that promoting racial equality was both morally and strategically right. As the party began to lose northern elections in the late 1860s, a debate ensued over the degree to which the electoral losses could be attributed to Reconstruction policies, and particularly to the fight over black voting

[10] Richard M. Valelly, "National Parties and Racial Disenfranchisement," in Paul E. Peterson, ed., *Classifying by Race* (Princeton: Princeton University Press, 1995), 188–216.

rights. With subsequent electoral defeats in both the North and South blamed on Reconstruction policies, the national party grew increasingly reluctant to fight for the protection of black voting rights. In the minds of many Republican leaders, reelection politics necessitated the party's surrender of southern blacks in the effort to maintain support from northern whites. Meanwhile, marginalized by electoral defeats, the Radical wing of the party lost control to the more "pragmatic" wing, resulting in a dramatic reduction in the federal enforcement of civil rights laws. The Radicals' influence did not decline in a steady fashion. Events occurred thoughout this period that provided Radicals with short-term control of the political agenda. Yet despite moments of Republican outrage stimulated by southern racism, electoral incentives continued to dominate the post-Reconstruction calculus, leading to a decline in the party's protection of equal rights in the South. The national party leadership's concerns about winning elections in the North, then, played a crucial role in the party's decline in the South.

Second, southern Republicans with an eye on winning local elections also played an important role in marginalizing black interests. Throughout the South, white and black Republicans divided over electoral strategy. Many whites, believing that they could not win elections with a coalition of largely black voters, left the party in favor of independent and fusion movements or the Democratic party. In many of these cases, national Republican leaders gave their support to the white independent movements over predominantly black Republican state coalitions. National leaders believed that this offered the best option for winning elections in the South. They also believed it would help reduce electoral problems in the North. This further weakened the Republican party in the South and marginalized blacks in southern and national politics. With blacks effectively captured in both the North and the South, party leaders actively distanced themselves from their interests.

Third, I argue that even when the Republican party no longer needed southern votes to win national elections, they continued to pursue white voters in the region. The electoral logic here is not easy to comprehend, since the realignment of 1896 in northern and western states had more or less given the party a stronghold throughout all major branches of government. Nonetheless, the pursuit of whites subsequently marginalized black interests even further, as party leaders believed that avoiding mention of black interests made the appeal to white voters in the South more effective. During Republican administrations from Theodore Roosevelt to Herbert Hoover, then, the race issue had largely disappeared from national electoral politics, and blacks found themselves to be more or less invisible as coalitional partners.

REPUBLICAN PARTY COMPETITION IN THE NORTH AND ITS
IMPACT ON SOUTHERN RECONSTRUCTION

Given the intensity of the Civil War conflict and the extreme division between the two national parties over the slave issue, it is not surprising that African American voters quickly joined the Republican party. To a small degree, some Democratic candidates in states such as Alabama, Arkansas, Louisiana, North Carolina, and South Carolina made appeals to black voters in the late 1860s, at times pledging to protect voting and civil rights for the former slaves, occasionally electing blacks to local offices and providing blacks patronage, and at times stressing their differences with the Republicans over economic policy.[11] Democrats nationally were divided during these early years over how to position themselves vis-à-vis black voters, with some believing that a general support of Reconstruction policies was necessary for electoral victories. Even when Democrats did appeal to black voters, however, they were often motivated by the longer-term goal of attracting white majorities. In some electoral areas in which blacks constituted the majority of the voting-age population, Democrats appealed to them by cynically attacking the Republican party for not promoting African American's more. As C. Vann Woodward has written, "By aiding the Negro leaders in maintaining control over their party and the Federal patronage, [Democrats] could thereby exclude capable native white leadership from control and thus minimize the danger of Republican victories. At the same time they could by these means identify the Republicans with the colored race, and more easily solidify their own party by the old cry of the white supremacy."[12] In many other areas, Democrats simply relied on coercion, intimidation, and the use of bribes to "win" black votes. Most black voters, recognizing these tactics and motivations, remained skepti-

[11] See Foner, *Reconstruction*, 415; Lawrence Grossman, *The Democratic Party and the Negro* (Urbana: University of Illinois Press, 1976), chap. 2 and particularly n. 67; Michael Perman, *The Road to Redemption: Southern Politics, 1869–1879* (Chapel Hill: University of North Carolina Press, 1984), 59; and Justus D. Doenecke, *The Presidencies of James A. Garfield and Chester A. Arthur* (Lawrence: Regents Press of Kansas, 1981), 108–9. On Arkansas specifically, see Fon Louise Gordon, *Caste and Class: The Black Experience in Arkansas, 1880–1920* (Athens: University of Georgia Press, 1995), 10. On North Carolina, see Eric Anderson, *Race and Politics in North Carolina, 1872–1901* (Baton Rouge: Louisiana State University Press, 1981), 87, 130–39. On South Carolina, see William J. Cooper, Jr., *The Conservative Regime: South Carolina, 1877–1890* (Baltimore: Johns Hopkins Press, 1968), chap. 3. According to Russell Korobkin, Democrats continued to make appeals for black votes well into the 1890s. See "The Politics of Disfranchisement in Georgia," *Georgia Historical Quarterly* 74 (1990): 29.

[12] C. Vann Woodward, *Origins of the New South, 1877–1913* (Baton Rouge: Louisiana State University Press, 1951), 103.

cal of Democratic party appeals and maintained support for the Republicans. Democrats soon recognized the difficulty of appealing to black voters and emphasized their differences with the Republicans over race in order to appeal to racially conservative whites.[13]

Republicans, meanwhile, galvanized by President Andrew Johnson's reconciliatory policies toward the Confederacy and by southern white defiance, vigorously undertook efforts to represent black interests. Congressional Republicans mustered the votes to pass the Fourteenth Amendment in 1866, as well as the first Reconstruction Act a year later, which provided blacks with military protection and voting rights. In the South, party conventions to draw up postwar constitutions were by and large dominated by blacks and Radical Republicans, further empowering the state governments to advance black interests in the political process.

The Republicans advocated black interests in the South while organizations such as the Ku Klux Klan grew increasingly active and violent. The Klan assassinated an Arkansas congressman in 1868 and intimidated both black and white Republican voters in Georgia and Louisiana, forcing the Republicans effectively to drop out of both states' presidential races. Eleven Georgia counties, in fact, recorded no votes at all for the Republican party ticket.[14] The white Republican governor of the state received death threats and a member of his administration was murdered while traveling back from Washington, D.C., where he had been requesting further government assistance to combat the violence.

The Republican party did make efforts to prevent this type of violence, and such efforts were motivated not simply by ideology. On a strategic level, African Americans were critical to the Republican party's effort to institute a powerful electoral presence in the South and to maintain majorities at the national level. This strategy was premised in part on simply the sheer number of potential black voters in the South. African Americans constituted majorities in three different states (Louisiana, Mississippi, and South Carolina) and in more than a third of the region's congressional districts. Blacks also represented near majorities of the population in three other states (Alabama, Florida, and Georgia) and in more than a dozen congressional districts. In the North, meanwhile, new black voters offered the potential of providing the margin of difference in closely contested electoral states such as Ohio, New York, Pennsylvania, and New Jersey. In New Jersey, for instance, while numbering only slightly more than four thousand voters, blacks could potentially determine outcomes, as two-party contests in this period were

---

[13] See Perman, *Road to Reconstruction*, chap. 3.
[14] Foner, *Reconstruction*, 342–43.

at times decided by fewer than three thousand votes.[15] Assuming an otherwise stable electoral coalition, Republican leaders could remain optimistic that a nationally competitive party based on a strong black presence in both the North and the South would be electorally profitable.

This electoral strategy met its first complications in northern elections in the late 1860s as the party discovered that the efforts of Radical Republicans to enforce Reconstruction in the South were hurting the party's electoral opportunities in the North. The conservative wing of the party, in particular, feared that Reconstruction policies would weaken the party's coalition-building opportunities among white southerners and would lead to black suffrage and equal rights in the North. In New York, Democrats resumed electoral prominence by attacking the Republican party's policies on a number of issues, particularly Reconstruction. Republican leaders in the state split over the suffrage question. A compromise plank was passed at their 1867 convention that called for suffrage in only vague terms and with no discussion of how it might be implemented.[16] Despite these last-second efforts to diffuse the race issue, the Republican vote in the state ended up declining in all but one county.[17] Around the nation that year, Republicans lost ground in almost all of the twenty northern state elections. In Connecticut, the party lost the governor's race and three of four House seats. In Ohio, voters rejected by a wide margin a black suffrage amendment, and in the process replaced a number of state legislators and a House member with Democrats.[18] Republican leaders in Maine, Vermont, and California also attributed their party's losses in state elections to the divisive issue of black suffrage.[19]

The losses in Connecticut, Ohio, Pennsylvania, and New York were particularly significant not only because these were important "swing" states for national elections, but also because party leaders interpreted them as a precursor to what might happen more widely in the North in the national elections of 1868 if the party continued to push black suf-

[15] William Gillette, *The Right to Vote: Politics and the Passage of the Fifteenth Amendment* (Baltimore: Johns Hopkins University Press, 1965), 113.

[16] Jerome Mushkat, *The Reconstruction of the New York Democracy* (Rutherford, N. J.: Farleigh Dickinson University Press, 1981), 121–31.

[17] See Phyllis F. Field, *The Politics of Race in New York* (Ithaca: Cornell University Press, 1982), 175.

[18] Voter majorities from twelve of the forty-five Republican counties in the state opposed the legislation. See Michael Les Benedict, "The Rout of Radicalism: Republicans and the Elections of 1867," *Civil War History* 18 (December 1972): 342.

[19] Not that other issues were not attributal to election losses. In Maine, for instance, a referendum on the prohibition of alcohol also split voters, while in Ohio, taxation issues were also on the voting agenda.

frage. Newspapers from Providence to Philadelphia all argued that the "lesson of Connecticut" was to slow down black suffrage.[20] Senator John Sherman said of the elections that "the chief trouble is the [Negro] suffrage question. It is clearly right. . . . It is easy to convince people so, but harder to make them feel it — and vote it." The *New York Times* warned specifically about the Ohio elections because the state provided "the key-note of the entire central West. If Ohio gives a decided vote, you need not expect any of the ten States, west and north of it, including Missouri and Colorado to go otherwise. These states give about one hundred electoral votes in the Presidential election."[21]

Republican leaders in New York once again tried to avoid the suffrage issue in 1868. After state Democrats took a strong stance at their convention in 1868 against black suffrage, the Republican convention voted to keep the suffrage issue separate from the party's convention, as they hoped to keep the issue from embroiling the presidential election.[22] State party leaders clearly believed that promoting equal suffrage risked alienating more white voters than attracting new black voters.[23] In fact, in a number of northern congressional districts both inside and outside of New York, the addition of black voters to the Republican Party between 1868 and 1870 led to larger victory margins for the Democratic party.[24] Meanwhile, Republican attempts to pass black suffrage laws in Colorado, Kansas, Michigan, Minnesota, Missouri, and Wisconsin all failed.[25] In Delaware, Maryland, Missouri, and West Virginia, state passage by the Republicans of the Fifteenth Amendment led to wide-scale losses and the Democratic party's recapture of their state legislatures between 1870 and 1872.[26]

The Republican losses in 1867 galvanized the party's conservative wing and made the nomination of a moderate on Reconstruction, Ulysses Grant, more or less inevitable. Grant, a war hero considered to be above partisan politics, was pushed most heavily by the conservative wing of the party, which hoped to strengthen ties with southern whites.

[20] See James C. Mohr, *The Radical Republicans and Reform in New York during Reconstruction* (Ithaca: Cornell University Press, 1973), chaps. 7–8.

[21] Quoted in Benedict, "Rout of Radicalism." 342–43.

[22] Field, *Politics of Race in New York*, 178.

[23] Mohr, *Radical Republicans*, 238. Also see LaWanda Cox and John H. Cox, "Negro Suffrage and Republican Politics: The Problem of Motivation in Reconstruction Historiography," *Journal of Southern History* 33 (1967), 319.

[24] Cox and Cox, "Negro Suffrage," 323–25.

[25] Gillette, *Right to Vote*, 42; Morton Keller, *Affairs of State: Public Life in Late-Nineteenth-Century America* (Cambridge: Harvard University Press, 1977), 144; Mohr, *Radical Republicans*, 242.

[26] Gillette, *Right to Vote*, 108–9.

He ran on a plank that left the suffrage issue up to individual states in the North.[27] Nonetheless, even with a war hero for a candidate and an opposition party that was weakened from internal fighting over their party nomination, the Republicans barely won the national popular vote (although they won twenty-six of thirty-four electoral college states).[28] They lost the crucial states of New York and New Jersey, as well as two of the seven southern states (Georgia and Louisiana) that were allowed to vote.[29]

Party leaders and activists fought over the interpretation of the presidential election results. Many Republicans called for further appeasement of southern whites and an easing of Reconstruction. Some argued that if Congress were to follow the electoral results, the issue of suffrage would be dead. Senator Thomas Hendricks of Indiana asked the Senate "to stand upon the pledge of honor that your party made to the people in the election last fall. . . . That the Democratic party, in casting its vote for Seymour and Blair, did not vote for negro suffrage, is plain enough. That the Republican party last fall in voting for Grant and Colfax cast a vote against universal suffrage is as plain. . . . If the people are against it what right have you to change the Government?"[30] Others believed that the party should try to immediately pass the Fifteenth Amendment as a way of taking "the everlasting negro question forever out of National politics."[31] Since no national election was to take place for another two years, now was the time for the Republicans to push through the constitutional amendment, and hope that it would lead Democrats to tone down their antiblack campaigns. The idea, according to Phyllis Field, was to take the issue out of politics by ending the matter once and for all: "The Republican party was already strongly identified with black suffrage and therefore always in danger of being hurt by the issue as long as it remained salient. . . . Successful evasion of the issue was not always possible, especially if Democrats were determined to keep it uppermost. . . . It was far more attractive to Republi-

---

[27] Ibid., 37. Also see Michael Les Benedict, *A Compromise of Principle: Congressional Republicans and Reconstruction, 1863–1869* (New York: W. W. Norton, 1974).

[28] As Eric Foner points out, the Democrats were still somewhat divided on the race issue as well. Two of the leading potential Democratic presidential candidates, George Pendleton and Chief Justice Salmon Chase, were supporters of black suffrage. See *Reconstruction*, 339.

[29] In the 1868 House of Representatives elections, Republicans lost three seats in New York and one seat in New Jersey. The party also lost three seats each in Ohio and Pennsylvania.

[30] *Congressional Globe*, Third Session, Fortieth Congress (January 28, 1869), 673.

[31] Quoted in Field, *The Politics of Race in New York*, 182.

cans to guarantee voting rights to *all* blacks, thereby removing the issue from politics altogether."[32]

Yet others in the Republican party, while perhaps recognizing the unpopularity of the bill, nonetheless pushed for its passage. As LaWanda and John Cox have argued, some Republican leaders pushed black suffrage "not because of political expediency but *despite* political risk."[33] For example, radical Senator Henry Wilson, a strong supporter of the Fifteenth Amendment, recognized that the battle for black suffrage had "cost the party . . . a quarter of a million votes. There is not to-day a square mile in the United States where the advocacy of the equal rights and privileges of those colored men has not been in the past and is not now unpopular." Nonetheless, "my doctrine is, no matter how unpopular it is, no matter what it costs, no matter whether it brings victory or defeat, it is our duty to hope on and struggle on and work on until we make the humblest citizen of the United States the peer and the equal in rights and privileges of every other citizen of the United States."[34] The author of the Fifteenth Amendment in the House, George Boutwell, recognized that "one tenth of the party are not in favor of [the Amendment], and they constitute the great obstacle in the way of perfecting this benign measure." He also believed the Republican party to have a "special duty which we owe to these black people" in the North who were not allowed to vote. Enabling blacks in the North to vote would not only provide 150,000 new voters in close northern states, but improve "his capacity to take care of himself in the South."[35] Senator Samuel Pomeroy responded to Wilson's comment regarding the loss of white votes by stating that "the strength of the Republican party consists in its adherence to principle, and to that embodiment of its principles, equality of the rights among men. . . . It was that for which it was organized; and instead of being a source of weakness it is, in my opinion, a source of strength and power."[36]

Still others in the party pointed out that Republicans continued to lose voters to the Democrats in 1868 despite a more moderate stance on the suffrage issue. Radical Republicans argued that the difference in Grant's popular vote margin was due to the overwhelmingly Republican African American vote.[37] One newspaper predicted that the ratification

---

[32] Ibid., 182.

[33] Cox and Cox, "Negro Suffrage," 317.

[34] *Congressional Globe*, Third Session, Fortieth Congress (January 28, 1869), 672. See also Benedict, *Compromise of Principle*, epilogue.

[35] *Congressional Globe*, Third Session, Fortieth Congress (January 23, 1869), 560–61.

[36] *Congressional Globe*, Third Session, Fortieth Congress (January 29, 1869), 708.

[37] Grant won the popular vote by a little more than 300,000 votes. Southern blacks

of the Fifteenth Amendment would assure the party electoral dominance in the future by adding close to one million new voters, while Charles Sumner argued before Congress that the party's difficulties in Connecticut would be resolved by giving suffrage rights to the state's three thousand black citizens.[38] Idealism, a still-strong belief within the party that black voters would add to Republican electoral totals, and a few significant concessions to moderate party members (allowing for state regulation of the suffrage) enabled the Radical Republicans to gather enough votes to pass the Fifteenth Amendment in February 1869.

If the elections of 1867 first notified Republican party leaders of potential trouble in the North, the elections of 1870 indicated the problems that they would face in the South, as an emboldened Democratic party made huge inroads in southern states such as Alabama and Georgia. These results followed elections in 1869, in which Virginians elected Democrats to the state legislature and governorship, and white Republicans in Tennessee successfully reached office by appeasing Democrats with the promises of refusing to enforce suffrage laws and of allowing former Confederates to vote.[39] Northern Republicans were divided over the necessary course of action. President Grant and the Republicans in Congress made some efforts to reinforce black voting in order to maintain electoral opportunities in the South. The Ku Klux Klan had used violence to intimidate a number of African Americans into abstaining from voting in states where blacks constituted large numbers of the population. In Alabama, Georgia, Mississippi, and South Carolina, violence was extraordinarily fierce, and election fraud was thorough.[40] In response, Congress and the president in 1871 passed the Enforcement Act, aimed to combat the Ku Klux Klan's terror over potential black voters. It gave the president power to call on federal troops and the courts the power to prosecute those who infringed black voting rights. Grant sent additional troops to many southern states in the attempt to protect the peace and potential Republican voters, and in most of these instances, the presence of troops was effective. Grant,

---

alone represented more than 450,000 voters. See William Gillette, *Retreat from Reconstruction, 1869–1879* (Baton Rouge: Louisiana State University Press, 1979), 40–41.

[38] Xi Wang, "Black Suffrage and Northern Republicans, 1865–1891" (Ph.D. dissertation, Columbia University, 1993), 101 and 87.

[39] Foner, *Reconstruction*, 413–14.

[40] See Edmund L. Drago, *Black Politicians and Reconstruction in Georgia* (Athens: University of Georgia Press, 1992), and in particular chapter 6; Vernon Lane Wharton, *The Negro in Mississippi, 1865–1890* (Chapel Hill: University of North Carolina Press, 1947); George Brown Tindall, *South Carolina Negroes, 1877–1900* (Columbia: University of South Carolina Press, 1952).

however, was generally reluctant to use force, preferring the states to handle problems locally.[41]

While the Enforcement Act was potentially an effective weapon, it increased division within the party over the long-term goals in the South. Voting rights supporters were powerful enough to pass another Enforcement Act in 1872, although the legislation, after suffering an initial defeat in the House, was limited in scope and effectiveness. For example, it prohibited federal marshals from making arrests at polling booths in rural areas with populations smaller than twenty thousand people.[42] The Liberal wing of the party, composed primarily of members from the northeast, wanted a more conciliatory policy toward southern whites. Liberals were upset with their party and with President Grant for a number of reasons, including tariff and civil service reform. But they targeted their anger at blacks, believing that they had misused their right to vote. They demanded literacy tests for national voters in order to rid the electoral system of what they saw as ignorant black voters in the South who were easily bribed.[43] They believed Grant was moving too slowly in his conciliation efforts with white southerners. Liberal Republicans opposed the Enforcement Acts and demanded an end to Reconstruction.

Liberal Republicans split from their party in 1872, endorsing Horace Greeley for president. Grant continued to use "bloody shirt" oratory to mobilize his party and won the election with the help of federal enforcement of Reconstruction policies in the South. Grant won all of the former Confederate states (albeit by close margins), with the exception of Georgia, Texas, and Tennessee. In House elections, the Republicans maintained the majority of seats in the delegations of seven southern states.[44] Nonetheless, after the election victory Grant began to promote further appeasement of southern whites. In his inaugural address of 1873, the president stated that "social equality is not a subject to be legislated upon, nor shall I ask that anything be done to advance the social status of the colored man, except to give him a fair chance to develop what there is good in him." In many instances, the administration gave out patronage in the South to white Democrats. In states with black majorities, Grant generally maintained support of black and Re-

---

[41] Gillette, *Retreat from Reconstruction*, chap. 4.

[42] Wang, "Black Suffrage," 170.

[43] See ibid., 160–64; William Gillette, "The Election of 1872," in Arthur M. Schlesinger, Jr., Fred L. Israel, and William P. Hansen, eds., *History of American Presidential Elections, 1789–1968* (New York: Chelsea House Publishers, 1971); and John G. Sproat, *"The Best Men": Liberal Reformers in the Gilded Age* (Chicago: University of Chicago Press, 1982).

[44] The seven states were Alabama, Florida, Louisiana, Mississippi, South Carolina, Tennessee, and Virginia.

publican voting rights. In states with white majorities, the president attempted to develop a coalition of white voters from both Republican and Democratic backgrounds, as well as some "independents." Often these coalitions, while providing opportunities for Republican party growth, were quite antagonistic to black voting rights.[45]

Virginia was perceived as the state where the Republican party had the greatest opportunity to make inroads among white voters. Grant's treatment of the emerging Radical Republican wing of the party suffered as a result. In 1870, Grant softened military enforcement in the state and agreed to accept a coalition of white conservatives to control the state legislature. While the president hoped that the conservatives would steer a moderate course between Radicals and Democrats while protecting black civil rights, the various independent movements quickly aligned with the Democrats' policy of "white man's rule." With Republicans outnumbered by a coalition of Democrats and moderate to conservative independents, Reconstruction policies were largely removed from the state legislative agenda. "Grant's policy of generosity, which amounted to appeasement," William Gillette writes, "succeeded only too well in disarming and destroying the Republican party in Virginia, which, along with its candidates, was obviously paralyzed by 1873."[46]

The 1874 elections continued a trend of northern voters turning against the Republican party in favor of the Democrats. Democrats took governorships in Ohio and Connecticut, giving them nineteen of twenty-five overall. The Republicans also lost control of the House of Representatives, as their power shifted from a majority of 110 to a minority of 60 seats. Academics still argue over whether voters were rejecting the Republican party's Reconstruction policies. Eric Foner, for instance, claims that the party's defeats were due more to an economic recession, while William Gillette claims that white voters used their votes as a referendum on Reconstruction.[47] Whatever the reason, the results led conservative Republicans to push more vehemently for restoration of southern governments, while Radical Republicans started to appear confused and fatalistic. While Henry Wilson remarked to William Lloyd Garrison at the time that "our Anti-slavery veterans must again speak out," most other Radicals were making concessions. Overt expressions of racism were becoming more commonplace in the public discourse of both parties, and more and more Republicans condemned Reconstruction as a failure.[48]

---

[45] Gillette, *Retreat from Reconstruction*, chaps. 4–7. With specific reference to South Carolina, see Thomas Holt, *Black over White: Negro Political Leadership in South Carolina during Reconstruction* (Urbana: University of Illinois Press, 1977), 177.

[46] Gillette, *Retreat from Reconstruction*, 83–85.

[47] Foner, *Free Soil*, 524–28; Gillette, *Retreat from Reconstruction*, 246–54.

[48] See Foner, *Free Soil*, 526–27. Wilson is quoted on 527.

President Grant's reaction to the continued widespread violence by the Klan was ambivalent. The Justice Department at this time curtailed prosecutions under the Enforcement Act. This occurred despite letters from black Republicans to Grant that made clear that without federal enforcement, widespread fraud and violence would allow for Democratic party victories. In some states, such as Louisiana, the president swiftly dispatched troops to put down white-on-black violence and uphold fair elections. In other states, such as Arkansas and Mississippi, the president resisted the request for federal troops while hundreds of potential black voters were killed in riots surrounding the 1875 election. One riot in Vicksburg, Mississippi resulted in the deaths of about three hundred African Americans.[49] The Republicans subsequently lost four of the state's House seats. With continuing violence by the Klan and voting fraud threatening Republicans in the 1876 election, the party once more tried to pass an enforcement act in 1875. This time they were defeated decisively by an opposition that included significant portions of their own party.

By 1876, the *New York Times* was commenting: "Wendell Phillips and William Lloyd Garrison are not exactly extinct forces in American politics, but they represent ideas in regard to the South which the great majority of the Republican party have outgrown."[50] The Supreme Court, moreover, was handing down a series of crushing decisions for the Reconstruction amendments. That year, *United States v. Reese* severely weakened any future efforts to enforce the Fifteenth Amendment and promote black suffrage in the region, as did the *Slaughterhouse-Cases*. Reconstruction officially ended, however, after the election of Republican Rutherford B. Hayes to the presidency. Hayes began the "let alone" policy toward the South. He withdrew federal troops from the region and continually proclaimed his support for local self-government, regardless of increasing reports of white-on-black violence. During his election campaign in 1876, Hayes rejected a "southern strategy"— Charles Nordhoff of the *New York Herald* had urged Hayes to confer "*quietly*" with "a few of the prominent old Whig leaders of the Southern states, . . . detach from the Democratic side down there the real Whig vote," and "without much trouble and with no embarrassing engagements, make sure of carrying Louisiana, North Carolina, Virginia, and Arkansas. . . . The darkies you'll have any how, the white

---

[49] After the riots, Grant did send troops to Vicksburgh. Williams C. Harris claims that "only a formal demonstration of military power was needed to reinstall (the government), reopen the courts, and dissolve the armed bands of whites in the country." See Harris, *The Day of the Carpetbagger: Republican Reconstruction in Mississippi* (Baton Rouge: Louisiana State University Press, 1979), 648.

[50] Quoted in Harvard Sitkoff, *A New Deal for Blacks* (New York: Oxford University Press, 1978), 3.

whigs are what you want to capture."[51] But once in office, the party lost the ability to enforce the voting rights of blacks in the region, and Hayes believed he had no choice other than to pursue different voters.

Hayes was ambivalent about the presence of federal troops in the South, at times vetoing efforts by congressional Democrats to rid the South of troops, but at other times arguing that only "peaceful methods" could "restore harmony and good feeling between sections and races."[52] In 1878, for instance, Hayes asked Congress for money to enforce election laws in the South. After being rebuffed, he backed down and remained optimistic that elections would be fair. Although he continually proclaimed support for black voting rights and pushed education policies to allow "intelligent" blacks to participate in southern politics, he initiated no legislative measures to protect these rights and generally prided himself on having "divided" the region's white vote for competition between the two major parties.[53] (The continuing failure of the Republicans to win, however, led Hayes to feel some regrets. After further violence, intimidation, and fraud led to more inroads for the Southern Democrats in the 1878 midterm elections, Hayes wrote in his diary, "if there had been free and fair elections in [all] the states during the last few years, there would now be Republican majorities in both Houses of Congress.")[54]

After successive attempts to veto Democrats' efforts at further weakening federal enforcement of African American voting rights, Hayes renewed efforts to compromise with southern whites. Similar to Grant, Hayes attempted to forge ties with various movements of moderate Republicans, Democrats, and independents in the region. These movements consisted of whites who were largely disgruntled with what they perceived to be extreme positions of both the Democrats and Republicans on the race issue. Hayes appointed General David Key as postmaster general in the hope of resurrecting old Whig elements in the region. In the fall of 1879, Republican leaders attempted to embrace William Mahone of Virginia. Mahone had only a year earlier led a revolt against the state's Democratic party and formed an independent "Readjuster" party. He was later elected to the U.S. Senate in 1880 with substantial Republican support and identified himself in the Senate as a member of the party. White Republicans, in particular, saw independent move-

[51] Quoted in Ari Hoogenboom, *The Presidency of Rutherford B. Hayes* (Lawrence: University of Kansas Press, 1988), 19.

[52] Quoted ibid., 60.

[53] See Rayford W. Logan, *The Betrayal of the Negro* (New York: Collier, 1954), 46. Also see Hoogenboom, *Presidency of Hayes*, chap. 3.

[54] From Charles Richard Williams, ed., *Diary and Letters of Rutherford Birchard Hayes* (Columbus, Ohio: F. J. Heer, 1924), 533–34.

ments like Mahone's as potential opportunities to shed themselves of the stigma of being attached to black Republicans and, in the process, to reach out to white Democrats disgruntled with their party's positions on nonracial matters. By removing race as a potentially contestable issue, white Republicans and independents hoped to win elections based on their differences with the Democrats on largely economic matters.

By the end of the Hayes administration, more and more southern Republicans had joined with conservative Democrats to form independent movements. Hayes helped bolster the independents against black Republican opposition by providing a great deal of patronage, including creating positions of election officials in charge of monitoring possible voting violations.[55] One of the severest critics of Hayes's policies in the South, William Chandler, argued at the time that reaching out to independents had effectively "resulted in the enforced dissolution of the Republican party at the South."[56] By 1880, while a majority of blacks continued to vote in all southern states except Mississippi and Georgia, an estimated 4 million southern blacks had been effectively disenfranchised. While the Republican party would remain internally divided over African American civil and voting rights, successive Republican presidents from Chester Arthur to Herbert Hoover continued to attempt to build coalitions among disgruntled southern white Democrats.[57]

THE COMPETITIVE REPUBLICAN PARTY
IN SOUTHERN STATE-LEVEL POLITICS

Throughout the 1870s, the national Republican party divided over the proper course of action to take toward the resurgence of southern white violence against blacks. As we saw in the last section, a significant part of this ambivalence was based on fears of electoral losses in northern states, which led to a mixed record of enforcement and aid to southern Republican movements. Such ambivalence on the part of the national party was often all that was necessary for southern Republican regimes faced with threats of violence to fall apart. The party in the South, meanwhile, already had divisions within its own ranks between whites and blacks, which made it additionally fragile. State party leaders in the

[55] Gillette, *Retreat from Reconstruction*, chap. 14.

[56] Quoted in Woodward, *Origins of the New South*, 100.

[57] See Stanley P. Hirshson, *Farewell to the Bloody Shirt: Northern Republicans and the Southern Negro, 1877–1893* (Bloomington: Indiana University Press, 1962), chaps. 5 and 8; Woodward, *Origins of the New South*, chap. 4; Vincent P. De Santis, *Republicans Face the Southern Question: The New Departure Years, 1877–1897* (Baltimore: Johns Hopkins University Press, 1957); and Logan, *Betrayal of the Negro*.

South, both black and white, recognized that they would need to reach out to white voters in order to maintain majorities in most areas. Moreover, they recognized that many southern white voters would resist a coalition that included a significant number of blacks. White Republican leaders feared that their party's emphasis on black issues would make coalition building difficult, if not impossible. For this reason, and because many of the leaders held strongly racist feelings toward their black colleagues, whites would fight internally with blacks. Party competition, then, served to exacerbate an already tense and difficult situation. As party organizations in the region broke down as a result of internal strife, northern Radical Republicans saw their strategic arguments for legitimating the enforcement of Reconstruction further weakened.

In state after state in the South, the Republican party was divided between black and white groups. Faced with a unified and overwhelmingly white opposition, white-dominated Republican movements in states from Arkansas to Florida to Texas formed and eventually split from predominantly black wings of the party.[58] Louisiana Republicans, for instance, began to split apart over the passage of a new constitution in 1868. At the time, a majority of blacks successfully overcame intimidation and violence as well as 90 percent turnout from white voters to pass laws intended to enforce integration. Soon after, however, a white Republican governor — despite being elected by a coalition that consisted of primarily black voters — vetoed a series of bills designed to prevent racial discrimination in public places out of fear that it would provoke widespread violence. After a great deal of internal fighting, the Republican party formally split in 1872 between the Radicals and the Reformers. Republicans lost two seats in the House in the 1874 elections and lost a third in 1876. At the state level, the Radicals initially survived the internal party fighting and maintained control over the state government until the election of 1876 and the subsequent end of Reconstruction. President Grant intervened in 1875, using federal troops to remove Democrats from the legislature. After the troops were removed from the state, the Democratic party wrested back control through both the use of extreme violence and simultaneous appeals to black voters that if elected, they would maintain peace. Only an occasional Republican would be elected in Louisiana after 1876.[59]

[58] See Perman, *Road to Reconstruction*, chap. 2.

[59] In the Senate, William Kellogg was the last Republican representative, leaving office in 1883. In the House, the Republicans elected four members after 1876: Chester Darrall from the third district in 1880; William Kellogg from the third district in 1882; Michael Hahn from the second district in 1884; and Dudley Coleman from the second district in 1888. See Roger A. Fischer, *The Segregation Struggle in Louisiana, 1862–1877* (Urbana:

Similar internal party fights occurred in South Carolina, as black Republicans fought for control of federal patronage while white Republicans feared a backlash against the nomination of too many blacks to political office. When white Republicans were defeated either at the polls or in party nominations, they often abandoned the party for the Democrats. Even though black and white party members had remained unified in a successful 1870 election, white Republicans left their state's nominating conventions in both 1872 and 1874, and held their own instead.[60] In 1874, Independent Republicans and Democrats came within 12,000 votes of defeating the regular Republican party in the gubernatorial race. In the two years following, Republican Governor Daniel Chamberlain moved further toward conciliation with white Republicans and Democrats, leading to additional splits with black members of the party. Chamberlain replaced a number of Republican officeholders with Democrats, refused to sanction the legislature's election of an abolitionist judge to the Charleston circuit, and generally overlooked the Democrats' steadily increasing control of the Republican party. In 1876, South Carolina's elections were obscured by violence and disputes over vote counts. Factions in the party, both black versus white and black versus black, weakened the party's substantial electoral majority. As Thomas Holt writes, "The desertions of [Republican] legislators and judges at critical junctures while the party was fighting for its political life point up the fundamental failure of the Republicans to unite their disparate forces and to create a political culture in which solidarity was a virtue."[61] After President Hayes decided not to send in troops to protect the Republican government, Reconstruction ended in South Carolina. Despite the fact that African Americans constituted majorities in all seven of the state's congressional districts, only two Republicans were elected to the House of Representatives after 1876. Both of these members were elected for only one term and both were from the state's seventh district, which was 81 percent black.

In Mississippi, where a majority black population seemingly offered opportunities for the Republicans' electoral success, blacks fought openly for control of the party with whites. When black party members asserted themselves in the mid-1870s and received the support of Governor Adelbert Ames, large numbers of white Republicans, aided by Democratic intimidation and ostracism, crossed over to the Democratic

---

University of Illinois Press, 1974); and Charles Vincent, *Black Legislators in Louisiana during Reconstruction* (Baton Rouge: Louisiana State University Press, 1976).

[60] See Hanes Walton, Jr., *Black Republicans: The Politics of the Black and Tans* (Metuchen, N.J.: Scarecrow Press, 1975), 108–12.

[61] Holt, *Black over White*, 175.

party.[62] At times, black voters were intimidated into voting for the Democratic party with threats of unemployment, violence, and even death. Riots against both black and white Republicans became a frequent part of Mississippi politics in the mid-1870s. Attempts by federal marshals to use the Enforcement Acts to protect black voters against corruption and intimidation generally failed.[63] When black politicians and Governor Ames requested protection, the federal government responded with indifference if not hostility to the idea of federal intervention. Ames recognized as much, writing at the time that "I am fully alive to the fact that my action [the call for troops] will be like an exploding shell in the political canvass in the North."[64] As Vernon Wharton recounts, "In the final moment of his decision, [President] Grant was visited by a delegation of politicians from Ohio, a pivotal state which was to have an election in October. Mississippi, these visitors declared, was already lost to the party; troops would arrive too late to save the state. Even worse, the order that sent troops to Mississippi would mean the loss of Ohio to the party. The Negroes must be sacrificed."[65] Grant ultimately refused the request for federal troops, and the state of Ohio would play a crucial role in Rutherford Hayes's defeat of Samuel Tilden in the 1876 presidential election. Hayes won the state's twenty-two electoral college votes by a total of 7,000 popular votes out of more than 650,000 cast. The subsequent violence and intimidation in the state of Mississippi were among the worst in the South, and the Democrats swept the state's elections. As one U.S. marshal, James Pierce, wrote at the time, "almost the entire white population of Mississippi is one vast mob. . . . If Republicans had been allowed to vote as they wished, and without being threatened in all manner of ways, beaten and killed, Mississippi would have voted for Hayes by [a] 20,000 majority."[66]

Republicans further contributed to their electoral problems in Mississippi by dividing over race and personal feuds. In some of the state's counties, the Republican party had two candidates running against each other. Black and white Republicans vied for control of local offices and patronage, leading in one instance to the death of two black politicians who were battling with white party members for control of their

---

[62] See Wharton, *Negro in Mississippi*, chap. 13.

[63] See Stephen Cresswell, "Enforcing the Enforcement Acts: The Department of Justice in Northern Mississippi, 1870–1890," *Journal of Southern History* 53 (August 1987).

[64] As quoted in Hayes, *Diaries and Letters*, 667.

[65] Wharton, *Negro in Mississippi*, 193. Also see John Roy Lynch, who claims that years later President Grant told him that Ohio was the decisive reason for not intervening: John Hope Franklin, ed., *Reminscences of an Active Life: The Autobiography of John Roy Lynch* (Chicago: University of Chicago Press, 1970), 144–45.

[66] James H. Pierce as quoted in Cresswell, "Enforcing the Enforcement Acts," 429–30.

county. In other counties, black politicians were divided among themselves, leading to a split of the black electorate. While President Grant debated sending troops to the state on Governor Ames's request, an anti-Ames faction countered this move with intense lobbying of their own. James Garner claims that by election time, "less than a baker's dozen of the prominent Republican leaders who had a substantial interest in the welfare of the state were supporters of Governor Ames in the election of 1875."[67] David Donald claims that "the greatest accession of Democratic strength came from the thousands of so-called scalawags — mostly former Whigs — who now denounced the Republican party and voted on the color-line."[68]

In Alabama, white Republicans also pushed for a moderate, white-dominated party. In 1870, the white Republican candidate for governor denounced black voters in an attempt to appeal to white Democrats. Federal intervention by President Grant at the time protected black interests and restored Republicans to power. A few years later, however, when faced with similar divisiveness between blacks and whites, the president did not send in federal troops. An attempt by black Republicans to hold their own convention and nominate their own candidates failed, and the party's white-dominated faction nominated a governor who ran on a platform declaring "the Republican party does not desire mixed schools or mixed accommodations for the colored people; but we ask for them that in all of these the advantages shall be equal."[69] As the Democratic party attacked the Republicans as a black party, Republicans responded with accusations that the Democrats also were pursuing black votes.[70] Democrats capitalized on the divisions within the Republican party and won the elections in 1874 with the additional help of rampant fraud and violence. Meanwhile, black Republicans made repeated requests for national government intervention, but received no response.

North Carolina Republicans, initially dominant in many areas of the state in the early 1870s, were continually plagued by interracial turmoil until the end of the century, when whites fled the party en masse for the Democrats. Often the Democrats stirred up Republican divisiveness. Democrats would encourage black leaders to take control of the GOP, and then point out with vigor the hypocrisy of white Republicans resisting their black colleagues. At the same time, Democrats used their in-

---

[67] James W. Garner, *Reconstruction in Mississippi* (London: Macmillan, 1901), 398.

[68] David H. Donald, "The Scalawag in Mississippi Reconstruction," *Journal of Southern History* 10 (1944): 459.

[69] Quoted in Allen Johnston Going, *Bourbon Democracy in Alabama* (Montgomery: University of Alabama Press, 1951), 12.

[70] Ibid., 15.

creasing power in the state legislature to disable Republican electoral opportunities. State Republicans, however, had plenty of internal divisions to deal with, regardless of Democratic efforts of manipulation. When a black Republican, James O'Hara, ran for Congress in North Carolina's second district in 1878, the party's whites and blacks divided into two competing electoral factions, leaving the district with its first Democratic representative in the post-Reconstruction era, despite an overwhelmingly Republican and black population. In response to the *New York Times* argument that the election was stolen by the Democrats through sheer corruption, O'Hara replied that "in my defeat, or rather my being counted out, the Republicans had more to do with it than the Democrats, and I say that the colored Republicans of the South have more to fear from the white Republicans than from the Democrats."[71] While black Republicans were able to maintain some degree of control over the district until 1900, the loss of white Republicans combined with the efforts of the white supremacy movements in the Democratic party eventually proved too much to overcome. In the 1892 election, white Republican leaders refused to support the state ticket because they believed it presented the party "as traitors to our race, aliens, an infamous, degraded set trying to put the state under Negro rule."[72] In the 1900 election, a leading white Republican announced that "when the test of his Republicanism was that he must vote for a negro then he was no longer a Republican."[73] Fewer than 40 of the party's 240 delegates at the state convention that year were black, and the party did little to maintain black voting rights in the face of Democratic party amendments at this time to restrict these rights.[74]

In Georgia, whites and blacks in the Republican party began to split in the late 1860s, shortly after the passage of Reconstruction measures in the region. Georgia was the site of intense violence by the KKK toward the Republican party, initially disenfranchising many blacks during the early stages of Reconstruction. A poll tax and registration requirements, coupled with the decision in September 1868 by a majority Republican legislature to expel elected black representatives, severely diminished black opportunities in the state. After the black elected officials were expelled, Democrats who had lost to them during electoral campaigns were named in their place. These decisions effectively gave

[71] Quoted in Anderson, *Race and Politics*, 73. For broader discussion of the period, see chaps. 2 and 3. O'Hara did eventually win congressional office from the district in 1882 and held office for two terms.

[72] J. J. Mott, quoted in Frenise A. Logan, *The Negro in North Carolina, 1876–1894* (Chapel Hill: University of North Carolina Press, 1964), 19.

[73] Quoted in Anderson, *Race and Politics*, 300.

[74] Ibid., 302–6.

the Democrats large enough numbers in the legislature to dominate any Republican program. White Republicans, meanwhile, tried to form their own party, claiming that blacks were corrupt and were the chief cause of party dissension.[75] As Edmund Drago writes, "With the expulsion of the blacks from the legislature, conditions in Georgia rapidly deteriorated. The expulsion emboldened the Ku Klux Klan to greater acts of violence, and the legislature passed several anti-Negro measures, including one that specifically excluded blacks from the jury box."[76]

After Grant lost Georgia in the 1868 presidential election, the Republicans began to look into strengthening voting rights enforcement and placed the state back under military rule. White Republicans in the state stressed that this would ruin their opportunities to continue to pursue white voters. In December 1869, Congress passed an act that returned Georgia to military jurisdiction and required that the black legislators return to their seats. Governor Bullock attempted to protect black rights while recognizing that such action was "intensely unpopular at the time, and . . . large numbers of white men who had accepted the reconstruction policy, condemned my course in behalf of the colored men and withdrew from the party."[77] Yet in elections at the state level in 1871, the Republicans lost badly, as they again found themselves internally split between blacks and whites, at times running two different candidates for office. State Republicans divided again the following year. Many party members joined Liberal Republicans in declaring their support in the national election for Horace Greeley and in the state gubernatorial race for the Democratic candidate.[78] Shortly after, the party would more formally split between "Lily-White" and "Black-and-Tan" factions. Meanwhile, President Grant and the national party were making fewer efforts to maintain the party's hold on the state, refusing to provide financial assistance for elections or protection for party politicians.[79] In 1874, the Democrats would win eight of nine congressional seats, after failing to win a single seat only two years earlier. Blacks maintained a substantial voting presence in the state until the early 1900s, when an increasingly competitive Populist party helped lead the

---

[75] Judson C. Ward, Jr., "The Republican Party in Bourbon Georgia," *Journal of Southern History* 9 (1943): 208.

[76] Edmund L. Drago, *Black Politicians and Reconstruction*, 51. Also see Foner, *Free Soil*; and Theodore Barker Fitz-Simons, Jr., "The Camilla Riot," *Georgia Historical Quarterly* 35 (June 1951): 116–25.

[77] Quoted in Russell Duncan, "A Georgia Governor Battles Racism: Rufus Bullock and the Fight for Black Legislators," in John C. Inscoe, *Georgia in Black and White* (Athens: University of Georgia Press, 1994), 45.

[78] See Olive Hall Shadgett, *The Republican Party in Georgia: From Reconstruction through 1900* (Athens: University of Georgia Press, 1964), chaps. 3–4.

[79] Gillette, *Retreat from Reconstruction*, 89–90.

charge toward the passing of disenfranchisement amendments in the Georgia legislature.[80]

I have presented in this section a rather elaborate state-by-state discussion of the Republican party in order to illustrate how critical racial divisions were in weakening an already fragile party organization in the South. The violence and racism associated with the region's Democratic party played only a role in the Democrats' achieving electoral dominance in the region. But Republicans, motivated by a combination of racism and a perception that their party's attachment to black voters and interests was hurting their electoral opportunities, consistently resisted entering into coalitions with black Republicans. Absent the ability to join a majority-based coalition, and often absent support from the national party leadership for help, black Republicans found themselves significantly disempowered as they attempted to fight the widespread Democratic party abuses in electoral politics. By the 1880s, with black Republican leaders marginalized and with fewer and fewer black voters participating in elections, national Republican leaders were able to futher legitimate the pursuit of electoral strategies that largely excluded black interests.

THE NATIONAL REPUBLICAN PARTY FROM GARFIELD TO HARRISON

The Republican party remained divided between Radicals and conservatives in the 1880 presidential election. A compromise choice, James Garfield, was selected on the thirty-sixth ballot after a long nomination fight between pro–civil rights enforcer James Blaine and the more conciliatory, former president Ulysses Grant. Garfield stressed the need to maintain voting rights enforcement in the South, arguing in his acceptance of the nomination that no peace could be restored until "every citizen, rich or poor, white or black, is secure in the free and equal enjoyment of every civil and political right guaranteed by the Constitution and the laws."[81] While Garfield struggled with what his role should be in protecting black voters, he also followed the Grant and Hayes administrations in exploring the various opportunities to woo disaffected southern white Democrats.

[80] See Korobkin, "Politics of Disenfranchisment," for a fascinating account of the disenfranchisement fight in the Georgia state legislature. Three competing groups, Populists, reform Democrats, and Democrats, all fighting for political power, worked both with and against each other in a political campaign designed to further each of their own electoral motives. The result was the disenfranchisement of blacks in 1908.

[81] Quoted in Wang, "Black Suffrage," 347.

The most prominent opportunity for the Republican party continued to be the independent movement in Virginia, the Readjuster party led by William Mahone. The alliance between the Republicans and Mahone allowed the Republicans to maintain a hold on the post-1882 Senate with thirty-eight Republicans (including Mahone), thirty-seven Democrats, and one Independent who generally voted with the Democrats. As Garfield debated whether to reach out to Mahone, the Virginia Republican party endorsed the senator, and later the Democratic Readjuster ticket in 1881. By this time, Chester Arthur, initially chosen by the Republican party as its vice presidential candidate to balance Garfield's secretary of state, James Blaine, had replaced the assassinated Garfield as the chief executive. Arthur and other Republican leaders reached out more aggressively to potential independents in the South and, in fact, went so far as to embrace them as the new leaders of the Republican party in the region.[82]

Arthur's first annual message as president focused primarily on foreign affairs. No mention was made of southern white intimidation in the voting booth, and what mention was made of southern blacks focused on an increase in education efforts.[83] More tangibly, Arthur wooed southern whites by providing federal patronage to independent movements, once again in an effort to split the white Democratic party. By the elections of 1882, Republicans felt that they needed twenty members of Congress from the South to maintain majority control of the House, and many in the Arthur administration felt this would be possible only through encouraging Independent Democrats to join the Republican party. Secretary of the Navy, William Chandler, the same man who had so actively opposed Hayes's policies in the South just a few years earlier, now had become convinced that "our straight Republican, carpet-bag, negro governments, whether fairly or unfairly, have been destroyed and cannot be revived. Without these coalitions or support of independents, we cannot carry Southern votes enough to save the House from Bourbon democratic control, and carry the next presidential fight. Beyond that, the safety of the colored race while exercising the suffrage depends upon the new departure. . . . You do not think that we can accomplish anything there without more white votes? How are we to get them if not by the practical movements now in progress?"[84]

Some northern Republicans resisted this logic, believing that few congressional seats or electoral votes were to be gained in the South and

[82] Vincent P. De Santis, "President Arthur and the Independent Movements in the South in 1882," *Journal of Southern History* 19 (August 1953): 346–63.

[83] Quoted in Wang, "Black Suffrage," 376.

[84] Quoted in De Santis, "Arthur and the Independent Movements," 350.

that support of the independent movements had hurt the civil rights of southern blacks. Arthur, however, was buoyed by the success of the Readjusters in Virginia, and he continued his support of the Independent Democrats as well as of many Greenback movements in the region. He believed that efforts of this sort to form new alliances deserved, and would receive, the blessing of the national party.[85] Some of the movements that Arthur supported did either directly or indirectly support black rights. The Readjuster-dominated Virginia legislature during this time passed laws designed to aid black education and voting rights in the state. But Arthur also assisted a number of former Confederates, angering black leaders in the process. Arthur, for instance, endorsed and provided federal patronage for General James Chalmers, the Independent leader in Mississippi. Chalmers was one of the leaders responsible for the "Fort Pillow massacre," where southern military men in 1864 murdered a regiment of Union black soldiers attempting to surrender. Secretary Chandler was convinced by white Republicans in the state to work toward making Chalmers the "Mahone" of Mississippi.[86] In Georgia, meanwhile, Arthur agreed to proposals that he shift federal patronage to an independent movement being led in part by General Longstreet and James Atkins, both of whom supported the expulsion of blacks from the state's Republican party. These independent leaders, in turn, worked to replace the black leader of the state Republican party, William Pledger, with a white member of the Independent party.[87] Arthur's appeal to independents did not have widespread success in the 1882 election. Overall in the region, eight independents were elected to the House in 1882, along with eight Republicans. These independents were enough, however, to provide the party with a slim congressional majority for the next two years.

The appeal by four consecutive Republican presidents to the various independent movements in the South is noteworthy because it reveals the degree that blacks' status as a captured group was not simply the product of electoral strategy. In this instance, Arthur and the Republican party clearly had alternative opportunities to win the additional twenty congressional seats. African Americans in 1882 constituted majorities in thirty-four congressional districts throughout the South, despite efforts by the Democrats to redraw the district lines in ways that

[85] In Mississippi, for instance, the Greenback party received over 50,000 votes to the Democrats' 77,700 in the 1881 governor's race. For discussion of Arthur's appeals to independents in the South, see Doenecke, *Presidencies of Garfield and Arthur,* 114–24.

[86] Woodward, *Origins of the New South,* 102–4. Chalmers was elected in 1882 to the House of Representatives.

[87] Shadgett, *Republican Party in Georgia,* chap. 7.

packed large numbers of African American voters into single districts. (It was not until the 1960s that the Supreme Court, in *Wesberry v. Sanders*, ruled that all congressional districts in a state had to be of roughly equal population. Prior to this decision, racial gerrymandering was a very popular way among southern Democrats to reduce black representation).[88] In ten other districts, blacks constituted more than 45 percent of the population (see table 3.1).[89] In the 1882 elections, Republicans won only three of these thirty-four House seats, and an additional seat from a district in which blacks constituted 48 percent of the population (Virginia's first district). Three of these seats were won by Readjuster candidates in Virginia, and the other was from the second district in North Carolina. The Republicans also won three other Readjuster seats in the Virginia elections, and these seven party victories allowed the Republicans to maintain the balance of power in the House of Representatives (147 to 135). As mentioned before, the Readjuster candidate, Mahone, provided the difference in a Senate body that was otherwise tied (37 to 37 to 1).

In the process, however, the national Republican party simply gave up roughly thirty House seats, not to mention six Senate seats from the three states in which blacks constituted a majority. Between 1877 and 1880, these House seats cost the Republican party majority control of the House. In 1884, the three states with African American majorities alone would have been enough to provide the balance of power in the presidential race. Note in figure 3.1, that these three states — Mississippi, Louisiana, and South Carolina — would have provided the twenty-six electoral college votes sufficient to give James Blaine the presidency over Democratic candidate Grover Cleveland.

The Republican party did not contest these states for a number of reasons. Violence and intimidation were intense in all three states, making it extremely difficult for the Republican party to survive, let alone win. Protection of black voters would have necessitated a much more forceful response. In states such as Mississippi, South Carolina, and Georgia, the battle to protect black suffrage had already been largely lost. What was left of the Republican party in these states was largely divided between black and white factions.[90] Northern Republicans,

---

[88] See J. Morgan Kousser, "The Voting Rights Act and the Two Reconstructions," in Bernard Grofman and Chandler Davidson, eds., *Controversies in Minority Voting* (Washington, D.C.: Brookings Institution, 1992), 144.

[89] Population data are gathered from Stanley B. Parsons, Michael J. Dubin, and Karen Toombs Parsons, *United States Congressional Districts, 1893–1913* (New York: Greenwood Press, 1990).

[90] Although it should be pointed out that blacks did continue to vote in some of these

TABLE 3.1

Southern Congressional Districts in 1883 with
Majority or Near Majority African American
Populations (percentages)

Majority Districts	Near Majority Districts
AL 1 55.3 (D)	FL 1 47.7 (D)
AL 2 50.4 (D)	FL 2 46.3 (D)
AL 3 54.9 (D)	GA 5 48.6 (D)
AL 4 80.5 (D)	MD 5 47.8 (D)
GA 1 53.3 (D)	MS 1 49.2 (D)
GA 2 55.9 (D)	NC 1 47.1 (D)
GA 3 55.1 (D)	NC 4 45.8 (D)
GA 4 50.5 (D)	VA 1 48.2 (R)
GA 6 56.6 (D)	VA 3 49.1 (D)
GA 8 59.0 (D)	VA 6 47.2 (D)
GA 10 61.0 (D)	
LA 1 59.5 (D)	
LA 2 65.6 (R)	
LA 3 50.0 (D)	
LA 4 59.1 (D)	
LA 5 67.8 (D)	
LA 6 56.8 (D)	
MS 2 53.7 (D)	
MS 4 53.8 (D)	
MS 5 51.6 (D)	
MS 6 52.6 (D)	
MS 7 64.5 (D)	
NC 2 61.2 (R)	
SC 1 69.9 (D)	
SC 2 63.0 (D)	
SC 3 52.3 (D)	
SC 4 56.0 (D)	
SC 5 57 1 (D)	
SC 6 56.6 (D)	
SC 7 81.7 (R)	
TE 10 55.9 (R)	
VA 2 55.3 (R)	
VA 4 64.7 (R)	

however, were continually divided about providing such support. Many
held racist opinions of blacks and believed that they were incapable of
making rational decisions anyway.[91] Perhaps Republicans, moreover, believed that defending the African American right to vote in the South
was simply too costly for vote-gathering efforts in the North. The Re-

areas. In Mississippi, for instance, black votes were significant in the defeat of Independent candidate James Chalmers. See Doenecke, *Presidencies of Garfield and Arthur*; Kousser, *The Shaping of Southern Politics*.

[91] Morton Keller, for instance, argues that one of the incentives for Republicans to
improve racial conditions in the South was their fear and opposition to blacks migrating
to the North. *Affairs of State*, 143. Also see Field, *Politics of Race*, 163.

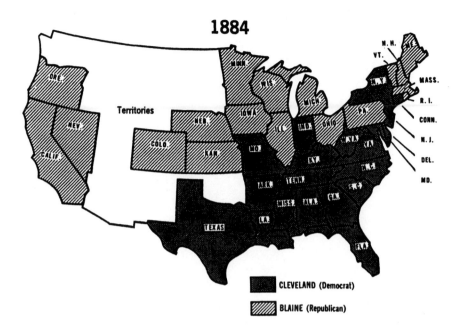

States	Electoral Votes	Cleveland	Blaine	States	Electoral Votes	Cleveland	Blaine
Alabama	(10)	10	-	Mississippi	(9)	9	-
Arkansas	(7)	7	-	Missouri	(16)	16	-
California	(8)	-	8	Nebraska	(5)	-	5
Colorado	(3)	-	3	Nevada	(3)	-	3
Connecticut	(6)	6	-	New Hampshire	(4)	-	4
Delaware	(3)	3	-	New Jersey	(9)	9	-
Florida	(4)	4	-	New York	(36)	36	-
Georgia	(12)	12	-	North Carolina	(11)	11	-
Illinois	(22)	-	22	Ohio	(23)	-	23
Indiana	(15)	15	-	Oregon	(3)	-	3
Iowa	(13)	-	13	Pennsylvania	(30)	-	30
Kansas	(9)	-	9	Rhode Island	(4)	-	4
Kentucky	(13)	13	-	South Carolina	(9)	9	-
Louisiana	(8)	8	-	Tennessee	(12)	12	-
Maine	(6)	-	6	Texas	(13)	13	-
Maryland	(8)	8	-	Vermont	(4)	-	4
Massachusetts	(14)	-	14	Virginia	(12)	12	-
Michigan	(13)	-	13	West Virginia	(6)	6	-
Minnesota	(7)	-	7	Wisconsin	(11)	-	11
				Totals	**(401)**	**219**	**182**

3.1 The electoral college vote in 1884. Congressional Quarterly, *Congressional Quarterly's Guide to U.S. Elections* (Washington, D.C.: CQ, 1975).

publican party recognized that reaching out to southern blacks not only
was extremely difficult, but that it could potentially disrupt their northern coalition.

As we will see in chapter 4, there is a degree to which the general una-
nimity of black support for the Republican party in the South hurt their
longer-term goals. Not that there was much choice: Democratic party
appeals to blacks at this time were generally exceptional and blacks
quite understandably were skeptical of such entreaties. A few African
American leaders also attempted to reach out to the Democratic party,
either out of frustration with the Republican party, or in an effort to
maintain some degree of political representation. Black leaders such as
Peter Clark in Cincinnati urged blacks in 1872 to vote not along party
lines but for candidates who offered jobs. In the mid-1880s, Clark felt
blacks would be mistaken to antagonize a Democratic party that held
power over the national government.[92] George T. Downing asked black
voters in Rhode Island in the 1870s, "Would any party treat a corresponding strength as the Republican party treats its black strength?"
Most African American leaders refused to support the Democrats because of the party's continued stance against the enforcement of civil
rights in the South. Frederick Douglass, for instance, responded to
Downing that "comparisons between the two parties are simply revolt-
ing."[93] Independent campaigns by black politicians also failed. Edward
Shaw, a prominent Memphis black leader, received only 165 votes
against a white Republican incumbent.[94] While Republican neglect did
drive blacks to vote for Democrats and Independents in some local and
state elections, and led others to support antigovernment self-help strategies, most for better or worse felt that they had little choice but to
remain "field hands" for the Republican party.[95]

By 1884, federal enforcement of election laws had declined significantly. Arrests for voting fraud in the South declined by more than 200
percent between 1880 and 1884.[96] With black voters in the region becoming increasingly scarce, the party tried to focus its attention on eco-

[92] David A. Gerber, *Black Ohio and the Color Line, 1860–1915* (Urbana: University of
Illinois Press, 1976), 233.

[93] Quoted in Grossman, *The Democratic Party and the Negro*, 39. Douglass would later
say during the Arthur administration that he was an "uneasy Republican."

[94] See Walter J. Fraser, Jr., "Black Reconstructionists in Tennessee," *Tennessee Historical
Quarterly* 34 (Winter 1975): 362–82.

[95] See Foner, *Free Soil*, 545. The term "field hands" comes from Frederick Douglass's
description of his own role during Reconstruction.

[96] Scott C. James and Brian L. Lawson, "The Political Economy of Voting Rights Enforcement in America's Gilded Age," *American Political Science Review* (forthcoming).

nomic issues in the national elections. Using such a strategy, Benjamin Harrison not only won the 1888 national election for the Republican party, he also received more southern votes than any Republican candidate prior. Harrison won the state of West Virginia and lost the states of Virginia, North Carolina, and Tennessee by extremely slim margins. Most of the credit for these southern votes went to the party's economic policies. The Republicans promised a tariff to bolster the national economy. A number of party leaders believed that this was the most electorally profitable way for the party to continue. In fact, many leading Republicans rejected attempts at keeping the "bloody shirt" slogan on the party platform, arguing that it would limit the party's ability to attract newcomers on the basis of the tariff. Prominent party leader Grenville Dodge commented, "I think if you keep on with this [bloody shirt] policy that you won't lose 8 to 10% of the Republicans . . . but will lose 25% of them."[97] In accepting the party nomination, Harrison stated that blacks desired only "the common rights of American citizenship" and were uninterested in special legislation that might protect their interests. Meanwhile, with the Republicans' victory in West Virginia, the *New York World* proclaimed that "the race question appears to have been eliminated from politics."[98]

The race question remained a pressing concern for some whites in the Republican party as late as 1890. Many Radical Republicans, in fact, viewed the national victory in 1888 as an opportunity to bolster electoral laws in the South, and their victories over both the House and Senate gave them the numbers to do so. The Radicals had become increasingly vocal about the fact that the Fifteenth Amendment over the years had resulted in thirty-eight new seats for the Democratic party as a result of black disenfranchisement in the South. William Chandler, back in the Senate and focusing attention on black suffrage shortly before the 1888 election, maintained that disenfranchisement had given the South and the Democratic party the opportunity to secure not only the three branches of national government, but "manufacturing and all other industries in the North. It means to hold in its hands the decision of all our national questions, those of foreign policy, tariff, finance, internal improvements, and all expenditures."[99]

Yet the majority of Republican leaders during the Harrison administration believed their party's efforts to avoid race were having a positive impact on southern whites, as Alabama Democratic congressman Wil-

---

[97] Quoted in Hirshson, *Farewell to the Bloody Shirt*, 208.

[98] Ibid., 156–67.

[99] William E. Chandler, *Congressional Record* (August 23, 1888), Fiftieth Congress, First Session, 7878.

liam Oates attested in 1889: "Sometimes I feel I am more of a Republican than Democrat. . . . If the Republican party can eliminate the race question from its politics, remove from our people the danger of local negro domination, it can have several Southern states for the asking."[100] Southern independents were also emboldened by the party's new stance and, with approval from Harrison, moved to take further control of the party's southern wing despite objections from black and Radical Republicans. As they had with previous attempts, the national party found that independent movements most often led to great Democratic party victories. Independent movements continued to divide the Republicans and had only limited success appealing to white Democrats.

The Federal Elections Bill of 1890 would be the last attempt by significant portions of the Republican party to enforce voting rights for southern blacks. Led by Henry Cabot Lodge and labeled by opponents as the "Force Bill," the legislation authorized federal officials to oversee any electoral district where a specified number of voters petitioned federal authorities for such oversight. The bill initially passed in the House of Representatives after acrimonious debate and received moderate support from President Harrison. However, Republicans in the Senate fought over the bill. While the state of Mississippi was simultaneously passing a new poll tax and literacy test for its voters, a combination of Democrats, Mugwumps, silver, southern, and business Republicans defeated the bill.[101] Among the prominent Republican voices in the campaign against the legislation were Senators James Blaine and Murat Halstead, who argued that the party was able to win the presidency in 1888 without the help of black votes and that it could and should continue to do so in order to bring more southern whites into the party.[102] Other members made statements similar to those of Republican Senator Wolcott, who argued that "there are many things more important and vital to the welfare of this nation than that the colored citizens of this nation shall vote."[103] With a loss of seats in the 1890 midterm elections, the party decided to focus again on the tariff and other economic issues.[104] Meanwhile, dissension within the southern ranks of the party

[100] Quoted in Hirshson, *Farewell to the Bloody Shirt*, 179.

[101] Key, *Southern Politics*, 535–39; Kousser, *The Shaping of Southern Politics*, 143–44; and Richard E. Welch, Jr., "The Federal Elections Bill of 1890: Postscripts and Prelude," *Journal of American History* 52 (1965): 511–26.

[102] See Hirshson, *Farewell to the Bloody Shirt*, 206–42.

[103] Quoted in Logan, *Negro in North Carolina*, 78.

[104] See Richard B. Sherman, *The Republican Party and Black America: From McKinley to Hoover, 1896–1933* (Charlottesville: University of Virginia Press, 1973), chap. 1; and Woodward, *Origins of the New South*, chap. 12. Also see Thomas Robert Cripps, "The Lily White Republicans: The Negro, the Party, and the South in the Progressive Era" (University of Maryland, Ph.D. dissertation, 1967); and Joseph H. Cartwright, *The Tri-*

also had an impact on the Force Bill vote. White southern members refused to acknowledge the oppression of blacks and claimed the bill would cause racial tensions and ultimately hurt the party's recent advancements among independent voters. A representative of Louisiana, for instance, said the party should give up attempts at enfranchising blacks and instead appeal to the former supporters of the Confederacy.[105] The Democrats swept the 1892 elections, and shortly after, federal funding for government marshals to supervise elections was completely cut off.

CAPTURED BLACKS AND REPUBLICAN COMPETITION FOR SOUTHERN WHITES, 1896–1932

By the turn of the twentieth century, blacks found themselves both captured and largely disenfranchised by the party system. The Republican party, meanwhile, survived the electoral turmoil of the Populist Era and built a dominant national coalition from 1896 to 1932, losing the presidency only twice (both times to Woodrow Wilson, in 1912 and 1916) and maintaining comfortable control of Congress for the large majority of these years. They were able to do this without southern support from whites or blacks.[106] Those party scholars who believe that the development of the one-party South led to black disenfranchisement claim that once the Republicans no longer needed southern electoral support, they focused their energy solely on nonsouthern and nonracial issues. As a consequence, disenfranchisement and segregation became far more severe in the region.

This is not, however, the only plausible explanation of Republican party behavior. It could be argued with equal plausibility that, no longer needing to appeal to southern white voters, the national Republican party could have finally freed itself to actively promote black interests without worry of electoral disadvantage. We have already seen that this could not happen, as party leaders continually worried that their electoral interests in the North would suffer from active promotion of black voting rights in the South. Interestingly enough, however, party leaders

---

umph of Jim Crow: Tennessee Race Relations in the 1880s (Knoxville: University of Tennessee Press, 1976), chap. 7.

[105] Wang, "Black Suffrage," 452.

[106] The Republican party did win the state of Tennessee in the 1920 presidential election, and five states supported Herbert Hoover and the Republicans in 1928 (Florida, North Carolina, Tennessee, Texas, and Virginia). In neither of these elections were southern states decisive for the Republican victory.

also limited their active appeals to blacks as they followed their continuing desire to pursue southern white voters. Republican leaders did not give up on the South, enabling only one party to exist for southern voters. Instead, Republican presidents from Roosevelt to Hoover actively courted southern whites in the hopes of strengthening their party's electoral possibilities. In the process, black interests became almost entirely invisible in the Republican's national policy agenda.

Theodore Roosevelt is often remembered for having dinner at the White House with prominent African American Booker T. Washington. He also continued the trend set by previous Republican presidents of pursuing the votes of southern white businessmen by excluding blacks from the party's coalition. While southern Republican conventions during this period already prohibited blacks from attending, Roosevelt agreed not to nominate blacks to federal positions in the South. Instead, he nominated southern Democrats to cabinet positions in an effort to appeal for their vote, and his administration took the first steps toward segregating departments of the federal government in Washington, D.C.[107] Roosevelt commented a few years after his presidency that "the disruption and destruction of the Republican party . . . has been brought about in large part . . . by refusing to face the truth, which is that under existing conditions there is not and cannot be in the Southern States a party based primarily upon the Negro vote and under Negro leadership or the leadership of white men who derive their power solely from Negroes."[108]

Roosevelt's dinner invitations to Washington, generally offered as example of the Republican party's support of its black constituents, actually were used quite effectively by Roosevelt and his successor, Howard Taft, to promote a white southern strategy. Taft in particular relied on Roosevelt's relationship with Washington as a way to appeal to southern white voters while maintaining support from northern black Republicans. "The colored people have been taught by their greatest leader, Mr. Washington," Taft told white southerners in a campaign stop in 1907, "that the way for the negro to build himself up is to make himself useful as a laborer — unskilled and skilled — as a farmer and as a business man in the community of which he forms part." As blacks were educated, Taft argued, their opportunities to vote "will be accorded them and they will exercise a far more useful influence as intelligent and

[107] See Sherman, *Republican Party and Black America*, chap. 2; Cripps, "Lily White Republicans," chap. 3; and Arthur S. Link, "Theodore Roosevelt and the South in 1912," in *The Higher Realism of Woodrow Wilson and Other Essays* (Nashville, 1971), 243–55.

[108] Quoted in Arthur S. Link, "Correspondence Relating to the Progressive Party's 'Lily White' Policy in 1912," *Journal of Southern History* 10 (1944): 487.

solid members of the community for the benefit of their race than the ignorant members of their race would have exercised, had they been allowed to vote." Thus, "we may still reach a result that will square with the requirements of the Federal constitution and will give to the negro every political and economic right, and will confer great benefit upon the colored race." The black man "understands his defects. He knows his virtues. And if the negro responds to the opportunities for improvement as Booker Washington points them out, we can be sure that he will grow in the estimation of his white fellow-citizens of the South, and that the great problem which has burdened the South, with its race issues, will be largely solved." As Taft assured southern whites, "If [a black man] lacks educational qualification, property qualification, or any other qualification that the state may lawfully impose as a rule of eligibility for its voters, then he may be excluded provided that everyone else who lacks similar qualifications is equally excluded. The 15th amendment . . . is not intended to give him affirmative privileges as a member of his race. Its strict enforcement does not involve the amalgamation of the races — does not involve social association or equality."[109]

Taft, in a speech made to northern blacks, made some effort to convince them that the appeals to the white South were appropriate. Despite losing their political influence after 1880, southern blacks, Taft stressed, had made important gains — an increase in land, farm, and home ownership, an increase in educational opportunities and attainment, and an increase in the number of black churches. "The impressive weight of the statistics which I have given above cannot be minimized by a partial or prejudiced view of those who do not take a broad, comprehensive view of the situation. There are many noble white men in the South." Education was vital because the Fifteenth Amendment had initially given the right to vote to those "that had not the education properly to conduct a government. And this led to the abuses which have been held up to execration by the lurid pictures of the reconstruction days. How far those pictures have been colored beyond the truth by partisan and racial prejudice it is not necessary for us to discuss, because one of the things which every lover of his country ought to refrain from doing is to say the things which are likely to stir up again the dying embers of race and sectional hatred. . . . In a population where illiteracy is proportionately very large, no one can object certainly under the Federal Constitution to the establishment of electoral educational or property qualifications. And I do not understand that the intelligent col-

---

[109] Taft speech in Lexington, Kentucky, "Southern Democracy and Republican Principles," (August 22, 1907).

ored men of the country object to the passage and enforcement of such a law."[110]

Taft's attempts to gain votes in the white South became an obsession for him, particularly given that those votes were not necessary to win national elections.[111] In 1908, with the help of the Populist divisions in the Democratic party, Taft gained white support for the Republicans from previous years, and came within 12,000 votes of winning North Carolina and within 9,000 votes of winning Tennessee. These gains occurred despite losses in votes from blacks, and party leaders believed further gains would come if the party erased its connection to any remaining pro-black policies. As William Garrott Brown wrote at the time,

> The drift of Southern opinion is clearly and strongly Republican. This drift was arrested in 1904 by the nomination of Parker and by the feeling against President Roosevelt because he had had Principal Washington to dinner, had appointed Crum Collector at Charleston, and had closed the post-office at Indianola. . . . The wisest course now open to the Republican party . . . is to consent, candidly and unequivocally, that it shall be safe for southern whites to support Republicans. . . . That [the Republicans have] substantially so consented, ever since the last Force Bill was killed, is what has made possible its recent gains. These became possible, not in spite of the laws which operate to disenfranchise the mass of the negroes, but because of those laws, and because the Republicans had virtually accepted them.[112]

With the 1908 election returns, Taft declared that "we have only just begun," and immediately embarked on a tour of the region. In a series of speeches entitled "The Winning of the South," he claimed that the best friends of southern African Americans were southern whites and that the fear whites had of federal enforcement of social equality was "imaginary."[113] He also agreed to avoid federal black appointments in the South: "I am not going to put into places of such prominence in the South, where the race feeling is strong, Negroes whose appointment will only tend to increase that race feeling. . . . There is no constitutional right in anyone to hold office. A one-legged man would hardly be selected for a mail carrier, and although we deplore his misfortune, nev-

---

[110] Taft speech in Brooklyn, New York, "The Progress of the Negro" (March 16, 1908).

[111] See *Nation*, (October 15, 1908), 349; and (October 22, 1908), 373.

[112] William Garrott Brown, *The New Politics and Other Papers* (Boston: Houghton Mifflin, 1914), 183–84.

[113] Woodward, *Origins of the South*, 468.

ertheless we would not seek to neutralize it by giving him a place that he could not fill."[114]

By 1912, the GOP made absolutely no reference to civil rights in its party platform. As Harvard Sitkoff points out, "Not a single word about civil rights appeared in the Democratic, Progressive, Republican, Prohibition, Socialist, or Socialist Labor" platforms during that election year.[115] Warren Harding, Calvin Coolidge, and Herbert Hoover continued the trend of appealing to southern whites at the expense of African American interests. None of these presidents, and no Republican Congress, made efforts to strengthen voting rights for black Americans during this time. In 1920, both Arkansas and Florida Republicans officially split between white and black factions. In Virginia of that year, Republicans led by Colonel Henry Anderson refused to seat blacks at the party convention. When Anderson ran for governor the following year, he declared that the Republicans despised blacks and did not want their votes.[116] Alabama also stopped allowing blacks into the Republican party that year. President Hoover culminated this period of Republican party dominance and the capture of African American voters by abolishing the Negro division of the Republican party, cracking down on any existing black patronage in the southern states, and choosing for his first nomination to the Supreme Court John Parker, a southern white segregationist with a record of opposition to black enfranchisement.[117]

CONCLUSION

Certainly there were a number of important Republican efforts to help expand African American civil and voting rights, especially in the years closely following the Civil War, but continuing also through the failed Force Act of 1890. A number of Republican leaders passionately held to the belief that voting and civil rights in the South were necessary and required northern enforcement. The various pieces of legislation passed

[114] Taft in correspondence with W. R. Nelson, February 23, 1909. Quoted in Henry F. Pringle, *The Life and Times of William Howard Taft: A Biography* (Hamden, Connecticut: Archon Books, 1964), 390.

[115] Sitkoff, *New Deal for Blacks*, 20.

[116] Ralph J. Bunche, *The Political Status of the Negro in the Age of FDR* (Chicago: University of Chicago Press, 1973), 518.

[117] See Nancy J. Weiss, *Farewell to the Party of Lincoln: Black Politics in the Age of FDR* (Princeton: Princeton University Press, 1983), 15–18; David S. Day, "Herbert Hoover and Racial Politics: The DePriest Incident," *Journal of Negro History* 65 (1980): 6–7; Sherman, *Republican Party and Black America*, 225–29; and Sitkoff, *New Deal for Blacks*, 28.

by the Radical Republicans in the 1860s and early 1870s should not be trivialized. Also not to be trivialized are the obstacles that the Republican party faced in maintaining civil rights. As scholars have well argued, to protect black civil rights against the degree of violence by the KKK and other white organizations necessitated a tremendous amount of coercive power from the federal government. In many ways, the federal government lacked the capacity to deal with such an enormous undertaking.[118] Moreover, the dissolution of the Republican party in the South undoubtedly hurt African American political interests both in the region and nationally. Once Republican leaders stopped actively fighting for African American equality in the late 1890s, the stage was set for racial discrimination and segregation to occur in all areas of the country and at all levels of society and the federal government.

Yet what I hope to highlight in this chapter is that the Republican party's efforts to expand its own electoral base made them quite complicitous in the disenfranchisement of black voters. While various factions of the party fought over proper direction, perceived electoral incentives won out. Having blacks in the Republican party's electoral coalition required efforts that diminished the party's chances with white voters in both the South and the North. Over time, black and Radical Republican demands for civil rights were delegitimated by other party actors who emphasized the need to win elections in a racist nation with a minority black electorate. As the party continued its pursuit of the median voter, blacks became a captured, and hence a largely silent, group on the national political agenda.

[118] See Richard M. Valelly, "Party, Coercion, and Inclusion: The Two Reconstructions of the South's Electoral Politics," *Politics and Society* 21 (March 1993); and George Rable, *But There Was No Peace: The Role of Violence in the Politics of Reconstruction* (Athens: University of Georgia Press, 1984).

CHAPTER 4

Capture inside the Democratic Party, 1965–1996

THE SECOND PERIOD of electoral capture occured shortly after the victories of the civil rights movement in the 1960s. In the national election of 1964, overwhelming numbers of African American voters cast their ballots in favor of the Democratic party candidate, Lyndon Johnson. The Republican party candidate of that year, Barry Goldwater, ran against the legislative centerpiece of the civil rights era, the Civil Rights Act of 1964. Since that election, black voters have consistently supported Democratic candidates in presidential elections at rates of over 80 to 90 percent. National Republican leaders, meanwhile, have made only sporadic and often halfhearted efforts to court black voters. Just as often, the party has utilized negative racial code words to appeal to swing voters and increase its base of primarily white voters.[1]

In some important ways, the post–civil rights era differs from the period following Reconstruction. While in the late 1800s opposition to civil rights was based on explicit expressions of genetic racism by a white public,[2] opposition to African American interests in the post–civil rights era is more subtle. Instead of openly expressing opposition to blacks, whites today express opposition to *policies* designed specifically to benefit blacks, such as affirmative action and busing. They defend these views by claiming they are opposed to government intervention or to programs that ostensibly conflict with individualistic values, or they claim that blacks are benefiting "unfairly" from these programs. Whereas in the 1800s, racist ideology often transcended broader left-right political distinctions, since the 1960s the two have subtly blended together.[3]

---

[1] On the use of racial code words by the Republican party, see Thomas Byrne Edsall and Mary Edsall, *Chain Reaction: The Impact of Race, Rights, and Taxes on American Politics,* (New York: Norton, 1991); Donald R. Kinder and Lynn M. Sanders, *Divided by Color: Racial Politics and Democratic Ideals* (Chicago: University of Chicago Press, 1996), chaps. 8–9.

[2] For just one account of white racial attitudes during this period, see George M. Fredrickson, *The Black Image in the White Mind: The Debate on Afro-American Character and Destiny, 1817–1914* (Hanover, N.H.: Wesleyan University Press, 1987), particularly chaps. 6–10.

[3] For trend analysis of racial attitudes just prior to and after the civil rights movement, see Howard Schuman, Charlotte Steeh, and Lawrence Bobo, *Racial Attitudes in America:*

The second difference between the two Reconstructions is that African Americans have found their political interests more firmly institutionalized in the post–civil rights era, both inside the Democratic party and inside government bureaucracies and private organizations.[4] Whereas African American interests in the post-Reconstruction era were severely compromised by the withdrawal of federal troops from the South, in the post-1960s they have been sustained through a series of changing legal, organizational, and cultural norms. African American political leaders have achieved a presence and stature in the country's cities, legislatures, and national parties that surpasses the highest moments of Reconstruction. The Democratic party is emblematic of this change. Not only has a prominent African American run a significant campaign for the party's presidential nomination, but African Americans have held positions at all levels of the party, including its highest post—the chair of the Democratic National Committee.

Nonetheless, the process by which African Americans found their interests captured by the Democratic party during this period also has significant parallels to the post-Reconstruction era.[5] Prior to both periods, leaders of the two parties generally avoided debating racial issues. Similar to the leaders of the second-party system created by Martin Van Buren, leaders of both the Republican and the Democratic party after the early 1890s generally kept appeals to blacks to a minimum in favor of economic and foreign policy. African American concerns were largely neglected during this time period. In both periods, the needs of black Americans eventually took center stage of the political agenda, despite the resistance of party leaders. During Reconstruction, a bloody civil war galvanized "Radical" Republicans in Congress to enact the civil rights reforms of the mid-1860s. During the "second Reconstruction," widespread violence by southern whites against black protestors gal-

---

Trends and Interpretations (Cambridge: Harvard University Press, 1985). See chap. 1 n. 70 for citations on the complexity of racial attitudes in modern society.

[4] See Adolph Reed, Jr., "Demobilization in the New Black Political Regime," in Michael Peter Smith and Joe R. Feagin, eds., The Bubbling Cauldron: Race, Ethnicity, and the Urban Crisis (Minneapolis: University of Minnesota Press, 1995), 183–84; and Hanes Walton Jr., When the Marching Stopped: The Politics of Civil Rights Regulatory Agencies (Albany: State University of New York Press, 1988).

[5] For other comparisons of the "two reconstructions," see J. Morgan Kousser, "The Voting Rights Act and the Two Reconstructions," in Bernard Grofman and Chandler Davidson, eds., Controversies in Minority Voting: The Voting Rights Act in Perspective (Washington, D.C.: Brookings Institution, 1982); Manning Marable, Race, Reform, and Rebellion: The Second Reconstruction in Black America, 1945–1982 (Jackson: University of Mississippi Press, 1984); and Richard M. Valelly, "Party, Coercion, and Inclusion: The Two Reconstructions of the South's Electoral Politics," Politics and Society 21 (March 1993).

vanized civil rights supporters in both parties in the mid-1960s to pass substantive legislative reforms.

As with the Republican party experience of the 1860s and 1870s, continued advocacy on behalf of African Americans by the Democrats would begin to decline once electoral politics returned to the "normalcy" of two-party competition. In the 1860s, a number of Republican leaders believed they could win national elections with the help of southern African American voters. They did not recognize the degree to which civil rights would anger white voters in areas outside the South such as Ohio and New York. In the 1960s, Democratic party leaders expected that advocating civil rights would lead to mass defections among the party's southern white voting bloc and to some opposition in the North. They were taken by surprise, however, by the large numbers of northern white Democrats and swing voters vehemently objecting to the goals and methods of the civil rights movement and to the government policies designed to implement its aims.[6] Government enforced busing, the perceived inadequacy and unfairness of the nation's welfare programs, and increasing urban violence angered many voters who had initially been at least mildly supportive of the civil rights movement. By the mid-1970s, these issues, plus the controversy surrounding affirmative action, were thought to have driven a wedge between African American Democrats and other important Democratic constituencies, including significant portions of organized labor and working- and middle-class whites.[7]

Also similar to the reaction in the Reconstruction era, the opposition party in the late 1960s reemerged as a nationally competitive organization, at least in part by taking advantage of widespread public dissatisfaction with the speed of civil rights reforms. Further damaging to the interests of civil rights supporters, the renewed competitiveness of the two-party system returned white ideological moderates, who were ambivalent or antagonistic to the continuing progress of the civil rights movement, to the center of electoral campaigns. Although white Republicans were opposed to white Democrats on a number of important issue dimensions, race was not one of them. By 1972, in fact, national

[6] There were warnings of a northern blue-collar vote backlash as early as 1964, as George Wallace did surprisingly well in a number of northern cities. See Richard L. Rubin, *Party Dynamics: The Democratic Coalition and the Politics of Change* (New York: Oxford University Press, 1976), 126.

[7] See Edsall and Edsall, *Chain Reaction*; J. Anthony Lukas, *Common Ground* (New York: Vintage, 1982); Jonathan Rieder, *Canarsie: The Jews and Italians of Brooklyn Against Liberalism* (Cambridge: Harvard University Press, 1985); and Thomas J. Sugrue, *The Origins of the Urban Crisis: Race and Inequality in Postwar Detroit* (Princeton: Princeton University Press, 1996).

survey data revealed that the majority of whites identifying with the Democratic party agreed with the majority of white Republican identifiers about most civil rights issues.[8]

In this chapter, I have two goals. First, I examine the process by which blacks found their votes and interests captured in the Democratic party during the post–civil rights era. As with the previous chapter, little of this history will be new to those familiar with the period. Considerable attention has been devoted to this period by journalists and scholars, centering largely on the civil rights movement's impact on Democratic party electoral opportunities. In fact, the story has been told so many times in the last few years that it borders on cliché: as the goals of the civil rights movement turned to programs such as affirmative action, increased welfare rights, school integration, and prisoner rights, many white voters, and in particular working-class voters living in urban areas, no longer felt represented by the Democratic party.

I do not offer here a new systematic historical account nor do I detail the party's legislative response (this latter subject will be taken up in chapter 6). Instead, I want to show how electoral incentives encourage party leaders to capture black interests. In sketching the process of electoral capture, I simplify a long, complicated history that defies a narrow linear progression. Party leaders often disagree about the best course of action to take. Even if they agree, party leaders may not initially respond to the incentives of two-party competition. They may lack information about which issues are most strategic to promote, or they may lack the institutional capacity to carry out what they believe to be the most strategic course of action. But as alternative efforts fail with mounting electoral losses, as leaders gain more information about correct courses of action to take, and as these leaders become increasingly legitimate in the party organization and come to dominate the party's electoral strategy, they are able to concentrate appeals on returning to the voter median. In the process, these strategic actors distance their party from African American leaders and interests. Despite the ideological battles and struggle between leaders over whether to represent or distance themselves from black interests, we can see an unfolding process by which party leaders slowly start following electoral incentives.

This leads to my second goal in this chapter: I want to pay attention to the attempts by Democratic party leaders during this period to reform their electoral organization. In particular, I want to examine the

---

[8] There was, however, quite a strong division between the party activists over racial issues. See Edward G. Carmines and James A. Stimson, *Issue Evolution* (Princeton: Princeton University Press, 1989). Also see Kinder and Sanders, *Divided by Color*, chap. 2.

party's presidential nomination process. The changing orientations of party reformers during this period illustrate a great deal about the role of electoral structures in determining whether a national party can represent black interests in a racially divided society. As we will see, a number of Democratic party leaders make sincere attempts to actively represent African American interests, whether for strategic or ideological reasons. After the 1968 presidential election, party leaders reformed the nominating process in order to unify their coalition, increase their electoral opportunities, and increase black representation (as well as the representation of a number of other politically underrepresented groups). Yet starting shortly after the party's landslide defeat in the 1972 presidential election, the leadership tried to re-reform the party organization — again in order to increase their electoral opportunities. This time, however, these reforms were designed to decrease the public presence of African American and other "special interest" groups, which were perceived as harmful to the party's electoral success. As the party continued to lose national elections for the next two decades, other party leaders and analysts focused the blame specifically on the party's close relationship with civil rights causes. The Democrats, they argued, were unable to elect candidates to the presidency because the leadership was too closely tied to the interests of blacks and other constituencies perceived to be far removed from the national median voter.

These party leaders had a great deal of difficulty in distancing the Democrats from black interests. This difficulty reflects, in part, the initial disagreement among these party leaders as to whether race is the primary problem for the party. It also reflects the power of organizational reforms to enable greater representation of black constituents. In many ways, the initial reforms worked as intended, and black Americans were among the chief beneficiaries. Jesse Jackson, for instance, would take advantage of the nominating process to run as an "outsider" candidate in the 1980s. He had a significant degree of success and influence over the general party direction and electoral message. The difficulty party leaders have had in counteracting these initial reforms reflects the fact that party politics is not simply played out on the basis of electoral incentives. As I have argued earlier, national parties in the United States are not controlled by a small group of leaders who make strategic decisions specifically with Downsian spatial models in mind. Parties are organizations with multiple interests, differing ideological positions, differing degrees of passion and activism, and differing opinions about how to win elections. Congressional members, urban mayors, state governors, and grass-roots activists, as well as any individuals who care to announce themselves as candidates in the party's presidential primaries can compete with other leaders to define the party's national message. That these actors often disagree over the proper course of party action is to be expected. Moreover, even the most strategic of party actors may not have accurate information about what is best for the party's electoral strategy.

Nonetheless, over time, electoral results provide party actors with more accurate information and more power to act strategically. We will see that party leaders by the mid-1970s begin to make what they believed to be necessary reforms to give them greater power. Electoral incentives, then, are ultimately determinative in the decision-making process of party leaders. This indicates that internal organizational reforms are not enough to solve the party's inabilities to be effectively democratic and are not enough to incorporate black interests over the long run. This point is relevant for both activists and scholars of party politics. Both groups have focused their dissatisfaction over the party's ability to be effectively democratic on organizational problems. As a result, they have continually promoted organizational reforms to make the parties more effective at democratic representation. In the 1950s and early 1960s, for instance, the decentralized nature of national party leadership in government was criticized by party scholars because it was seen as preventing the translation of majority support for civil rights reform into actual legislation. For this reason, a number of scholars promoted institutional reforms that would centralize power in the hands of party leaders. "Responsible" party advocates wanted to transform parties into strong, cohesive institutions that would enact distinctive policies once the party was in office.[9]

Since then, other scholars and activists have criticized the parties' presidential nomination process. They have called for organizational reforms that, depending on the viewpoint, would either decentralize the process and allow for more constituency activism through party primaries and caucuses or centralize the process and allow leaders to have more control over the party message.[10] Both sides argue that organizational design is the problem, and that their vision of reforms would enable blacks and other historically disadvantaged groups to be better represented. I argue in this chapter that both contentions are problem-

---

[9] See E. E. Schattschneider, *Party Government* (New York: Holt, Rinehart and Winston, 1942); and the American Political Science Association, "Toward a More Responsible Two-Party System" (Report of the Committee on Political Parties) *American Political Science Review* 59 (March 1965).

[10] Among those desiring decentralized parties, see John S. Saloma III and Frederick H. Sontag, *Parties: The Real Opportunity for Effective Citizen Politics* (New York: Alfred A. Knopf, 1972). For centralized parties, see James Q. Wilson, *The Amateur Democrat* (Chicago: University of Chicago Press, 1962); and Nelson W. Polsby, *The Consequences of Party Reform* (New York: Oxford University Press, 1983).

atic. The problem is that they focus their attention on the wrong place. The incentives inherent in the majority-based *electoral structure* (i.e., the need to win elections in a winner-take-all electoral system) mean that the need to appeal to the voting majority will trump the power of organizational reforms. These incentives, combined with the perception by party leaders that the median voter is hostile to specific black interests, continues to pit the goal of African American representation against party electoral interests, leading over time to organizational counterreforms that eclipse African American interests.

THE MOVEMENT OF AFRICAN AMERICANS
INTO THE DEMOCRATIC PARTY, 1933–1965

The captured status of African Americans in the Republican party of the late 1800s and early 1900s ended not so much with the opposition party reaching out and making specific appeals to their political interests, but with the rise of a new, dominant issue-dimension that successfully appealed to voters regardless of racial distinction. The Great Depression of the late 1920s created widespread economic despair previously unseen in the United States. Black voters, like most groups in the country at that time, expressed dissatisfaction with the Republican party's efforts to combat the Depression. Nonetheless, black voters by and large remained loyal to Herbert Hoover in 1932, perhaps in part because Franklin Roosevelt did not address civil rights or black voters during the course of the campaign.[11] The Roosevelt administration, while making appeals to blacks on economic grounds, was not in a position to directly promote civil rights legislation and anger the party's southern segregationist wing. The white South continued to dominate each party's electoral aspirations, and recognizing this, leaders of both parties attempted to appeal to blacks while keeping race from dominating the political agenda. Roosevelt generally refused to support race-specific legislation such as antilynching laws, arguing that blacks were better off when economic issues, not civil rights issues, were the focus of legislative debate.[12] While he supported party efforts to mobilize black

[11] See Harvard Sitkoff, *A New Deal for Blacks: The Emergence of Civil Rights as a National Issue, the Depression Decade* (New York: Oxford University Press, 1978), chap. 2; and Nancy J. Weiss, *Farewell to the Party of Lincoln* (Princeton: Princeton University Press, 1983), chap. 1.

[12] See Weiss, *Farewell to the Party of Lincoln*; John B. Kirby, *Black Americans in the Roosevelt Era: Liberalism and Race* (Knoxville: University of Tennessee Press, 1980); and John Frederick Martin, *Civil Rights and the Crisis of Liberalism: The Democratic Party, 1945–1976* (Boulder, Colo.: Westview Press, 1979), 60. Martin quotes President Roose-

voters in the North, little effort was made to disturb the existing order in the South.[13]

The need for Roosevelt to appease southern whites not only limited his ability to propose civil rights legislation. It also significantly limited the ability of his economic programs to aid black Americans. Since none of his administration's measures could be passed without the support of southern Democrats in Congress, many of whom controlled powerful committees in the House and Senate, a number of prominent economic programs contained provisions that effectively prevented blacks from receiving their share of government relief programs. By official pronouncement, Roosevelt forbade discrimination in New Deal programs. Yet many of the programs contained significant loopholes that allowed for unequal access and benefits to black Americans. The Social Security Act, for instance, included a provision excluding farmers and domestic employees, accounting for roughly 65 percent of all black workers. In the subsequent debate over Aid to Dependent Children (ADC), southern committee members called for states' rights provisions to allow for their states to discriminate when handing out public assistance. African Americans as a result ended up receiving smaller amounts from ADC.[14] The National Labor Relations Act, meanwhile, failed to include a clause written to prohibit union discrimination;[15] the government's program to help farmers, the Agricultural Adjustment Administration, displaced black sharecroppers and tenant farmers from their land; and the National Recovery Act excluded many categories of employment that were heavily concentrated with black workers.[16]

Regardless of the discriminatory intent, New Deal legislation provided black voters a substantive option, allowing them to leave their captured status inside the Republican party. African American voters had a unique opportunity to benefit from bipartisan competition, but this opportunity existed precisely because their specific issues were not championed in a way that might divide either political party. In the 1936 elections, black voters began to move to the Democratic party, in part because of economic policy and in part because of increased ap-

---

velt, explaining his neutrality to an antilynching bill: "If I come out for the anti-lynching bill now, [southern congressional Democrats who were chairmen of most House and Senate committees] will block every bill I ask Congress to pass to keep America from collapsing."

[13] Sitkoff, *New Deal for Blacks*, 310.

[14] See ibid.; and Robert C. Lieberman, "Race and the Organization of Welfare Policy," in Paul E. Peterson, *Classifying by Race* (Princeton: Princeton University Press, 1995).

[15] See Ira Katznelson, Kim Geiger, and Daniel Kryder, "Limiting Liberalism: The Southern Veto in Congress, 1933–1950," *Political Science Quarterly* 108 (1993): 283–306.

[16] See ibid.; and Weiss, *Farewell to the Party of Lincoln*, 55–57.

peals by the Roosevelt campaign in the North. The Roosevelt campaign recognized not only that blacks benefited enough from New Deal economic policies but that they would have reason to leave the Republicans. The campaign also recognized that large numbers of new black voters were moving during this period from southern to northern states such as New York, Illinois, Ohio, Michigan, and Pennsylvania—all which were crucial for winning presidential elections. While the Democrats continued a trend of not mentioning civil rights issues in their party platform, African Americans did attend the national convention as delegates for the first time in party history, and party mobilization efforts doubled the number of registered Democratic voters in northern urban areas such as Harlem and Philadelphia.[17] Republicans also stepped up appeals to black voters, offering various forms of civil rights legislation, often without much substantive bite but with symbolic significance nonetheless. Their presidential candidate in 1936, Alfred Landon, broke with the more ambivalent Republican platform by pledging that "if ever in this country there is an attempt to persecute any minority on grounds of race, religion, or class, I will take my stand by the side of the minority."[18]

In 1940, African Americans were mentioned for the first time (albeit in ambiguous terms) in the Democratic party platform. As the migration of many African Americans from the South to northern cities continued throughout the decade, party leaders increasingly perceived the black vote as potentially pivotal in many important northern states. Although still a small portion of the electorate overall, their votes were concentrated in strategic areas. As Henry Lee Moon suggested in 1948, "The Negro's political influence in national elections derives not so much from its numerical strength as from its strategic diffusion in the balance of power and marginal states whose electoral votes are generally considered vital to the winning candidate."[19] Truman administration official Clark Clifford similarly pointed out "that the Negro vote today holds the balance of power in Presidential elections for the simple

[17] See Patricia Sullivan, *Days of Hope: Race and Democracy in the New Deal Era* (Chapel Hill: University of North Carolina Press, 1996), 93; Thomas T. Spencer, "The Good Neighbor League Colored Committee and the 1936 Democratic Presidential Campaign," *Journal of Negro History* 63 (1978): 307–16. The 1936 convention also marked a historic vote by which party delegates ended the need for "two-thirds" of the delegates to win the party nomination. While the two-thirds necessity had helped protect southern white interests in the party nomination process for more than 100 years, there was little resistance in the 1936 convention by southern whites. For further discussion, see Rubin, *Party Dynamics*.

[18] Quoted in Sitkoff, *New Deal for Blacks*, 93.

[19] Henry Lee Moon, *Balance of Power: the Negro Vote* (Garden City, N.Y.: Doubleday, 1948), 198.

arithmetical reason that the Negroes not only vote as a bloc but are geographically concentrated in the pivotal, large, and closely contested states such as New York, Illinois, Pennsylvania, Ohio, and Michigan. . . . As always, the South can be considered safely Democratic."[20]

Clifford's comment is of interest. Perhaps it is because racial issues had for so long remained invisible on the national political agenda that he forgot the intensity of southern white opposition to civil rights. Or perhaps it is because he believed that southern whites were themselves a captured group with nowhere else to turn. Regardless, Clifford miscalculated, underestimating the disruptive effects of civil rights advocacy, both in the short term and the long run. Efforts by President Truman and other leading Democrats to aggressively promote a national civil rights agenda nearly backfired during the presidential election of 1948. After appointing a presidential Committee on Civil Rights to review racial conditions, Truman endorsed the committee's findings that black citizens were grossly discriminated against in American society. The president proclaimed his support for the Fair Employment Practices Commission, stricter antilynching laws, anti–poll tax measures, and the prohibition of discrimination in interstate transportation facilities.[21] Southern Democrats were furious at the president's pro–civil rights stand and a group of "Dixiecrats," led by South Carolina governor Strom Thurmond, walked out of the party convention in 1948 in opposition to civil rights measures in the party's platform. In the subsequent fall election, Thurmond's third-party campaign received 56 percent of the vote in the Deep South, winning the electoral college votes of Alabama, Louisiana, Mississippi, and South Carolina.

Although Truman and the Democrats won the election without Dixiecrat support, they were not ready to abandon southern whites in favor of civil rights. By 1952, the Republican party started making inroads in the South, and nervous Democratic party leaders attempted to appease this potential rift in the party by nominating a racial moderate, Adlai Stevenson, in both 1952 and 1956. Stevenson appeared acceptable to pro–civil rights voters, but not so liberal on civil rights that he would lose the South. Southern conservatives could accept him.[22] While campaigning, Stevenson pushed for southern whites to be "given time and

---

[20] Quoted in David McCullough, *Truman* (New York: Simon and Schuster, 1992), 590.

[21] See Barton J. Bernstein, "The Ambiguous Legacy: The Truman Administration and Civil Rights," in *Politics and Policies of the Truman Administration* (Chicago: Quadrangle Books, 1970); Monroe Billington, "Civil Rights, President Truman and the South," *Journal of Negro History* 58 (1973); and Donald R. McCoy and Richard T. Ruetten, *Quest and Response: Minority Rights and the Truman Administration* (Lawrence: University of Kansas Press, 1973).

[22] John Bartlow Martin, *Adlai Stevenson of Illinois: The Life and Times of Adlai Stevenson* (New York: Doubleday, 1976), 554.

patience" on civil rights, and opposed the use of federal troops or the withholding of federal aid to enforce court-ordered desegregation in the region.[23]

The fears of pushing too far on the civil rights issue were also evident during the Kennedy administration, as the president emphasized voting rights over civil rights legislation in an effort to appease both civil rights activists and southern whites.[24] Attorney General Robert Kennedy commented after his brother's death that the president had no expectation of gaining votes in the South through civil rights programs and, in fact, had feared that for every vote gained, two would be lost: "We were alienating so many people." He also worried that civil rights would cost the party votes "even in the suburbs" and "the big cities in the North."[25] The Kennedys, Kenneth O'Reilly argues, "pursued voting rights as the least objectional and least intrusive course of action. If it had not been for the pressure brought by the civil rights movement, in all probability the Kennedys would not have moved at all."[26]

Nonetheless, as he looked ahead to the 1964 election campaign, President Kennedy slowly began to increase pressure on southern whites to end legal discrimination. The president faced not only constant pressure from civil rights protestors, he faced pressure from international allies trying to ward off communist movements in their nations. Television broadcast images across the world of white violence against civil rights demonstrators. International leaders and U.S. advisers told Kennedy at the time that the treatment of blacks was perceived by many in the decolonized world as indicative of how capitalist nations were treating people of color. As the United States struggled against communist expansion in Africa, Asia, and South America, Kennedy felt increasing pressure to end the violent conflict in the South.[27] He and Robert Kennedy sent federal marshals and militia to protect African Americans from angry mobs of white racists. At the same time, he and Congress began to work on significant civil rights legislation.

Despite the Kennedy brothers' fears, increased civil rights enforcement benefited the party's national electoral fortunes. Pollster Louis

[23] See Harvard Sitkoff, *The Struggle for Black Equality, 1954–1980* (New York: Hill and Wang, 1981), 25.

[24] See Aldon D. Morris, *The Origins of the Civil Rights Movement* (New York: Free Press, 1984), 234–36; and Allen J. Matusow, *The Unraveling of America: A History of Liberalism in the 1960s* (New York: Harper Torchbooks, 1984), chap. 3.

[25] Robert Kennedy quoted in Kenneth O'Reilly, *Nixon's Piano: Presidents and Racial Politics from Washington to Clinton* (New York: Free Press, 1995), 229.

[26] Ibid., 209.

[27] See John David Skrentny, "The Effect of the Cold War on African American Civil Rights: America and the World Audience, 1945–1968," *Theory and Society*, (forthcoming); and Mary L. Dudziak, *Cold War Civil Rights: Civil Rights and Foreign Affairs of World War II* (Princeton: Princeton University Press, forthcoming).

Harris reported in the fall of 1963 that Kennedy had lost 4.5 million voters over his stand in favor of civil rights, but had gained an estimated 11 million people who had voted for Nixon in 1960.[28] Large portions of northern whites approved the president's civil rights programs, and a general feeling among many party leaders and intellectuals was that racism and racial conflict were nearing an end.[29] The nonviolent protest strategies of civil rights activists had captured the hearts of many Americans, millions of whom watched on television Martin Luther King's famous "I Have a Dream" speech at the Lincoln Memorial in 1963. Between 1961 and 1965, the "Negro question" was consistently identified in public opinion polls as the most important issue on the national agenda. As Doug McAdam writes about the shift in public opinion, "No longer could the cost of openly racist rhetoric or policies be measured only in terms of the loss of black support that inevitably followed from such actions."[30] Party leaders, looking for electoral opportunities, began to promote civil rights in Congress and in campaigns. Lyndon Johnson, for instance, with his eye increasingly on winning the presidency, changed from a supporter of southern segregation to a civil rights advocate. Johnson, according to Robert Sherrill, "got the message: victory lay in the cities, victory lay within the union blocs, the black blocs, the immigrant blocs, the big city bosses, with the independent voters, and if possible with farm blocs, though that was the last to worry about. Johnson saw that he who gets the South gets naught."[31] (At the same time, and in a very different electoral setting, George Wallace came to believe that running for office in the South as a relative moderate on civil rights was strategically disadvantageous. After losing a 1958 Senate race in Alabama—where even though he won black votes lost large portions of the white vote—he reportedly told reporters that "no other son-of-a-bitch will ever out-nigger me again.")[32]

[28] Harris poll is from "How Whites Feel about Negroes: A Painful American Dilemma," *Newsweek* 62 (October 21, 1963), 44–57.

[29] For trends in public opinion during this time, see Schuman, Steeh, and Bobo, *Racial Attitudes in America*. Among intellectuals, see Gunnar Myrdal, *An American Dilemma: The Negro Problem and Modern Democracy* (New York: Harper and Brothers, 1944); and Bayard Rustin, "From Protest to Politics: The Future of the Civil Rights Movement," *Commentary* 39 (1965): 25–31.

[30] Doug McAdam, *Political Process and the Development of Black Insurgency* (Chicago: University of Chicago Press, 1984), 159. Also see Paul Burstein, "Public Opinion, Demonstrations, Media Coverage, and the Passage of Anti-Discrimination Legislation" (manuscript, Yale University, 1978); and James Q. Wilson, "The Negro in Politics," in Talcott Parsons and Kenneth B. Clark, eds., *The Negro American* (Boston: Houghton Mifflin, 1965), 423–47.

[31] Robert Sherrill, *The Accidental President* (New York: Grossman, 1967), 193.

[32] Wallace is quoted in Dan T. Carter, *The Politics of Rage: George Wallace, the Origins of the New Conservativism, and the Transformation of American Politics* (New York: Simon and Schuster, 1995), 95.

Kennedy's death, the civil rights movement's ability to galvanize public opinion and place pressure on the national government, and fears of foreign policy officials that the communist and potentially communist world was watching helped provide the necessary incentives for the Democratic-controlled government to finally pass a number of significant pieces of legislation in the mid-1960s. Most prominent among these were the 1964 Civil Rights Act, the Voting Rights Act in 1965, and the Fair Housing Act in 1968. Although they met fierce southern opposition on the floor and in committees, all three bills passed both houses with widespread bipartisan support. In addition, President Johnson made numerous public gestures on behalf of African Americans, speaking many times in favor of civil rights, appointing blacks to high government agencies, and issuing executive orders eliminating discrimination in the federal government.[33]

Nonetheless, most party leaders did not anticipate the impact of aggressive promotion of civil rights on the party. Johnson and others expected the party to suffer losses in the South: the Republicans, in fact, gained electoral votes from the region in 1964 and began to invest resources toward building a strong infrastructure in the region. The Voting Rights Act of 1965 would do little to counteract this, despite its potential to mobilize hundreds of thousands of new black voters. Unlike in the 1870s, no southern state had a black majority. In 1960, blacks accounted for between 12 and 42 percent of the population in southern states. Moreover, as Earl and Merle Black have found, far more whites than blacks registered to vote in the South between 1960 and 1980. "During the 1960s, the period of the strongest advance in black voter registration, three new whites were enrolled in the Deep South for every two new blacks."[34] Less expected was the consequence for electoral politics in the North. National support for civil rights during the mid-1960s was quite high and rising. White support for integrated schools rose between 32 percent in 1942 to 70 percent in 1965. Large majorities supported the notion of equal employment opportunity for all races, and slight majorities now supported the principle of desegregation.[35]

Yet by the midterm elections of 1966, as with the midterm elections of almost a hundred years prior, the promotion of civil rights was perceived as a liability for the Democratic party in northern states. In the fall of that year, a majority of white voters responded in a public opinion poll that President Johnson was moving too fast on civil rights re-

[33] See Matusow, *Unraveling of America*, chap. 7; and Edsall and Edsall, *Chain Reaction*, chap. 3.

[34] Earl Black and Merle Black, *Politics and Society in the South* (Cambridge: Harvard University Press, 1987), 138–39.

[35] See Schuman, Steeh, and Bobo, *Racial Attitudes in America*, chap. 3.

forms. "Go . . . into any home, any bar, any barber shop and you will find people are not talking about Vietnam or rising prices or prosperity," commented Chicago congressmember Roman Pucinski. "They are talking about Martin Luther King and how [blacks] are moving in on us and what's going to happen in our neighborhoods."[36] In an effort to stave off midterm losses, President Johnson slowed down promotion of the open housing legislation. The Democrats, however, lost forty-seven House seats in that election. In California, Republican Ronald Reagan appealed to white anger over urban riots to defeat Democratic incumbent Pat Brown. The *New York Times* attributed Democratic party defeats to racial backlash not only in the South and California, but in Illinois, Maryland, Michigan, New York, and Pennsylvania.[37] Civil rights leaders, meanwhile, were finding themselves more and more in public disagreement over the continuing tactics and goals of the movement.[38]

By 1968, pollster Richard Scammon was telling Lyndon Johnson that "the American voter today is un-young, un-black, and un-poor. . . . Campaign strategy should be carefully aimed at the white, middle-aged, middle-class voters — the people . . . who bowl regularly."[39] Johnson was faced not only with Republican presidential candidate Richard Nixon's "southern strategy" and emphasis on the "silent majority." He was also faced with third-party candidate George Wallace, whose racist appeals were gaining significant portions of the white vote in the South and Midwest and northern cities. With mounting pressures from public disapproval to the Vietnam War, the president subsequently withdrew himself from the Democratic party nomination, opening the party up to a challenge at the National Convention in Chicago that would have implications for electoral politics long after 1968.

RICHARD NIXON RESPONDS TO THE
END OF THE CIVIL RIGHTS ERA: FROM AFFIRMATIVE
ACTION TO A SOUTHERN STRATEGY

With the 1966 elections, leaders of both parties began to perceive the implications of the divisiveness over civil rights and what that meant for expanding their party's coalitions. Nonetheless, party leaders reacted to

[36] Matusow, *Unraveling of America*, 214.

[37] See "Backlash Voting across Nation Helps Republicans to Gain, Especially in the South," *New York Times* (November 9, 1966), 25, 26, and 29; and John Herbers, "White Backlash Evident in Voting," (November 9, 1966), 31.

[38] See Clayborne Carson, *In Struggle: SNCC and the Black Awakening of the 1960s* (Cambridge: Harvard University Press, 1981), pt. 3; and McAdam, *Political Process.*

[39] Quoted in O'Reilly, *Nixon's Piano*, 262.

the midterm results in a number of different ways. Many leaders of both parties spoke forcefully for the need to continue with civil rights reforms. It remained quite unclear where the civil rights movement would head, and what impact it would have on national party coalitions. While white backlash was blamed for a number of Democratic party losses in 1966, pro–civil rights Democrats and Republicans also won a number of significant elections that year, leading both sides of the issue to have some hope and popular legitimation for their views. Many in the Republican party moved to take advantage of white backlash. Campaign adviser Kevin Phillips told Richard Nixon in 1968 that "substantial Negro support is not necessary to national Republican victory. The GOP can build a winning coalition without Negro votes. Indeed, Negro-Democratic mutual identification was a major source of Democratic loss — and Republican or American Independent Party profit." Resources would need to be spent on making the public perceive the Democrats as "a black party." Once this occurred, "white Democrats will desert their party in droves."[40]

Liberal elements in the Republican party, however, did maintain some legitimacy. Liberals were weakened by Goldwater's campaign in 1964 and the significant number of new conservative candidates elected to office in 1966. However, even in 1966, liberal Republican George Romney saw his victory in Michigan as a potential propeller of his views, if not his own nomination, into the party's presidential politics of 1968.[41] A smaller but still significant number of the party's constituents were sympathetic to liberal civil rights causes and a number of their elected officials still associated themselves with the legacies of the Abolitionists, Abraham Lincoln, and the Radical Republicans.[42] African Americans, meanwhile, still gave hints that they would support Republican candidates who made direct appeals for their vote. As recently as 1960, nearly a majority of middle-class blacks and a third of all black voters had given their support to Richard Nixon against John Kennedy. Although by 1964, fewer than a fifth of black voters supported Barry Goldwater, they continued to selectively offer support to Republican candidates at the state and local level. In 1965, a near majority of black voters supported Republican John Lindsay for mayor of New York City, as they did Nelson Rockefeller for governor of the state in 1966 — prompting the *New York Times* to note that the "Republicans appeared

[40] Phillips is quoted ibid., 285.

[41] See Walter Rugaber, "Romney Edges toward Race for '68 Nomination," *New York Times* (November 10, 1967), 28.

[42] See Nicol C. Rae, *The Decline and Fall of the Liberal Republicans, from 1952 to the Present* (New York: Oxford University Press, 1989); and A. James Reichley, *Conservatives in an Age of Change* (Washington, D.C.: Brookings Institution, 1981).

to have recaptured some of the Negro voters who have been going Democratic in recent years."[43] New York Senator Jacob Javits received three times as many votes from black voters as Nixon in 1968, and Senate candidate Henry Bellmon received a great deal of support from blacks in Oklahoma. Huge majorities of black voters, meanwhile, supported Republican Winthrop Rockefeller in his campaign for governor of Arkansas.[44]

As a result, a number of Republican leaders maintained that African Americans, or at least significant minorities of black voters, remained an integral part of their coalition. Gerald Ford, minority leader in the House, pushed the party in Congress to avoid making commitments to southern Democrats, fearing that Republicans would fail to attract potential black supporters. The Ripon Society, an influential Republican-allied think tank of the time, argued that Republicans needed to pay attention to a rising black middle class that could potentially operate as a swing group as they looked to both parties for potential interest. Finally, Richard Nixon recognized that in the late 1960s, white backlash was neither strong nor legitimate enough to allow for an across-the-board civil rights rollback. Despite several years of racial tensions and the beginnings of a white backlash, the national discourse remained centered on government involvement in social problems, including racial problems. Nixon, historically a moderate on civil rights, felt that he needed some civil rights accomplishments to counter potentially severe and damaging criticism that he was a racist and not a legitimate national leader in the post–civil rights era.

As a result of such thinking, Nixon initially made a surprising number of appeals to black voters.[45] While a "southern strategy" was osten-

---

[43] "Backlash Voting across Nation," 26.

[44] Rae, *Decline and Fall*. The Ripon Society found further evidence of the willingness of African American voters to support racially progressive Republican candidates in the 1972 elections in Chicago. While strong majorities of the city's black voters supported Democrat George McGovern for president, significant portions split their tickets for progressive Republicans in both the Senate (Charles Percy) and governor's (Ogilvie) races. See Ripon Society, *Jaws of Victory: The Game-Plan Politics of 1972, the Crisis of the Republican Party, and the Future of the Constitution* (Boston: Little, Brown, 1973), 196–99.

[45] Nixon's situated position vis-à-vis a weakened but still vital liberal establishment fits nicely within a theoretical category of presidential authority that Stephen Skowronek has labeled "preemptive politics." He argues that presidents are bound by the historical period in which they enter office; institutions, public discourse, and the president's relation to them are important in determining his political fate. Politicians such as Nixon who enter office during the "preemptive" period are "limited by the political, institutional, and ideological supports that the old establishment maintains. Intruding into an ongoing polity as an alien force, they interrupt a still vital political discourse and try to preempt its agenda by playing upon the political divisions within the establishment that affiliated presidents instinctively seek to assuage. . . . Opportunities for preemption are never diffi-

sibly incompatible with the promotion of civil rights, Nixon went to great lengths to try to make them fit. In a radio address to the nation during the 1968 campaign, Nixon proposed a "new alignment," which would combine southern whites with some "black militants" and "thoughtful critics like Daniel Moynihan and Richard Goodwin—both liberals."[46] In 1970, the president attempted to pass through Congress the largest affirmative action program in U.S. history, the Philadelphia Plan. Like many strategic actors at the time, Nixon was unclear about the best possible direction for the Republican party and thus tried a number of strategies, learning from both the failures and the successes.[47]

By late 1970, however, Nixon and the Republicans clearly believed that appealing to blacks would hamper broader coalition-building efforts. African American voters and political leaders reacted skeptically to the Philadelphia Plan. Democrats in Congress were sharply divided over school busing. Nixon grew fascinated with the potential of race as a wedge to bring white labor and blue-collar workers over to the Republican party. In one administration memo, Nixon's staff related that the "September 5 News Summary" reported that "the majority of people in the West between the Alleghenies and the Rockies" had a whole series of beliefs about social issues, all basically conservative, such as "the rebellious kids are both wrong and a menace" and, notably, "Negroes have rights but forced integration will leave everybody worse off." Nixon official John Ehrlichman described how the Philadelphia Plan worked to break apart the Democratic coalition: "While anti-labor and pro-black, the legislative battle drove a wedge between Democrats and labor which has stretched the membrane."[48] As another Republican official commented in 1971, "The civil rights issues have a two-edged impact. Actions deemed desirable by the Blacks leave many whites unhappy, and vice versa. . . . The Blacks, it is true, are not very friendly

---

cult to find, but the political terrain to be negotiated is always treacherous. These presidents will in effect be probing for reconstructive possibilities without clear warrant for breaking cleanly with the past." See *The Politics Presidents Make: Leadership from John Adams to George Bush* (Cambridge: Harvard University Press, 1993), 43–44.

[46] Quoted in Reichley, *Conservatives in an Age of Change*, 54. Moynihan and Goodwin were the authors of Lyndon Johnson's famous civil rights speech at the 1965 Howard University commencement, which compared African Americans to shackled runners in a race with whites, and for whom equal opportunity necessitated special help.

[47] See Paul Frymer and John David Skrentny, "Coalition-Building and the Politics of Electoral Capture during the Nixon Administration: African-Americans, Labor, Latinos," *Studies in American Political Development* (Spring 1998).

[48] Both quotes are from John David Skrentny, *The Ironies of Affirmative Action: Politics, Culture, and Justice in America* (Chicago: University of Chicago Press, 1996), 213 and 214. For a general discussion of Nixon's efforts to promote the Philadelphia Plan, see chap. 7.

toward the Administration, and it is not expected that vote-getting potentials are very large."[49]

The Republicans began to see race issues as a wedge, and they had the institutional capacity to react quickly. As the Democratic party coalition divided, the Republicans were in a perfect situation to pick up new voters. Goldwater's anti–civil rights platform in 1964 made the party immediately appealing to whites upset about the progress of the civil rights movement. The victories in 1966 gave new Republican leaders like Ronald Reagan a great deal of leverage in party circles, diminishing the size and power of the pro–civil rights wing of the party. As Nixon recognized the benefits of a "southern" and "silent-majority" agenda, pro–civil rights officials in his administration like Leon Panetta and George Romney were easily marginalized or pushed out of office. By Nixon's reelection campaign in 1972, liberal Republicans had little strategic legitimacy.

DEMOCRATS INSTITUTIONALIZE AFRICAN AMERICAN REPRESENTATION INTO THE PARTY

While leaders in the Republican party attempted to distance themselves from black voters, many Democrats began to recognize the potential threat posed by civil rights to their coalition. One of the issues at the heart of this divisiveness was busing. School segregation was largely a southern issue until the late 1960s, when courts ordered northern cities to use busing to integrate the public schools. Protests and violence emerged over busing in cities from Boston to Denver. These battles spilled over into Congress, where northern Democrats began to split as members supporting white urban constituents lodged passionate protests against school busing and even offered a constitutional amendment to forbid busing for the purpose of desegregation. Southern Democrats like John Stennis tried to take advantage of northern Democratic unwillingness to bus in an effort to slow down desegregation efforts in the South. The Stennis Amendment in 1970 sought to ensure that federal desegregation would be applied throughout the nation uniformly and, hence, would alienate northerners and lead to a decline in federal enforcement of civil rights in the South. Although later diluted in conference committee, the Stennis Amendment passed the Senate 56 to 36. Gallup polls showed that close to 80 percent of the white public was opposed to busing.

Unlike leaders in the Republican party, however, Democratic leaders,

---

[49] Quoted in Frymer and Skrentny, "Coalition Building," 159.

who saw how divisive the continuing civil rights debate was in the North, were not in a favorable position to dictate party strategy. While the Republican party of the 1960s was infused with white backlash candidates, the Democratic party was infused with civil rights activists. Internal party battles during this period only further fueled activist behavior. In 1964, a group of African American Democrats from the state of Mississippi (calling themselves the Mississippi Freedom Democrats) contested the state's selection of white, prosegregationist delegates to the national party convention. The initial conflict at the convention resulted in a compromise in which two black delegates were seated at the convention. Although black Democrats at the time were dissatisfied with this compromise, they hailed the party leadership's decision to create a Special Equal Rights Committee and to take "affirmative steps" to incorporate black party members into delegate politics.

Then in 1968, the party's convention ended in chaos and violence, as activists outside the convention hall were beaten by police officers under the direction of Chicago Mayor Richard Daley. Upset with the nomination of Hubert Humphrey, many party activists tried to take greater control of the process. In particular, reformers wished to "seek as broad a base of support for the Party as possible by implementing the anti-discrimination standards adopted by the national committee; and overcome the effects of past discrimination by taking affirmative measures to encourage the representation of minority groups, young people and women in reasonable relationship to their presence in the population of the state."[50] While Nixon may have won in 1968 with a "southern strategy" and the help of a prosegregationist third party, the civil rights legacy remained legitimate among Democrats. Many party activists and leaders argued that a mobilized black electorate in 1968 would have (theoretically) provided the Democratic party a runaway victory in that year's presidential electoral college, as black voters had the potential to determine the vote in twenty of the thirty-seven states the party had lost to either Nixon or Wallace. Blacks and women in the party pushed for quotas and other reforms to decrease discrimination in the party and allow for increased representation at the delegate level, and as William Crotty points out, "The party had no intention of ignoring or jeopardizing the contribution."[51]

After the furor surrounding the 1968 convention, the Democratic party agreed to the demands of the new party activists and sat down to

[50] Quoted in Ronald W. Walters, *Black Presidential Politics in America: A Strategic Approach* (Albany: State University of New York Press, 1988), 55.

[51] See William J. Crotty, *Decision for the Democrats: Reforming the Party Structure* (Baltimore: Johns Hopkins University Press, 1978), 137.

reform their nominating process with the McGovern-Fraser Commission. As a result of their successful push, black representation more than doubled in the party delegations between 1968 and 1972, to about 15 percent. The change was most notable in states with large black populations. In Arkansas, Florida, Mississippi, North Carolina, and Tennessee, for instance, over 40 percent of their party delegations in 1972 were black.[52] Black political leaders generally endorsed the reforms as a means of giving blacks a potentially powerful voice in party electoral strategy.[53] The McGovern-Fraser reforms, moreover, attempted to increase the role of party activists and grass-roots movements and to make it significantly more difficult for party leaders to control the nomination process without including key constituency groups. Among the most significant reforms of the Commission was the mandating of an increased number of party primaries. The reliance on primaries and caucuses for the party nomination considerably weakened the ability of party leaders to select a nominee who could most effectively appeal to the national median voter.[54] For a candidate to win the primary, he or she need not reach the median in the nation, but only win the median in his or her party's constituency. Large concentrations of black voters in specific regions of party politics gave black leaders an opportunity to influence the primary results in these states, especially when low voter turnout historically gave mobilized groups great advantages, when rules allowed delegate allocation to be based on proportional vote shares, and (as was frequent in party primaries) when more than two candidates were involved in the race. This was further complicated by the format and financial structures of the primary process. Candidates who could win early on could use financial resources and media momentum to carry them to the nomination without having to appeal to a majority of the overall party's voters.

Although the intent of the reforms was to bring blacks and other historically underrepresented voters more directly into the presidential selection process, many scholars have attacked the reforms as signaling the party leadership's cession of control over the nomination process to party activists and various interest groups. As a result, it is argued, the Democratic party leadership lost its ability to advance electorally viable candidates and bring together broad groups of people into a coalition.[55]

[52] See ibid., 76.

[53] See Julian Bond, *A Time to Speak, A Time to Act: The Movement in Politics* (New York: Simon and Schuster, 1972).

[54] See Polsby, *Consequences of Party Reform*, chap. 3.

[55] See ibid.; and Byron E. Shafer, *Quiet Revolution: The Struggle for the Democratic Party and the Shaping of Post-Reform Politics* (New York: Russell Sage Foundation, 1983).

Nelson Polsby claims that the reformed selection process promotes candidates who represent intense minorities instead of those popular with broad majorities of the party, and as a result leads to crazes, manias, fads, and ideology.[56] If given power, these ideological amateurs saddle their candidates with unpopular issues and weaken the party's ability to be electorally competitive. As Byron Shafer claims, "at bottom, the result of all these reforms was *the diminution, the constriction, at times the elimination, of the regular party in politics of presidential selection*" (emphasis in original).[57] In many ways, these scholars are correct. Party leaders had lost a great deal of control over the process, and African Americans would be among the groups in the party to benefit. However, as the Democrats suffered continuing electoral losses, party leaders were slowly able to regain a significant degree of their lost influence.

George McGovern took advantage of the party's nomination reforms to become the party's candidate in 1972. Black leaders within the party, for the most part, supported McGovern's candidacy. Few in the Democratic primaries endorsed African American congresswoman Shirley Chisolm.[58] The party presented one of the more progressive agendas in electoral history, and was perceived by most national voters as too far removed from the median. After a landslide defeat in the presidential election of that year, party leaders began efforts to wrest back control from the party's activist wing. One reform of the subsequent Mikulski Commission was to keep "affirmative" procedures for blacks and other underrepresented groups incorporated into the party nominating delegation, but to make it easier to get around such procedures. Quota language was eliminated entirely by the Charter Commission, despite the disagreement of many of the black members of the committee and black California delegate Willie Brown's walkout from the meeting.[59] Southern Democrats, meanwhile, looking for more influence, pushed for a regional primary to occur early on in the nomination process. The party continued to battle over electoral strategy into the 1980s with no clear winners. In 1976, the Black Democratic Caucus eventually agreed on a compromise with other Democratic leaders over the party's affirmative action policies. Despite Jimmy Carter's victory in 1976 as a moderate southern Democrat who could appeal to southern white voters and receive the support of African American voters, many party

---

[56] Polsby, *Consequences of Party Reform*, 147. Also see James L. Sundquist, *Dynamics of the Party System* (Washington, D.C.: Brookings Institution, 1973), 307.

[57] Shafer, *Quiet Revolution*, 525.

[58] See Rubin, *Party Dynamics*, 133–36, for a discussion of the black Democratic leadership's position and black Democratic voters toward McGovern's candidacy.

[59] See Walters, *Black Presidential Politics*, 55–68.

leaders — blacks and whites — remained unhappy with their lack of control over the nomination.

When Carter lost reelection in 1980, some party leaders stressed the need to return to a "coalition, which is still there among intellectuals, liberals, labor, minorities, women, and the handicapped." It was pointed out that Ronald Reagan had won in 1980 by a very close margin. Had the turnout levels of blacks, Latinos, and poor and working-class whites been higher, the party might very well have carried the necessary electoral college states to win the election. In eleven states (North Carolina, Louisiana, Mississippi, New York, South Carolina, Virginia, Massachusetts, Alabama, Arkansas, Kentucky, and Tennessee), the number of unregistered black voters was greater than Reagan's victory margin. For these Democrats, increased voter mobilization provided the answer for both maintaining party representation of black interests and creating a more competitive party in the electoral arena.[60] Walter Mondale was among those arguing that "these Americans, so crucial to our party, have been explicitly written off by the Republican party. For us to ensure their participation is not only good government, it is also good politics. I am convinced that this registration campaign can make the margin of victory in 1984."[61]

The mobilization viewpoint received a boost in a number of the congressional and state elections shortly after 1980. In 1981, black voters were crucial to the Democratic party's key victories in North Carolina, Mississippi, Tennessee, and Texas, as well to Charles Robb's victory in the gubernatorial race Virginia. The victory by a Democratic candidate, Wayne Dowdy of Mississippi, in a 1981 congressional election — again with the aid of an overwhelmingly loyal black voting bloc — led one prominent Republican pollster to comment that Dowdy's election "put a stop to many Republicans' thinking that in the South we had a strategy built around Ronald Reagan that would last any time." When Democrats gained twenty-six congressional seats in 1982, nine of which were aided by significant blocs of black voters, some Republicans felt that their party had moved too far against the interests of blacks and other disadvantaged groups. Michael Horowitz, the general counsel of the Office of Management and Budget, wrote in an internal memo in 1982 that "we are being savaged by the fairness issue. Our moral and, correspondingly, our political base has been truly eroded. The toll has been acute."[62] Reagan's response, while not akin to Richard Nixon's

---

[60] See Rhodes Cook, " 'Have-Not' Surge to Polls: Major Force in 1984 Elections," *Congressional Quarterly Weekly* (July 23, 1983), 1503–7.

[61] Quoted in Milton Coleman, "Democrats Plan a $5 Million Drive to Register Minorities," *Washington Post* (May 28, 1983), A2.

[62] Both quotes are from Milton Coleman, "To Blacks, GOP Offers Little," *Washington Post* (December 7, 1983), A1.

reaching out for black voters, was to soften his stand on racial issues in an attempt to retain white moderate voters. The president changed his mind about supporting a national holiday for Martin Luther King and eventually supported various revisions to the Voting Rights Act in 1982.

Despite this, most leaders of both parties continued to argue that a distancing themselves from black interests was most strategic. Within the Democratic party, the defeat of a number of liberals in Senate and House elections led the chairman of the Democratic National Committee, John White, to advocate a new centrist agenda for the party. "The political needs of our traditional supporters—white ethnics, urban dwellers, labor, blue-collar workers, small businessmen—have changed but we haven't changed with them. We must realize that this is a new America, with new constituents and a new culture." House Speaker Tip O'Neill argued that while "in the 1970s, the preoccupation was with procedural concerns, opening the process and making it more democratic[,] in the 1980s, ideology and regionalism will be a greater concern."[63] Public opinion polls seemed to back this up, as not only were more Americans identifying themselves as Republicans, but a growing gap was occurring between black and white voters on economic matters.

Further movement was underway by party leaders to regain control of the nomination process. Carter supporters, for instance, proposed a southeast regional primary that would include Georgia, Alabama, and Florida. The regional primary would benefit southern moderate candidates (like Carter) by creating a barrier early in the process against northern liberal candidates trying to gain momentum in the run toward the party nomination. A second response, the Hunt Commission reforms, gave party leaders more control over the nomination process by creating "superdelegates." These delegates allowed party leaders to either place their support for the candidate of their choice regardless of the primary vote, or allowed them to go to the national convention uncommitted to any candidates. Superdelegates would give party leaders some more autonomy from the primary voters, and in the event of a close national convention, could be important in swinging the nomination to a more electorally viable candidate. The Hunt Commission also pushed for the "front-loading" of states that were strategically important for the party to nominate a candidate that would represent the "whole" party and not just certain factions or interest groups. Placing southern states near the beginning of the primary season, for instance, was thought to make it difficult for ideologically liberal candidates to win the nomination. Since the bulk of the party's southern primary vot-

[63] Both quotes are from Philip A. Klinkner, *The Losing Parties: Out-Party National Committees, 1956–1993* (New Haven: Yale University Press, 1994), 156 and 158.

ers are ideologically moderate, having these primaries early on in the nomination campaign would greatly advantage moderate candidates in their quest to win the presidential nomination. Finally, party leaders moved that delegate awards from individual primaries be determined in a winner-take-all fashion — a move that hurt party candidates who represented more narrow constituencies, and a move that would be fiercely contested by Jesse Jackson.

Efforts by strategic party leaders to steer the party in the direction espoused by White and other DNC leaders were hampered, however, by their continued inability to control the nomination process. The Hunt Commission took steps toward increased leadership influence, but party officials were still beholden in significant ways to primary voters and to any potential candidates who could gain the support of these voters. Although one of the party leadership's candidates, Walter Mondale, eventually won the party nomination, it was not before Mondale and the party endured a bruising battle with the first prominent African American candidate in American history, the Reverend Jesse Jackson. Jackson had entered the campaign, he claimed, to send a "message to white Democrats that black voters can no longer be taken for granted because they have 'no where else to go.' "[64]

On the one hand, concentrated efforts to mobilize more minority voters received a further boost in the 1984 election when Jackson, despite the resistance of most white and many black party leaders, emerged as a serious contender for the party's presidential nomination. According to at least some reports, Jackson's involvement in the campaign created enormous jumps in black participation.[65] A number of black leaders supported Jackson's candidacy, most notably former presidential candidate Shirley Chisolm; Washington, D.C., mayor Marion Barry; and about half the members of the Congressional Black Caucus.[66] Most black leaders, however, were skeptical, if not disapproving, of the Jackson candidacy. Detroit mayor Coleman Young declared that "Jesse, first of all, has no experience. And he has no platform. And he has no chance. . . . He is no answer to our problem."[67] Andrew Young agreed

[64] Quoted in Walters, *Black Presidential Politics*, 179.

[65] See Thomas E. Cavanaugh and Lorn S. Foster, *Jesse Jackson's Campaign: The Primaries and Caucuses* (Washington, D.C.: Joint Center for Political Studies, 1984). For a contrasting view, see Adolph L. Reed, Jr., *The Jesse Jackson Phenomenon* (New Haven: Yale University Press, 1986), chap. 2.

[66] See Manning Marable, *Black American Politics: From the Washington Marches to Jesse Jackson* (London: Verso, 1985), 253–56; Roger Wilkins, "Why Blacks May Not Follow in Droves behind White Democrats," *Washington Post National Weekly Edition* (August 6, 1984), 24.

[67] Quoted in Martin Schram and Dan Balz, "Jackson's Run Poses Dilemma for Black Leaders," *Washington Post* (November 27, 1983), A1.

that "blacks ought to be in any campaign where the candidate is likely to be elected president." Bayard Rustin worried that a Jackson campaign would "heighten racial tensions."[68] Congressman Charles Rangel agreed to serve as national vice chairman of the Mondale campaign.

For party leaders trying to reassert their control over the party and its message to white swing voters, Jackson was a disaster.[69] Although the civil rights leader surprised both whites and blacks by achieving a great deal of success in the campaign, party leaders did not view him as a legitimate national contender.[70] At the party convention, the Jackson campaign protested that their votes were not being fairly represented in the delegate process. This led to further division within the leadership over Jackson's role in drafting a party platform. Civil rights leader Andrew Young was booed by Jackson supporters for trying to work with the Mondale campaign to compromise demands by Jackson for more representation.[71] Jackson was also perceived as divisive to crucial elements within the party, particularly Jewish and white blue-collar voters, and an encumbrance in appeals to white swing voters. His reference to Jews as "Hymies" and to New York as "Hymietown," his refusal to disassociate himself from Reverend Louis Farrakhan, and his public embrace of Palestine Liberation Organization leader Yasir Arafat all deeply angered Jewish voters in the party's coalition. According to historian Steven Gillon, Mondale advisers were urging their candidate to publicly break with Jackson at the National Association for the Advancement of Colored People convention over the issue of Jackson's anti-Semitism. Mondale's refusal to do so was considered by at least one party adviser to be, "the last opportunity to draw a line that middle-America could discern as being significant."[72]

In the national election, Walter Mondale received more than 90 percent of the black vote, but received only one-third of the white vote. Despite providing sizable minorities of the vote in the South, black voters were unable to help Mondale win a single state in the region; he

---

[68] Young and Rustin are quoted in Marable, *Black American Politics*, 254–55.

[69] See Walter Karp, "Playing Politics," *Harper's* (July 1984), 51–60.

[70] See William Crotty, "Jesse Jackson's Campaign: Constituency Attitudes and Political Outcomes," in Lucius J. Barker and Ronald W. Walters, eds., *Jesse Jackson's 1984 Presidential Campaign: Challenge and Change in American Politics* (Urbana: University of Illinois Press, 1989), 64–65.

[71] See Robert G. Newby, "The 'Naive' and the 'Unwashed': The Challenge of the Jackson Campaign at the Democratic Party National Convention," in Lucius J. Barker and Ronald W. Walters, eds., *Jesse Jackson's 1984 Presidential Campaign: Challenge and Change in American Politics* (Urbana: University of Illinois Press, 1989), 160–76.

[72] The quote is from William Galston, and is in Steven M. Gillon, *The Democrats' Dilemma: Walter F. Mondale and the Liberal Legacy* (New York: Columbia University Press, 1992), 350.

received only 28 percent of the southern white vote. Contrary to the conventional wisdom that electoral groups benefit from their concentrated numbers in key electoral college states, the influence of black voters over the electorate did not increase in states where their numbers were highest. With the exception of Washington, D.C., which in 1984 had a voting population comprised of 65 percent African Americans, the relative size of the African American vote had no impact on the overall votes received by Ronald Reagan (see table 4.1). Courting the black vote in these states, then, seemed irrelevant for winning the overall election.

Thus, while party leaders had made a number of attempts to regain the control lost from the McGovern-Fraser reforms, the Jackson candidacy frustrated these efforts and posed continuing constraints on party leadership control. Shortly after Mondale's defeat, one party leader commented, "Blacks own the Democratic party. . . . White Protestant male Democrats are an endangered species."[73] Many commentators saw southern whites being scared away from the party by Jackson's candidacy.[74] Senator Daniel Moynihan claimed that the party was now seen by national voters as primarily one for minority voters.[75] In the aftermath of the election, Democratic leaders went back to the drawing board with yet another attempt to gain institutional control of the party.

SUPER TUESDAY AND THE RISE OF THE DEMOCRATIC
LEADERSHIP COUNCIL

In an analysis prepared for the Democratic party in Michigan, pollster Stan Greenberg found that the white Democrats "express[ed] a profound distaste for blacks, a sentiment that pervades almost everything

[73] Quoted in James R. Dickenson, "Democrats Seek Identity after Loss," *Washington Post* (December 17, 1984), A6.

[74] See Everett Carl Ladd, "On Mandates, Realignments, and the 1984 Presidential Election," *Political Science Quarterly* (Spring 1985): 13; Samuel P. Huntington, "The Visions of the Democratic Party," *Public Interest* 79 (1985); and Wilson Carey McWilliams, "The Meaning of the Election," in Gerald M. Pomper, ed., *The Election of 1984* (Chatham, N.J.: Chatham House, 1985), 174.

[75] John Herbers, "Party Looks Inward for Ways to Regain Majority," *New York Times* (November 8, 1984), A24. Whether Jesse Jackson did cause a white backlash is a different question. John F. Zipp has argued that the Jackson campaign was not responsible for the white support for Reagan. See Zipp, "Did Jesse Jackson Cause a White Backlash against the Democrats? A Look at the 1984 Presidential Election," in Lucius J. Barker and Ronald W. Walters, eds., *Jesse Jackson's 1984 Presidential Campaign: Challenge and Change in American Politics* (Urbana: University of Illinois Press, 1989), 208–26.

TABLE 4.1

Black Voting Size (by State) versus Vote for Reagan, 1984
(percentage)

	Black Voting Population	Vote for Reagan
DC	64.8	13.7
MS	31.4	61.9
LA	27.5	60.8
SC	27.3	63.6
GA	24.4	60.2
MD	23.9	52.5
AL	23.2	60.5
NC	20.2	61.9
VA	17.8	62.3
DE	16.4	59.8
TN	14.7	57.8
NY	14.5	53.8
IL	14.2	56.2
AR	13.6	60.5
MI	13.2	59.2
NJ	12.7	60.1
FL	11.8	65.3
TX	11.2	63.6
OH	10.0	58.9
MO	9.7	60.0
PA	8.6	53.3
CA	7.5	57.5
IA	7.5	53.3
IN	7.5	61.7
CT	7.1	60.7
KY	6.9	60.0
OK	6.0	68.6
NV	5.9	65.8
KS	5.2	66.3
MA	4.2	51.2
WI	3.9	54.3
CO	3.6	63.4
AK	3.3	66.6
RI	3.2	51.8
NE	3.0	70.6
WV	2.9	54.7
AZ	2.4	66.4
WA	2.3	56.2
HI	1.8	55.1
NM	1.6	59.7
OR	1.4	55.9

TABLE 4.1 *(cont.)*

	Black Voting Population	*Vote for Reagan*
MN	1.3	49.5
WY	0.7	69.1
ID	0.6	72.4
NH	0.6	68.6
UT	0.6	74.5
ND	0.5	64.8
SD	0.4	63.0
ME	0.3	60.8
VT	0.3	57.9
MT	0.2	60.5

they think about government and politics. Blacks constitute the explanation for their vulnerability and for almost everything that has gone wrong in their lives; not being black is what constitutes being middle class; not living with blacks is what makes a neighborhood a decent place to live. . . . These sentiments have important implications for Democrats, as virtually all progressive symbols and themes have been redefined in racial and pejorative terms."[76] A similar study conducted by the DNC found even more damning results from interviews with forty-three party focus-group sessions. They were subsequently destroyed on the orders of party chairman Paul Kirk.[77]

The election results and the conclusions drawn by Greenberg's and the DNC's surveys further emboldened those in the party leadership who wanted to make a concerted effort to refocus on attracting moderate white voters.[78] With division among African American party leaders over party strategy, the Democrats in 1986 passed new nominating rules in an attempt to provide a more moderate message.[79] The Democratic National Committee gave Paul Kirk the opportunity to reformulate the party's message, even if it meant alienating black voters and other groups labeled as "special interests" in the party. As Kirk commented, the attitude of the party interest groups was "Got a cause, get a caucus. As a result, white male Americans say, 'Do we have to have a caucus to

[76] Stanley B. Greenberg, "Report on Democratic Defection" (report to the Democratic party, April 15, 1985), 13.

[77] Gillon, *Democrats' Dilemma*, 395.

[78] See Phil Gailey, "Political Memo: Slouching toward the Center (Post-Reagan)," *New York Times* (September 18, 1985), 18; and Gailey, "Democratic Group, On Trip, Seeks Political Mainstream," *New York Times* (May 19, 1985), 13.

[79] Phil Gailey, "Democrats, with Little Dissent, Approve New Nominating Rules," *New York Times* (March 9, 1986), 28.

have a vote in the party?' Enough is enough." Kirk then broke with party tradition and refused to endorse the DNC black caucus's choice for party vice chair, Mayor Richard Hatcher of Gary, Indiana. Jesse Jackson called Kirk's effort an attempt "to prove its manhood to whites by showing its capacity to be unkind to blacks."[80]

While party leaders saw their proposals increasingly applauded, some leaders continued to disagree with this right turn. They resisted calls for a total abolition of interest group caucuses and racial quotas, maintaining that the party needed to stay true to its principles. Kirk himself stated that eliminating quotas "is not what the Democratic party is all about. I don't think we can turn our back on our heritage. . . . one of the great strengths of our party is diversity." Kirk also refused to take advantage of a party-commissioned survey that claimed to show that the party was alienating white moderates by appealing too much to special interests.[81] Still, party leaders made other efforts to boost their own influence over the nomination process. Kirk developed the Democratic Policy Commission, designed to reclaim "mainstream values." Probably the most significant component of this reform effort was the creation of "Super Tuesday," a one-day primary in fourteen southern and border states, which would be held early on in the presidential nomination process. By grouping these southern primaries together early on in the nomination season, party leaders hoped to attract a candidate who could appeal to conservative white voters and, hence, could be a more appealing candidate in the national election. If a conservative southern candidate ran in Super Tuesday, he or she would most likely exit with a commanding lead over other Democratic candidates, providing momentum for later primaries. Even if no southern candidate ran for president, the importance of Super Tuesday would force all candidates to adopt policy stands consistent with the interests of southern voters. As Georgia senator Sam Nunn stated shortly after the 1984 election, "The moderate and conservative Democrats didn't make it past the first round in its primaries in 1984 and we want to change that."[82]

Meanwhile, the Democratic Leadership Council (DLC) was created after the defeat of Walter Mondale in the 1984 presidential election. While officially autonomous from the party, the DLC consisted of a large number of elected official from the party's moderate and conservative wing, and was largely influenced by the party's southern wing. Much of the DLC's focus was on strengthening the ability of party leaders to resist the message popular in the party primaries and instead

[80] Gailey, "Slouching Toward the Center," B8; and Klinkner, *Losing Parties*, 180–83.
[81] See Klinkner, *Losing Parties*, 187–88.
[82] See *New York Times*, March 1, 1985.

to promote a message perceived as more suitable for winning national elections. Mondale, as Gerald Pomper writes, "personified the problem of the Democratic party generally, the need to define a more general vision from the clash of competing factions."[83] Jon Hale writes that Mondale's "call for a tax increase to reduce the deficit was portrayed by Republicans as an attempt to make the white middle class pay more taxes for government programs that benefited an array of special interests — especially blacks — in the Democratic party."[84] Other party leaders, however, were skeptical about whether such reforms would work. As former DNC chair Robert Strauss commented, "The defeat will mean nothing to them. The hunger of these groups will be even greater. Women, blacks, teachers, Hispanics. They have more power, more money than ever before. Do you think these groups are going to turn the party loose? Do you think that labor is going to turn the party loose? Jesse Jackson? The others? Forget it."[85] And given what would happen in 1988, Strauss was in many ways correct.

Super Tuesday, for instance, was a disaster as far as party leaders were concerned. Efforts to provide the white South with a more prominent ability to shape the party's message and candidate backfired when Jesse Jackson and northern liberal Michael Dukakis became the two most popular party candidates on Super Tuesday. Part of the problem was due to a formality that the party would straighten out in 1992. Many states had their party's primaries on different days from the Republican primary, allowing voters to vote in the Republican presidential primary and in the Democratic party's state primary — a move that reflected the split-ticket behavior of many southern white voters during the 1980s. As Norman Ornstein commented shortly before the primaries, "at the very least this could skew voter turnout and take away a lot of mainstream voters the Democrats need to win and hold through the general election."[86]

Moreover, with four prominent candidates running in the primaries, a majority of the primary vote was not needed to win a state on Super Tuesday. This reality benefited those candidates with tightly mobilized constituencies. Jackson, with an enthusiastic and mobilized black vote,

[83] Gerald M. Pomper, "The Nominations," in *The Election of 1984* (Chatham, N.J.: Chatham House, 1985), 16.

[84] Jon F. Hale, "The Democratic Leadership Council: Institutionalizing a Party Faction," in Daniel M. Shea and John C. Green, *The State of the Parties: The Changing Role of Contemporary American Parties* (Lanham, Md.: Rowman and Littlefield, 1994), 250.

[85] Quoted in Thomas Ferguson and Joel Rogers, *Right Turn: The Decline of the Democrats and the Future of American Politics* (New York: Hill and Wang, 1986), 9.

[86] Quoted in Phil Gailey, "Washington Talk: Politics; Some Second Thoughts on 'Super Tuesday,'" *New York Times* (March 24, 1987), A24.

carried every state that had been covered by the Voting Rights Act of 1965, winning a total of 286 delegates to the convention. In no state did Jackson win a majority of the popular vote. News organizations estimated that he received more than 90 percent of the black vote.[87] Meanwhile, the multitude of candidates hurt DLC favorite Al Gore, who finished second to Jackson in most southern states, and finished third to Dukakis and Jackson in the key states of Florida and Texas. Gore was the leader among white voters, and succeeded particularly in districts with many Republican leaners, but with two other candidates actively competing for the white moderate vote, Gore lost badly needed voters. With his relatively poor showing on the primary day designed for his type of candidacy, his race was all but over.[88] A second moderate candidate, Dick Gephardt, also was eliminated from the race as a result of his poor showing on the day. Thus, an organizational effort by party strategists had backfired. As Lee Atwater, George Bush's campaign manager commented, Super Tuesday was the "biggest political boo-boo of the decade."[89]

With Jackson's prominence in the Democratic primaries, Michael Dukakis was soon attempting to distance himself from the Jackson campaign in an effort to appeal to national swing voters, primarily the group of Reagan Democrats surveyed by Greenberg after the 1984 election. During the campaign, Dukakis made few appeals to blacks, rarely visiting black audiences or inner-city neighborhoods. At the Democratic convention, elaborate efforts were taken to make sure that Dukakis and Jackson were never standing alone together in order to assure that pictures linking the two would not show up in national newspapers.[90] Jackson, boosted at the convention by the large number of delegates aligned with his candidacy, was angered when Dukakis failed to inform him, after promising otherwise, of his pick for the vice presidency. The rift between Jackson and Dukakis was one of the dominant themes of media coverage during the convention, exposing to the national public the sizable degree of influence Jackson continued to have over party politics. Whether Dukakis liked it or not, Jackson delegates were vocal at the party convention, giving Jackson the leverage that could not be denied.

[87] Charles S. Bullock, III, "The Nomination Process and Super Tuesday," in Laurence W. Moreland, Robert P. Steed, and Tod A. Baker, *The 1988 Presidential Election in the South: Continuity amidst Change in Southern Party Politics* (New York: Praeger, 1991), 9–10.

[88] Ibid., 11.

[89] Quoted in Michael Oreskes, "Turnout in South Seen as Boon for the G.O.P.," *New York Times* (March 10, 1988).

[90] Kinder and Sanders, *Divided by Color*, 237.

Republicans, meanwhile, made every effort they could to link Du-kakis with Jackson. Both President Reagan and party nominee George Bush insinuated at their party convention that Jackson was a third member of the Democratic party ticket. Bush referred to the Democrats as "three blind mice." California voters received letters from the Repub-lican party claiming that "if [Dukakis] is elected to the White House, Jesse Jackson is sure to be swept into power on his coattails."[91] The Bush campaign later made national headlines with their attempt to link Dukakis with Willy Horton, an African American prisoner who had raped and murdered while on a weekend release program that Dukakis had supported when he was governor of Massachusetts. Dukakis, at-tempting to distance himself from Horton and Jackson, said very little about racial discrimination or inequality. Regardless, he saw a large lead early in the year evaporate into the party's third consecutive presi-dential election defeat.

RON BROWN, BILL CLINTON, AND THE "NEW" DEMOCRATS

In 1989, the Democratic party elected Jesse Jackson's campaign man-ager, Ron Brown, as the party chairman—the first African American chair of a national party in United States history. Although southern and moderate Democrats initially opposed Brown's selection as too closely tied to the Jackson wing of the party, he gained their trust by endorsing a white candidate in Chicago's heated mayoral race in 1989 and by appearing at the DLC's annual meeting to show his commitment to a more moderate party message. In 1990, the DLC, empowered by large increases in its ranks, selected Bill Clinton as its chair.[92]

The decision to pick Brown proved to be advantageous. His close working relationship with Jackson allowed him to have some influence over Jackson's decision not to run in 1992. Jackson and his followers, deflated by continuing party losses throughout the 1980s, realized they would have to temper their ideological proclivities. Civil rights suppor-ters suffered further public setbacks in two 1990 state races where prominent up-and-coming stars of the party suffered defeats in cam-paigns that highlighted divisions over affirmative action. In the North Carolina senate race, African American Democratic candidate Harvey Gantt lost a narrow lead late in the campaign when Republican incum-bent Jesse Helms ran a campaign ad in which a pair of white hands crumpled a rejection letter while the narrator said: "You needed that

[91] See ibid., 233.
[92] See Dan Balz, "Democrats' Perennial Rising Star Wants to Put New Face on Party," *Washington Post* (June 25, 1991).

job, and you were the best qualified. But they had to give it to a minority because of a racial quota. Is that really fair?" In the California governor's race, Republican Pete Wilson attacked Democrat Dianne Feinstein with an ad that asked voters, "Can we afford a governor who puts quotas over qualifications?"

By 1992, with the combination of Brown and Clinton, as we saw in chapter 1, the Democratic party's moderate wing took center stage. When Clinton attacked Jackson at a NAACP speech with the reference to Sister Soulja, few party leaders—including key African American leaders—came to Jackson's defense. The Democrats, still reeling from the perceived consequences of Willy Horton, defended Clinton's attack, and his general avoidance of black issues in the campaign, as strategically necessary in an electoral system dominated by white interests. Even black Congressman John Lewis said at the time, "In the communities I deal with, people want to win, they want to see a Democrat in the White House. . . . They understand that in order to win, it's necessary to bring back those individuals who had left the party." Wayne County Commissioner Bernard Parker was more blunt: "As a politician, I understand why Clinton is playing down. It's because he is trying to reach white middle America. I'm not bothered by his strategy. I think the strategy is paying off. . . . I am bothered by the racism of this country that forced him to do that."[93] After withstanding twelve years of Republican presidents, the moderate wing of the party made the most noise and captured the greatest degree of legitimacy. Most of the party's African American leaders offered support for Clinton. Jackson did as well, only after reaching out to Ross Perot at one point during the campaign and being largely rebuffed by the independent candidate. Although black voting turnout rates declined from 1988, those who did vote identified with the Democrats.

Meanwhile, the party's reform efforts had in many ways effectively come full circle. While still faced with a much different nominating structure than the 1960s, the Democrats nonetheless enhanced the power of their national leaders to control party candidates and the party's public message. With increased control over the party message, and with the legitimation of the DLC with Clinton's nomination, the Democratic party took perhaps its greatest strides in returning to the voter median and, in the process, distancing itself from its African American constituency.

[93] Both quotes are from Thomas B. Edsall, "Black Leaders View Clinton Strategy with Mix of Pragmatism, Optimism," *Washington Post* (October 28, 1992), A16.

CHAPTER 5

Party Education and Mobilization and the Captured Group

ONE of the underlying arguments of this book is that the manner in which parties compete with each other in order to get their candidates elected affects how individuals and groups think about themselves as political actors. I dispute the contention that parties are little more than umbrella organizations that bring together diverse groups of society into broad, competitive electoral coalitions. Even if parties see themselves as umbrella organizations, they nonetheless communicate messages to the voters about who matters and who does not. When party leaders focus their appeals on white swing voters, those messages, with their valorization of whites, are communicated to the national electorate. Furthermore, when party leaders assume that messages focusing on black concerns will detract from their pursuit of the median white voter, the resulting silence regarding black concerns has significant consequences for national electoral behavior. Perceptions by party leaders, then, lead to certain types of behavior that in turn influence how voters think about policies and how they participate in the political arena.

One of the most important ways that parties create, mold, and often redefine people's political identities, is campaign mobilization. According to the predominant scholarship on parties, campaign mobilization is a natural by-product of a party attempting to elect candidates to office. As long as there are two competitive parties, no voter will be neglected. The parties will always attempt to outdo each other in an effort to expand their electoral coalition to include a majority of voters. Since no group is discriminated against in the party's quest to increase its electoral majority, mobilization efforts are politically neutral. Majoritarian parties will promote the interests of the many voters who are left out of a political system dominated by powerful interest groups.

As this chapter explains, competitive parties often fail to mobilize African American voters in the way that scholars have predicted. It is not surprising that one national party makes little effort to mobilize their votes. After all, why would a political party mobilize a group of potential voters who would most likely vote against the party come election time? What is surprising, however, is that despite the fact that African American voters since the mid-1960s have supported the Democratic party at rates of over 80 percent, Democratic campaign leaders often exclude them from widespread mobilization efforts. Tactical and strategic reasons explain much of this behavior. Party leaders and consultants believe that the party should concentrate its efforts on those most likely to vote. Poor African American communities historically have low turnout rates. Second, the party will focus on persuading and mobilizing swing voters — rather than using precious resources to mobilize those voters who are firmly loyal to the party, as well as those who are effectively captured. As a captured group, then, blacks are often left out of not only Republican party mobilization drives but Democratic party efforts as well. Third, many Democratic party leaders believe their victory is threatened by their association with large numbers of African American voters. This leads them to minimize the public appearance of their candidates with these voters. If Democratic party leaders believe wide segments of the public are ambivalent about black interests, they will disassociate themselves from black voters.

This activity by party leaders has important consequences for the attitude and behavior of both the targeted white voter and the captured black voter. Party candidates, strategists, and activists focus their attention on voters deemed important. These voters are informed repeatedly about their issues. They are listened to when the party forms its political and legislative agenda, and they are mobilized both to vote and to participate in campaign activities. Those voters who are deemed unnecessary and sometimes threatening to party electoral pursuits are ignored, neglected, and, as a result, left politically demobilized, marginalized, and uninformed. It is also important to recognize the link between mobilization and the policies that parties support once in office. In the process of mobilizing a group of voters, that group's expectations are raised and they come to believe that their interests will be represented in the party's legislative agenda. If groups are not mobilized, then their political interests will not be promoted because their votes are not crucial to winning campaigns. Mobilization efforts, then, do not just reflect the way campaigns are run. They also reflect the policies that are pursued. If party leaders believe that mobilizing African American voters will increase the visibility of blacks, and if they believe that this visibility will make it more difficult for the party to appeal to white swing voters, they will avoid mobilizing blacks.

PARTY MOBILIZATION AND VOTER PARTICIPATION

There has long been a close relationship between party mobilization efforts and high participation rates. Beginning with the development of the Democratic party in the late 1820s, there have been dramatic increases in voter mobilization whenever political parties have actively sought out new constituencies.[1] National turnout in presidential elections between the 1830s and 1890s hovered around 80 percent.[2] On a number of occasions, parties mobilized groups with direct policy appeals. During the Populist and New Deal campaigns, as well as the Alfred E. Smith campaign in 1928, the Democratic party mobilized working-class and rural voters by putting forth substantive agenda proposals.[3] On other occasions, parties have mobilized ethnic and racial minorities with promises of legislation on their behalf.[4] On still other occasions, party mobilization efforts have emphasized cultural and nationalistic appeals.[5]

When the ability of mass parties to mobilize voters was weakened around the turn of the twentieth century, voting turnout began to decline dramatically.[6] In the 1800s, when party organizations naturalized and registered scores of immigrants, there were few limitations on the party's ability to mobilize. By the turn of the century, barriers to voting made it increasingly difficult for working-class and poor voters to participate. Party competition was responsible for many of these barriers. Democrats and Republicans, for instance, competed (as we saw in chapter 3) to disenfranchise African Americans in the South. At the same

[1] See Richard P. McCormick, *The Second American Party System: Party Formation in the Jacksonian Era* (Chapel Hill: University of North Carolina Press, 1966); and John H. Aldrich, *Why Parties? The Origin and Transformation of Party Politics in America* (Chicago: University of Chicago Press, 1995), chap. 4.

[2] Joel H. Silbey, *The American Political Nation, 1838–1893* (Stanford, Calif.: Stanford University Press, 1991), 145.

[3] See Martin Shefter, "Party, Bureaucracy, and Political Change in the United States," in Louis Maisel and Joseph Cooper, eds., *Political Parties: Development and Decay* (Beverly Hills, Calif.: Sage Publications, 1978), 211–65; James L. Sundquist, *Dynamics of the Party System* (Washington, D.C.: Brookings Institution, 1973); and Walter Dean Burnham, *Critical Elections and the Mainsprings of American Politics* (New York: Norton, 1970).

[4] See Steven F. Lawson, *Black Ballots: Voting Rights in the South, 1944–1969* (New York: Columbia University Press, 1976); Paul Kleppner, *Chicago Divided: The Making of a Black Mayor* (DeKalb: Northern Illinois University Press, 1985); Manning Marable, *Black American Politics: From the Washington Marches to Jesse Jackson* (London: Verso, 1985); and Earl Black and Merle Black, *Politics and Society in the South* (Cambridge: Harvard University Press, 1987).

[5] See Silbey, *American Political Nation*; and Michael E. McGerr, *The Decline of Popular Politics: The American North, 1865–1928* (New York: Oxford University Press, 1986).

[6] See Shefter, "Party, Bureaucracy, and Political Change"; Walter Dean Burnham, *The Current Crises in American Politics* (New York: Oxford University Press, 1986); Steven Erie, "The Two Faces of Ethnic Power: Comparing the Irish and Black Experiences," *Polity* 13, no. 2 (Winter 1980); and Frances Fox Piven and Richard A. Cloward, *Why Americans Don't Vote* (New York: Pantheon, 1988), chap. 2.

time, northern Republicans passed strict voter registration laws in an effort to limit the Democrats' ability to mobilize immigrant voters.[7] But antipartisan movements also played their role. The Progressive movement of the early 1900s, for instance, imposed a number of barriers on the ability of party machines and organizations to continue mobilizing large portions of the mass public. Reforms of the mid-1900s further weakened the ability of the party organization to undertake mobilization efforts. While local campaigns sporadically mobilized communities of voters, national party mobilization declined and voting rates declined with it.

In recent years, however, the national party organization has had a rebirth of sorts. Parties have become increasingly influential in organizing the campaigns of congressional candidates, coordinating the advertising and mobilizing of party positions, and controlling the political agenda. They have taken back control from consultants, the media, and PACS by nationalizing their authority and centralizing fund-raising and voter registration efforts. They are taking a more active role in encouraging candidates to run for office and supplying candidates with survey data, media and other consulting services, and campaign training.[8] Paul Herrnson claims that the national parties "now assist in campaign functions requiring technical expertise, in-depth research, or connections with campaign elites that possess many of the skills and resources needed to communicate with the electorate."[9] The ability of parties to involve themselves in campaigns by providing the technology and expertise deemed necessary to win has given them a degree of leverage over campaigns that they have not had in many years.

The Democratic National Committee (DNC), for instance, now has influence over what can be called a "family" of both coordinated and semiautonomous organizations that help the national party remain electorally competitive. This influence extends to officially autonomous campaign consultant groups such as the National Committee for an Effective Congress (NCEC). Though technically a political action committee, the NCEC engages in campaign consulting exclusively for the Democratic party. It provides electoral targeting analysis to nearly all of

[7] See Erie, "Two Faces of Ethnic Power"; and Scott C. James and Brian L. Lawson, "The Political Economy of Voting Rights in America's Gilded Age," *American Political Science Review* (forthcoming).

[8] A. James Reichley, "The Rise of National Parties," in John E. Chubb and Paul E. Peterson, eds. *New Directions in American Politics* (Washington, D.C.: Brookings Institution, 1985), 175–200. Also see Robert Blaemire, "The Party as Consultant," *Campaigns and Elections* (July/August, 1987): 30–33.

[9] Paul S. Herrnson, *Party Campaigning in the 1980s* (Cambridge: Harvard University Press, 1988), 122.

the Democratic candidates who run for Congress. The Democratic Congressional Campaign Committee (DCCC) and the Democratic Senate Campaign Committee (DSCC), together with the DNC, refer potential candidates to the NCEC. Candidates are first contacted by either the DNC or DCCC, who offer media services and technical assistance and who link the candidate with quality Democratic consultants. The DCCC and DSCC also aid House candidates in mobilization efforts by training campaign workers on how to "Get Out the Vote" (GOTV) on the day of the election. Thus, in making themselves more competitive, the Democrats should at least have enhanced their capability to reach out to disadvantaged voters.[10]

One of the most important ways that parties have historically mobilized disadvantaged voters is through the party canvass. As Huckfeldt and Sprague point out, "When a party worker knocks on a citizen's door, calls a citizen on the telephone, or affronts him with a yard sign, an effort is being made . . . to provide information that will influence the behavior of another individual."[11] In this realm, parties are much more active now than they were three to four decades ago. Rates of contact have risen dramatically since the 1950s, although contact has been declining over the last four national elections.[12] These studies show that parties encourage voters to participate by contributing financially to a campaign and volunteering time.[13] Evidence from National Election Study data illustrates that canvassing is especially effective for mobilizing those citizens generally not active in the political system. In the 1988 election, for instance, 90 percent of those contacted by a person from one of the major parties voted. This is close to 40 percent more than those who were not contacted by anyone from a political party, (53.4 percent).[14] The numbers are more dramatic among low-income

[10] Some would argue that the party is not stronger but instead has given power to non-party-affiliated consultants. The enhanced power of these consultants is consequently different than having enhanced power in the party. See Marshall Ganz, "Voters in the Crosshairs: How Technology and the Market Are Destroying Politics," *American Prospect* (Winter 1994).

[11] Robert Huckfeldt and John Sprague, "Political Parties and Electoral Mobilization: Political Structure, Social Structure, and the Party Canvass," *American Political Science Review* 86 (1992): 70.

[12] See Peter W. Wielhouwer and Brad Lockerbie, "Party Contacting and Political Participation," *American Journal of Political Science* 38 (February 1994): 211–29.

[13] See, for instance, ibid.; Daniel Katz and Samuel J. Eldersveld, "The Impact of Local Party Activity upon the Electorate," *Public Opinion Quarterly* 25 (1961): 1–24; Gerald H. Kramer, "The Effects of Precinct-Level Canvassing on Voter Behavior," *Public Opinion Quarterly* 34 (1971): 560–72.

[14] In the NES sample, 60.5 percent of the overall sample responded that they voted in the 1988 election.

TABLE 5.1
Party Contact and Voting by Income Group
(percentage voting)

Income Level	Contacted	Not Contacted
Bottom fifth	72.9	33.4
Second fifth	88.4	44.8
Third fifth	87.8	56.1
Fourth fifth	91.7	68.1
Top fifth	96.4	86.2

voters. Table 5.1 shows the percentage of people in 1988 who voted by income, comparing those who were contacted by one of the political parties with those individuals who were not.[15] The belief that parties can increase voter turnout among low-income voters, then, seems quite justified. When party members contact citizens, especially poor citizens, they have an enormous impact on whether they participate in elections. What remains unclear is whether parties will mobilize voters, and if they do, which voters they will mobilize.

MOBILIZATION OF AFRICAN AMERICANS

There are many reasons why the Democratic party would want to target blacks for mobilization drives. Blacks represent nearly a quarter of the party's voters and vote for Democratic presidential candidates at rates near or above 80 percent. Their turnout rates have been consistently low, significantly lower than whites, and the absence of these black voters can hurt the Democratic party's electoral chances. In Democratic party presidential victories since 1964, for example, the black voting population helped provide the margin of victory in a number of crucial electoral college states.[16] Large election-day turnout of black voters contributed to party victories in the 1976, 1982, and 1998 national campaigns, as well as many local campaigns. In elections that the Democrats lost, the absence of black voters often proved critical. Based on election data from the 1984 election, the Joint Center for Political Studies claims that increased registration of black voters might have

[15] The specific question asked by the NES is: "The political parties try to talk to as many people as they can to get them to vote for their candidate(s). Did anyone from one of the political parties call you up or come by to talk to you about the campaign? Which party was that?"

[16] Ronald W. Walters, *Black Presidential Politics in America: A Strategic Approach* (Albany: State University of New York Press, 1988), chap. 2.

brought the Democrats victories in New York, Massachusetts, Georgia, Maryland, and South Carolina.[17] Low turnout also contributed to Michael Dukakis's loss of a number of important states in 1988. Given the enormous potential for increased Democratic party votes, the party ought to intensify its mobilization efforts in African American communities.

Yet National Election Study data indicates that Democrats have primarily focused their mobilization efforts elsewhere. Michael Krassa finds that between 1964 and 1984 whites were about two times more likely to be contacted by one or both of the major political parties.[18] That African-Americans are less likely to be contacted by the two political parties combined is not surprising. With little support for Republicans (in 1984, less than 5 percent of surveyed African Americans classified themselves as "Republican" or "strong Republican"), it makes some sense for Republicans to stay clear of these primarily Democratic neighborhoods. What is surprising is that black citizens are less likely to be contacted than whites even by Democratic party campaign workers. Krassa finds that in every election between 1964 and 1984, a substantially higher percentage of whites were contacted by the Democratic party than blacks. While the Democratic party is more than twice as likely as the Republican party to contact blacks, in some elections it is also twice as likely to contact whites over blacks.

One possibility for this difference is that lower-income groups are less likely to be contacted than groups with higher incomes and more education. Some political scientists, for instance, have argued that because of a lack of resources, parties concentrate on those voters who are most likely to vote. As Rosenstone and Hanson point out, "Because political leaders cannot afford to mobilize everyone, they concentrate their efforts on people they have the greatest chance of mobilizing."[19] For this reason, they argue, the poor, the unemployed, and the uneducated are less likely to be contacted — because they are less likely to benefit the party by their political participation. "Intent on creating the greatest effect with the least effort, politicians, parties, interest groups, and activists mobilize people who are known to them, who are well placed in

[17] Joint Center for Political Studies, *Blacks and the 1988 Democratic National Convention* (Washington, D.C.: Joint Center for Political Studies, 1988).

[18] Michael A. Krassa, "Getting Out the Black Vote: The Party Canvass and the Black Response," in Lucius J. Barker, ed., *New Perspectives in American Politics* (New Brunswick, N.J.: Transaction, 1989), 58–75.

[19] Steven J. Rosenstone and John Mark Hansen, *Mobilization, Participation, and Democracy in America* (New York: Macmillan, 1993), 31.

social networks, whose actions are effective, and who are likely to act. Their efforts to move the organized, the employed, the elite, and the advantaged into politics exacerbate rather than reduce the class biases in political participation."[20] This has had a significant impact for African American voters. Rosenstone and Hansen find that curtailed registration and mobilization efforts account for nearly two-thirds of the drop in black voter participation since 1968.[21] In interviews with a number of party campaign leaders, I also heard comments consistent with Rosenstone and Hansen's findings.[22] The bulk of a campaign's time and resources are targeted at those who have voted before because there is an expectation that they will do so again. Many campaign managers argue that when mobilization drives of poor communities have been attempted, they result in only a 1 or 2 percent difference in turnout. Campaigns have more success, they argue, when they focus on people who have previously voted and who lack strong affiliation to either political party.

Yet there are a number of reasons to question this argument. For one, as Krassa finds, even when educational status is controlled for, blacks are less likely to be mobilized. There are strategic and ideological reasons for why black voters are not contacted. As the following section will point out, the incentive to focus on middle-of-the-road voters leads parties to focus their efforts on primarily non–African American communities.

"PERSUADABLE VOTERS"

As is expected of competitive parties, the Democratic party and its strategists focus almost exclusively on swing voters (among those considered likely to vote) who lie in between the parties. In the effort to attract swing voters, they all but ignore captured voters. Party strategists are unanimous in pointing out that roughly 80 to 90 percent of campaign resources—money, propaganda efforts, candidate visits, door-to-door canvassing—is spent in pursuit of "persuadable" voters. A persuadable voter is generally defined as one who has voted in the past few elections and has had a history of splitting his or her ballot. At times, the voter

[20] Ibid., 33.

[21] Ibid., 224.

[22] Representatives from the DNC, the DCCC, and the DSCC were interviewed during the winter of 1994. I also conducted interviews with four prominent national Democratic party consultants, a representative of the NCEC, and party campaign managers in the states of California, Connecticut, and Massachusetts.

has supported Democratic candidates and at times the voter has supported Republican candidates. A consultant with the DCCC terms persuadable voters as those voters who are "not regular Democrats, but
are not regular Republicans either." Thus, the voter is "persuadable"
because (*a*) this person does vote and (*b*) this person has not exhibited
past loyalty to either party.

The DNC, DCCC, and DSCC direct their candidates to consultants
such as the NCEC. The NCEC supplies nearly all of the party candidates in any given election. They consider their electoral targeting analysis to be "a resource allocation tool that helps campaigns spend their
time and money more efficiently."[23] The targeting consists of primarily
statistical data from the district, broken down by precincts, that pin-
points which precincts have high percentages of persuadable voters as
opposed to those with predominantly loyal Democrats or Republicans.
Once the NCEC provides this information, the candidate and campaign
organization decide what to do with it. However, all but two of the
campaign workers I spoke with said that the NCEC data was a primary
source of campaign strategy. The two that did not use NCEC data
nonetheless claimed that similar types of data were used instead.

Campaign mobilization efforts, then, depend in large part on the percentage of persuadable voters within a certain district. "These voters are
the principal targets of voter contact programs including direct mail,
phone banks, phone-mail systems, lit-drops, surrogate and volunteer
door-to-door canvassing, etc., between now and election day."[24] One
consultant at the DSCC contended that about 80 percent of campaign
mobilization efforts are spent on persuadable voters. A director of the
Clinton campaign in central California said that up until the final weekend before the campaign, almost no time was spent on nonpersuadable
voters. Not until the final weekend, and especially the day of the election, are efforts made to get out the vote in predominantly Democratic
neighborhoods.

By the definitions offered in these targeting analyses, most African
American voters are not considered persuadable. Since these voters have
a combination of high solidarity to the Democratic party and low voting rates, Democrats attempting to reach out to persuadable voters do
not tend to look to these communities for extra votes. The Third Congressional District in the state of Connecticut provides a nice example
of the consequences for African Americans of a party's focus on persuadable voters. Like many cities today, the central city area of New
Haven has high percentages of African Americans, many of them in

[23] Author's interview with analyst at the NCEC, March 1994.
[24] From NCEC report for unnamed House candidate in the 1992 election.

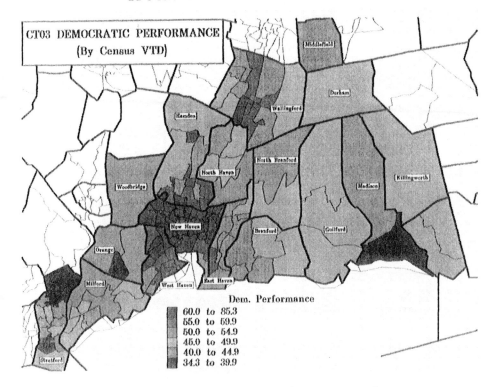

5.1 Third congressional district, Connecticut, democratic performance

working-class and poor communities. This area is surrounded by a predominantly middle-class and white population. As we see in figure 5.1,
the central city area of New Haven also contains strong and loyal Democratic voters. This reflects, of course, the strong national levels of support among African Americans for the Democratic party. The surrounding communities, as is reflective of many suburbs across the nation,
have much lower levels of Democratic support.

Now look at figure 5.2. The New Haven area that is so predominantly Democratic is also the area with the lowest level of persuadable
percentages. All of the wards in the central area of New Haven have
persuasion rates of less than 10 percent. Many have persuasion rates of
less than 2 percent. Compare this to the congressional district average
of 16 percent or to the average communities in predominantly white,
middle-class Wallingford (according to the 1990 census, only 1 percent
of Wallingford residents are African American), which has nearly a 30
percent persuasion rate.

Figure 5.3 examines the relationship between the percentage of per-

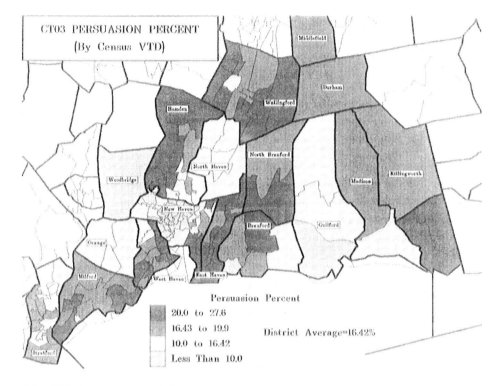

CT03 PERSUASION PERCENT
(By Census VTD)

Persuasion Percent

20.0 to 27.6

16.43 to 19.9   District Average=16.42%

10.0 to 16.42

Less Than 10.0

5.2   Third congressional district, Connecticut, persuasion percentage

suadable voters in New Haven precincts and the percentage of blacks living in these precincts. Because the United States Census does not provide racial breakdowns by voting precincts, these data are limited to the city of New Haven proper, and not to other communities in the Third Congressional District.[25] Nonetheless, the relationship is striking. Predominantly black precincts have significantly fewer persuadable voters than those of predominantly white precincts. A simple regression analysis of the relationship concurs. The greater the number of blacks in a precinct, the lower the number of persuadable voters.

Regression Analysis:

Percentage Persuadable Voters = 14.80 (Intercept) - 14.70 (% Race)

$$(4.81) \qquad\qquad (2.99)$$

[25] In Connecticut's Third Congressional District, only the city of New Haven keeps records of racial demographics by voting precinct.

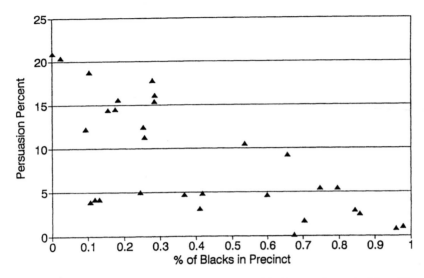

5.3 Percentage persuadable by percentage black (precincts in New Haven, 1992)

Income level data is available for all of the precincts in the Third District, and figure 5.4 examines the relationship between the percentage of homes with incomes between $0 and $20,000 and the percentage of persuadable voters in the district. In the scatterplot, we again see a clear relationship: as the percentage of lower-income households decreases, the percentage of persuadable voters increases. Clearly, then, both African American and other lower- and working-class citizens who are loyal Democrats are not included in party mobilization efforts.

CONSEQUENCES FOR VOTER EFFICACY

What are the consequences of this type of campaigning for African American voters? One campaign targeting report claims that "not mailing packages aimed at swaying (solid Democrats and Republicans) would save the campaign resources." Yet by not targeting these potential voters, the party is not informing them or attempting to integrate them into the political system. By saving campaign resources for largely white, middle-class, persuadable voters, the Democratic party is neglecting those who would most benefit from party contact. This becomes a reoccurring cycle. Those who are marginalized from the political system do not vote; those who do not vote are neglected even further.

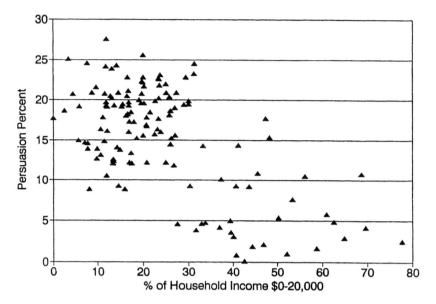

5.4   Persuadable voters by income level

In order to look at changes over a particular time period, isolating for the effect party contact has on potential voters, I used the American National Election Study's 1980 Panel Study. This study was conducted in four waves during the electoral campaign from January to November. Overall, 1,003 people were interviewed in the first wave; 763 people participated in all four waves of questioning. Again, the key variable I focused on is party contact. What impact does direct party contact have on how much people know about campaign issues, how interested they are in the campaign, and how involved and comfortable they feel with the political process in general?[26]

Beginning with a set baseline of January 1980, we can gain at least some sense of the impact of party contact on the electorate. Of course, even without direct party contact, political parties have a major bearing on how much the electorate knows about politics and how interested they are in the campaign. Just from each party presenting a candidate to the voters, and the increased media publicity that surrounds that process, parties are educating and stimulating some interest even in those who they do not contact directly. Door-to-door contact, however, more immediately engages people with the political campaign. People may

[26] The specific question for party contact is: "Has anyone from one of the political parties or candidates for president called you up or come around and talked to you about the election this year?"

feel more appreciated and included in the political system when they see that political leaders and activists care enough to knock on their door. Moreover, unlike a television news story, a person at one's door forces a potential voter to pay attention (albeit briefly) to campaign concerns. He or she may learn about key issues as well as various party activities that are occurring in the neighborhood, and where to register and then vote on election day. Finally, if party contact is so influential in mobilizing people to vote, then we should expect a similar difference for whether one is interested in the campaign and whether one learns more about the issues.

Previous studies have found that people who are contacted by a party are more likely to donate money to a campaign and to participate in some way on behalf of the candidate (i.e., wearing a campaign button, attending a political rally, or working for a campaign).[27] I focus specifically on three variables in the 1980 panel study that are designed to tap the general level of interest people have in the campaign: one asks how interested the respondent is in the campaign, and two other related questions ask how much they follow the campaign and whether they have spoken to friends about the campaign.

A number of studies have linked education and income to rates and styles of participation. Wolfinger and Rosenstone, for instance, argue not only that education is the best indicator of whether one votes or not, but also of one's interest in politics and understanding of politics and voting procedures.[28] We should expect, then, that party contact will be more significant for those in society who are otherwise removed from politics: the less educated, less involved, less likely to vote, and less likely to learn about politics through the media, friends, or activities. Parties are supposed to be most influential for bringing these people into the political process; as we saw in the previous chapter, however, they are the group more often left out of party mobilization drives. For these reasons I also control for educational level.

The results of the first set of variables examining respondent interest in the campaign are significant. Of those contacted by a political party, 65 percent expressed a strong interest in the campaign ($n = 143$). Of those not contacted, only 40 percent expressed a similar interest ($n = 620$). Educational differences are also important. For instance, among those not contacted by a party, 63 percent of those with a college degree reported an interest in the campaign, roughly the same percentage as

---

[27] See Wielhouwer and Lockerbie, "Party Contacting"; Huckfeldt and Sprague, "Parties and Mobilization"; and John F. Zipp and Joel Smith, "The Structure of Electoral Political Participation," *American Journal of Sociology* 85: 167–77.

[28] Raymond E. Wolfinger and Steven J. Rosenstone, *Who Votes?* (New Haven: Yale University Press, 1980).

TABLE 5.2
Effects of Party Contact on Campaign Interest
(percentage and standard deviation)

	Party Contact	
	Whites	*Blacks*
Follow campaign	.252 (.048)	.399 (.086)
Take interest in campaign	.388 (.046)	.648 (.223)
Talk to friends	.331 (.059)	.315 (.123)

Note: Figures in parentheses are significant at .05.

those who were contacted. The findings are similar for those respondents who were contacted by a party but were without a high school degree: 67 percent ($n = 24$) reported a strong interest. There is a dramatic difference, however, for those without a high school degree who were not contacted by a party: only 25 percent ($n = 161$) of these respondents reported a strong interest in the campaign. Party contact, at least in this instance, appears to have the ability to make up for educational disadvantages, disadvantages that otherwise lead to a great disparity in overall interest.

Similar differences occurred with the other two related questions. Only 4 percent of those contacted directly by a political party replied that they followed none of the election campaign. A full 36 percent of those not contacted made the same statement. Of those contacted, 65 percent reported caring at least somewhat about the campaign and 70 percent reported speaking with friends about the campaign, ($n = 143$). For those not contacted, 54 percent claimed to care at least somewhat about the campaign and 41 percent spoke to friends about the campaign ($n = 652$). On both questions, we see differences of roughly 30 percentage points, depending on party contact. Educational differences were also noticeable with these two variables. Only 22 percent of those without a high school diploma who were not contacted by a party claimed to follow the campaign at all ($n = 161$). This nearly doubled to 42 percent among those contacted with the same educational background ($n = 26$).

Table 5.2 presents the party contact coefficients for the three issues, broken down by racial subgroups and controlled for educational level. Although the small number of African Americans sampled in the panel study ($n = 106$) makes it difficult to make further breakdowns by educational level, we can see nonetheless that direct party contact significantly affects the level of interest in the campaign for both blacks and whites.

TABLE 5.3
Change in Respondent Interest, Controlling for Party Contact
(percentage difference)

	Later Contacted	Not Contacted
Follow campaign	+59.4	+42.9
Take interest in campaign	+31.3	+16.5
Talk to friends	+55.2	+36.3

What is problematic here is the age-old chicken-and-egg problem. Are those contacted already more involved in politics and more informed on the issues? For instance, some research has found that parties target those who already have a history of participation and involvement in politics.[29] The electoral maps earlier in this chapter provide further evidence for this phenomenom. Parties devise mobilization strategies around already integrated voters. Given that this is the case, the findings here are not as dramatic as they appear. It is not that party contact is so influential, but that parties are contacting those already knowledgeable and interested in the issues.

Nonetheless, parties do have an impact if they target those less involved. In table 5.3, I test the degree of impact party contact has specifically on those who were previously uninterested in the campaign. By isolating for those respondents who claimed in the initial panel wave that they were uninterested, we can more accurately gauge the degree to which party contact makes someone interested in the campaign. As table 5.3 reflects, while the campaign itself tends to have a positive impact on people's interest, party contact heightens it. Respondents who were not interested in the first panel were almost twice as likely in the fourth panel to claim that they were very interested in the campaign if they had been contacted by a worker from a political party. Contacted respondents were also more likely to have spoken to friends about the campaign and to have followed campaign events than those who were not contacted.

The second set of questions I examine deals with the respondents' overall relationship to the American political system. Three questions in the panel study attempt to determine respondents' levels of political efficacy: whether they believe politics is confusing, whether they feel that they generally have a say in politics, and whether public officials care about their concerns.[30]

---

[29] See Rosenstone and Hansen, *Mobilization.*

[30] These three questions were asked only once in the panel survey, during the June 1980 interviews. For consistency, I employ the party contact variable only from the same June panel.

TABLE 5.4
Effects of Party Contact on General Political Efficacy
(Logit Coefficients and Standard Deviation)

	Party Contact
Confused by politics	−.325 (.144)*
Believes officials don't care	−.285 (.161)
Believes individuals have no say in politics	−.386 (.174)*

*Significant at .05.

The results are similar to those discussed above. There is a 20-point difference in the percentage of people who say that they are confused by politics, depending on whether they have been contacted or not—54 percent (n = 66) for those contacted as compared to 74 percent (n = 760) for those not contacted. Only 26 percent of those contacted claim that they do not have a say in the current political system, while 46 percent claim that political officials do not care (n = 66). Comparatively, 48 percent of those not contacted believe that they have no say and 65 percent feel that political officials do not care about their concerns (n = 763). Table 5.4 offers logit coefficients for these variables, again controlling for the impact of educational achievement.

One problem with this panel study is that these questions were not asked after the second wave of questioning in June. As a result, fewer respondents at this time reported being contacted by a political party, and the smaller sample size makes breaking the data results down into various demographic categories more difficult. Educational differences are in particular more difficult to detect because of the especially low number of people contacted as of June who do not have a high school degree (yet another indication of the failure of political parties to target those groups who need more sustained mobilization efforts). Similar problems exist for breaking this down by racial groups. For many of the variables, only five African Americans claimed to have been contacted by a party, making any type of statistical comparison useless. Only if we examine those not contacted by the parties can we make comparisons based on education or race. The results, as might be expected, are not overly conclusive. I do find, however, that the problems associated with the lack of party contact are more exaggerated within the African American community, and are especially pronounced among less-educated whites. In general, 51 percent of noncontacted whites (n = 488) believe that political officials do not care about them, compared to 68 percent among noncontacted African-Americans (n = 82) and 73 percent among noncontacted whites without a high school degree (n =

155). A similar difference exists on the question of whether one has a say in the political system: 37 percent of noncontacted whites (n = 508) feel they do not have any say, compared to 47 percent of non contacted blacks (n = 86) and 50 percent of noncontacted, less-educated whites (n = 161). Both noncontacted whites and blacks feel about equally that they are confused by the political process — 68 percent among whites (n = 506) and 74 percent among blacks (n = 86). This rises to 90 percent among noncontacted, less-educated whites (n = 159).

FURTHER IDEOLOGICAL REASONS
FOR THE LACK OF MOBILIZATION

So far in this chapter, I have argued that national Democratic party campaigns avoid large-scale mobilization efforts of black voters. There are important exceptions to this, not brought out by the above data, when large numbers of black voters have been mobilized by Democrats. Quite often this mobilization has centered around election day Get Out the Vote efforts, as the recent 1998 campaign exemplifies, or has centered around the specific campaigns of black party candidates, (the Harold Washington and Jesse Jackson campaigns are particularly notable in this regard). Moreover, Democrats have other avenues for promoting black voter participation, for instance federal enforcement of the Voting Rights Act. As I have emphasized many times throughout this book, however, party organizations have many facets that often participate in conflicting activity. National election incentives matter because they push forth dominant trends and behavior. From both the data and interviews presented above, it seems clear that centering campaigns around swing voters has become, and will remain, a dominant strategy for party candidates. And if we maintain that party mobilization dramatically impacts voter participation and efficacy, then these strategies and tactics have important short- and long-term consequences.

As an electorally captured group, though, we should also expect more racially-specific electoral incentives for why the Democrats would avoid appealing to African American voters. If party leaders believe that mobilizing black voters hurts their chances with moderate white voters, then they should attempt to avoid such mobilization efforts. While data similar to the above discussion is impossible to attain, both Democratic and Republican party campaigns are littered with examples of attempts to avoid association with African American voters. The Republican examples have received a greater share of both public and academic attention, yet, the Democratic party efforts have in many ways been similar. [31] In 1984, central Democratic party strategists fought with Jesse Jackson over his efforts to mobilize increased numbers of African American voters out of fear that the party electoral percentages would suffer at election time. [32] During the 1988 Democratic primaries, Al Gore became the first national candidate to raise the issue of Willy Horton, a black rapist who raped and murdered a white couple while out on a weekend prison furlough granted by then-governor of Massachusetts Michael Dukakis. Dukakis would be criticized for the Horton incident again during his national campaign against George Bush. Perhaps in response, Dukakis tried to deflect race from his campaign. He generally avoided central city areas with large black populations, and he made a well-publicized campaign stop at Philadelphia, Mississippi, where he avoided mentioning to a nearly all-white crowd that the day marked the anniversary of the murder of three civil rights activists in that area. In the 1992 election, Bill Clinton made his highly publicized bus tour of America through predominantly white communities, while black leaders complained about being neglected, as they have complained to the media in every election going back to Jimmy Carter's campaign in 1976.

In a number of interviews that I conducted with Democratic campaign leaders, people expressed frustration at the unwillingness of the party's presidential and congressional candidates to enter into black communities. Part of this is due to the strategic reasons of going after persuadable voters. When most persuadable voters are white and when 80–90 percent of campaign energy is spent on persuadable voters, black communities are left out. One campaign worker pointed out that the liberal House candidate he worked for visited an African American church twice during the campaign, while spending sometimes five to six days a week in suburban supermarkets. Other complaints ranged from black city council members excluded from the stage at Democratic party rallies to black incumbent House members resisting voter registration drives out of fear of creating new and unknown constituencies. No campaign leader claimed that specific efforts were made to mobilize black communities with the exception of GOTV efforts on election day. Almost all agreed that such mobilization efforts were not a priority.

All of those I interviewed, meanwhile, agreed that the lack of contact had negative consequences for African American participation. As one campaign director complained about Michael Dukakis's unwillingness

---

[31] See Thomas Byrne Edsall and Mary D. Edsall, *Chain Reaction: The Impact of Race, Rights, and Taxes on American Politics* (New York: W. W. Norton, 1992); and Keith Reeves, *Voting Hopes or Fears? White Voters, Black Candidates, and Racial Politics in America* (Oxford: Oxford University Press, 1997).

[32] Jonathan Moore, ed., *Campaign for President: The Managers Look at 1984* (Dover, Mass.: Auburn House, 1986), 33.

to go into black communities in Los Angeles, "Bringing Dukakis in would have gotten people excited. They would have felt that the campaign was *happening*. Without [Dukakis] it was hard to get them to take an interest. At least he would have gotten them to come outside for a change."[33] A consultant at the DCCC denied any explicit racial reason for party targeting strategy, but added that "sometimes short-term desires have long term consequences that are not so desirable." As John Corrigan, a Dukakis campaign adviser, has pointed out, race "definitely exacerbates not only the fundamental tension in American politics but in the country itself. So highlighting racial tension (in a campaign) is never a good idea."[34]

CONCLUSION

E. E. Schattschneider has pointed out that "politics deals with the domination and subordination of conflicts."[35] What he and other party scholars have not entirely come to terms with, however, is the degree to which the two-party system, and its inherent electoral incentives, works to subordinate the interests of black Americans. If a nation is divided by race, with one group indelibly in the minority, the two-party system places the center of conflict and attention around the majority group. In turn, the minority group becomes further demobilized and, in the process, loses most semblances of representation in American politics.

[33] Author's interview with Marshall Ganz, March 1994.

[34] As quoted in David R. Runkel, ed., *Campaign for President: The Managers Look at '88* (Dover, Mass.: Auburn House, 1989), 230.

[35] E. E. Schattschneider, *The Semi-Sovereign People* (New York: Holt, Rinehart, and Winston, 1960), 66.

CHAPTER 6

Black Representation in Congress

THUS FAR, I have demonstrated the thesis of electoral capture with evidence drawn primarily from the politics and policies of the executive branch. At the congressional level, electoral incentives apply somewhat differently, leading party leaders in Congress to behave somewhat differently. For starters, there are 435 individual members in the House of Representatives, representing districts with radically different demographics. Some of these members represent districts where African Americans are the majority. Others represent districts where African Americans are a sizable plurality. Still others represent districts where there are very few African American voters. Representatives from black majority districts, in turn, pursue policies that reflect the interests of these constituents. Those that represent few black constituents pursue policies that reflect the interests of their own constituents. Thus, while national party leaders tend to elide the interests of African American voters in order to build a national political coalition, some individual members of Congress are motivated to pursue vigorously the concerns of African Americans.

Parties in Congress have historically reflected the district-based incentives of their members. Since members are accountable to local constituencies, congressional party leaders generally do not interfere with how members vote.[1] During election campaigns, this often means that the national party maintains a low profile in specific congressional races if the candidates are likely to benefit from such a low profile. As Richard Fenno has shown, many congressional candidates rely on "home style" appeals to their districts, and these appeals rarely entail a mention of the candidate's national party.[2] Members also have a great deal of control over their own committee assignments and legislative jurisdiction, especially when a specific assignment allows them to better represent their district.[3] Members of Congress have been further insulated from

---

[1] See David R. Mayhew, *Congress: The Electoral Connection* (New Haven: Yale University Press, 1974).

[2] Richard Fenno, Jr., *Home Style: House Members in Their Districts* (Glenview, Ill.: Scott, Foresman, 1978).

[3] See Richard L. Hall, *Participation in Congress* (New Haven: Yale University Press, 1996).

the national party leadership through the benefits of seniority on committees and subcommittees and by the emphasis in the Senate on "unanimous consent" agreements that force the parties to listen to the individual concerns of all one hundred senators.[4]

Since the 1960s, however, congressional parties have tried to intervene more often in individual members' affairs. While members are still elected from individual districts with different constituencies, the parties have gained some leverage through a variety of mechanisms. First, they have revitalized congressional election committees (the DCCC and RNCC in the House, the DSCC and RNSC in the Senate). Both parties have benefited from improved targeting of campaign funds, greater influence over large PAC contributors, and the general use of "soft money" to influence congressional races — with the hope, of course, that congressional candidates will in turn feel a greater debt to the party leaders once they enter office.[5] Second, party leaders (e.g., the Speaker, majority leader, and minority leaders) have gained more influence over the legislative process. Instead of automatically honoring seniority for committee chairs and allowing these chairs a great deal of individual autonomy, party leaders now can intervene and select a chairperson more responsive to the majority of the party. In the House, the Speaker now has much more influence over the Rules Committee, allowing him to control the timing of a bill's vote and the method by which the bill will be discussed and potentially amended. "Special" rules utilized by the Speaker allow party members to support their district's local concerns while simultaneously offering support for their national party's legislative priorities. In the Senate, the ability of blocs of members to filibuster has been weakened now that cloture requires only sixty votes. The reforms seem to have had some success, as the two congressional parties in the last few decades have become much more cohesive on legislative roll call votes.[6]

The revitalization of congressional parties is pertinent for a number of reasons. First, it is interesting to note that one of the leading causes for the resurgence of congressional party power was the fight in the

[4] For discussion on the House specifically, see Nelson W. Polsby, "The Institutionalization of the U.S. House of Representatives," *American Political Science Review* 62 (1968): 144–68.

[5] See Paul S. Herrnson, "National Party Organizations at the Century's End," in L. Sandy Maisel, ed., *The Parties Respond: Changes in American Parties and Campaigns* (Boulder, Colo.: Westview Press, 1998).

[6] See Walter J. Oleszek, *Congressional Procedures and the Policy Process* (Washington, D.C.: Congressional Quarterly Press, 1996); and David W. Rohde, *Parties and Leaders in the Postreform House* (Chicago: University of Chicago Press, 1991). For a counterview, see Keith Krehbiel, "Where's the Party?" *British Journal of Political Science* 23 (April 1993).

1960s over civil rights. For nearly three decades prior to the civil rights era, significant numbers of northern Democratic and Republican members of Congress tried to pass civil rights policies. Southern Democrats blocked this legislation, as well as legislation on labor, welfare, social security, and other New Deal economic policies. They were able to do so because congressional rules enabled them to trump congressional majorities. Southern members dominated over two-thirds of the committees in the House (including such powerful committees as Rules, and Ways and Means) by utilizing rules that guaranteed committee chairmanships to the most senior congressional members. In the Senate, southern Democrats blocked civil rights legislation by utilizing a variety of antimajoritarian measures, the most notorious of which was the filibuster.[7] For national Democratic party leaders who were unable to pass policies in a legislative body where they held a numerical majority, the dominance of southern members became particularly problematic when a solid majority of the nation's public began to demand stronger civil rights laws. Both civil rights advocates and party leaders interested in election strategy at this time found it in their interests to oppose the antimajoritarian rules used by southern members of Congress.[8]

Second, it is generally believed that the strengthening of congressional parties has improved the representation of black interests in Congress. In the mid-1960s, large majorities of Democratic and Republican members of Congress combined with President Lyndon Johnson to overcome the Democratic party's southern wing and pass some landmark legislation: the 1964 Civil Rights Act, the 1965 Voting Rights Act, and the 1968 Fair Housing Act. Shortly thereafter, the Democratic Study Group in the House pushed its party's rank-and-file members to pass a series of reforms (as mentioned above) to weaken the Conservative Coalition's general domination of the legislative process and of civil rights legislation in particular. A number of scholars have argued that this increased cohesiveness and party strength has had important ramifications for the representation of black interests in Congress. David Rohde, for instance, maintains that the declining influence of southern white conservatives has allowed the party to offer a more united and liberal front on civil rights issues.[9] James Carmines and Edward Stimson contend that the Democratic party since 1964 has "showed not the slightest remorse

---

[7] See Richard Franklin Bensel, *Sectionalism and American Political Development* (Madison: University of Wisconsin Press, 1984), chap. 5; and Charles Whalen and Barbara Whalen, *The Longest Debate: A Legislative History of the 1964 Civil Rights Act* (New York: New American Library, 1985).

[8] See Bensel, *Sectionalism and Political Development*; and James MacGregor Burns, *The Deadlock of Democracy* (Englewood Cliffs, N.J.: Prentice-Hall, 1963).

[9] Rohde, *Parties and Leaders*, 64–65.

concerning its past support for civil rights and indicated no hesitation about present and future support. The Democratic party had gradually but unmistakably become the home of racial liberalism."[10]

Much of this scholarly research is premised on a comparison between the Democratic party with either the current Republican party or with the party prior to the civil rights movement. Carol Swain's study of black representation in Congress, for instance, focuses on a modern-day comparison of the two parties. She finds that on indicators of black interests, "Republicans are less responsive to black interests than are Democrats."[11] Carmines and Stimson find a similar difference between the parties based on their comparison of congressional roll call votes and national party platforms.[12] Rohde, meanwhile, uses roll call scores to illustrate that the Democrats have become more unified and more liberal on a wide range of legislative matters, including civil rights. Roll call votes also indicate that many southern white Democrats have become less conservative, particularly on civil rights issues, as they have been forced to be more responsive to their party's leadership or to the rise of new black voters in their districts.[13]

It is clear that the weakness of the Democratic party in the 1960s was detrimental to the passage of civil rights. The emphasis on individual autonomy in Congress gave southern whites an ability to dig in against attacks on the racist status quo. Civil rights legislation was revolutionary policy, and it demanded strong, unified action by the congressional parties. Moreover, with a few exceptions, the Democratic party over the last three decades has consistently made stronger efforts to promote black interests than has the Republican.[14] African American voters of all socioeconomic backgrounds appear to recognize this and vote at dramatically high rates for the party's congressional candidates.[15] These points, however, do not capture the full story of black representation in Congress. Representation entails more than one party doing a better job than the other, or both parties responding in historically exceptional moments. It means a group playing a fundamental role in the decision-

[10] Edward G. Carmines and James A. Stimson, *Issue Evolution: Race and the Transformation of American Politics* (Princeton: Princeton University Press, 1989), 52.

[11] Carol M. Swain, *Black Faces, Black Interests: The Representation of Black Interests in Congress* (Cambridge: Harvard University Press, 1993), 13–19.

[12] Carmines and Stimson, *Issue Evolution*, chaps. 2–3.

[13] Rohde, *Parties and Leaders*, chap. 3.

[14] Some exceptions are the Philadelphia Plan promoted by the Nixon administration in the early 1970s and the concept of enterprise zones espoused in the mid-1980s by Reagan administration officials such as Jack Kemp.

[15] See Michael C. Dawson, *Behind the Mule: Race and Class in African American Politics* (Princeton: Princeton University Press, 1994), chap. 5.

making process, and the process in turn responding to the group.[16] As Lani Guinier writes: "A fair system of political representation should include mechanisms to ensure that a disadvantaged and stigmatized minority group also has a fair chance of having its needs and desires satisfied. . . . Each voter should enjoy the same opportunity to influence political outcomes."[17] This chapter takes a closer look at the degree to which the Democratic party has championed black issues in the legislative process in the post–civil rights era.

I find that African American interests have clearly fared better in congressional politics than in presidential politics. Controversial issues such as affirmative action, employment policy, opposition to apartheid, and voting rights were raised and championed by members of Congress well before they entered national political discourse. Black voters have also benefited from congressional attention to constituency service and bureaucratic oversight. The crucial question is: Is this representation in Congress a product of a unified Democratic party? Or does it merely reveal that the House is composed of 435 individual representatives — some of whom represent black majority districts — and that congressional rules empower these members to represent their constituents? Black voters have benefited from legislation supported by congressional majorities. Some of this legislation has been the product of a cohesive Democratic party defeating a cohesive Republican party. At times, this is the result of Democratic party leaders pushing their members to vote in favor of something their constituents might oppose. More often, however, black voters have benefited from institutional arrangements that weaken congressional parties. In fact, antimajoritarian norms and procedures such as self-selection for most committee assignments, committee autonomy, seniority, the filibuster, and racial gerrymandering have been among the most crucial and successful methods of black representation in Congress.

To be sure, many of these antimajoritarian procedures were created with the support of both the Democratic and Republican parties. Rules

---

[16] What group representation does mean, however, is quite ambiguous in the scholarly literature. Most scholars of legislative and electoral politics focus narrowly on whether voters are adequately represented by the specific people they elect to office. In turn, the discussion deals primarily with the classic distinction of descriptive versus substantive forms of representation, based on the work of Hannah Fenichel Pitkin, *The Concept of Representation* (Berkeley: University of California Press, 1967). Others focus on constitutional issues: see Iris Marion Young, *Justice and the Politics of Difference* (Princeton: Princeton University Press, 1990); Anne Phillips, *The Politics of Presence* (Oxford: Oxford University Press, 1992); and Will Kymlicka, *Multicultural Citizenship* (Oxford: Oxford University Press, 1995), chap. 7.

[17] Lani Guinier, "The Representation of Minority Interests," in Paul E. Peterson, ed., *Classifying by Race* (Princeton: Princeton University Press, 1995), 25.

about seniority, committee autonomy, and the filibuster are the result of both the institutionalization of congressional individualism and the votes of party caucuses.[18] The degree to which black interests benefit from these procedures also depends strongly on the Democratic party being the majority party in Congress. Many institutional rules benefit only members in the majority party, particularly in the House. Moreover, a strategy of relying on antimajoritarian procedures works primarily as a method to defend the status quo, not to pursue an active legislative agenda.

Yet the fact that black representation does rely on these procedures indicates the limits of strong congressional parties. Black representation relies on antimajoritarian procedures because civil rights interests are often threatened by majorities. In the post–civil rights era, members representing black interests have been on the defensive much more than they have been on the offensive. This has led them to defend many of the methods used by the Conservative Coalition to prevent the passage of civil rights measures in the 1940s through 1960s. African American members of Congress now endorse seniority, committee autonomy, and racial gerrymandering despite their recognition that all three hurt the overall coherence and power of the Democratic party. Antimajoritarian procedures coupled with the election of members of Congress from predominantly black districts has also meant that black interests are now on the agenda more often than they are during presidential elections. That they win on many constituent-oriented and low-profile issues is reflective of the design of Congress. That they lose on many high-profile pieces of legislation is reflective of the fact that black interests remain captured in the national party system. When majorities are needed to pass legislation, the same tensions that exist at the national level work to defeat legislation at the congressional level.

DETERMINING THE DEMOCRATIC PARTY'S LEGISLATIVE PERFORMANCE

In discussing the degree to which blacks are represented in Congress, we are confronted with a number of methodological and interpretive challenges. For instance, is there a definable "African American" political interest? If so, given the complexity of the legislative process, how can

---

[18] For different perspectives on why these procedures exist, see Polsby, "Institutionalization of the House of Representatives"; Krehbiel, "Where's the Party?"; and Gary W. Cox and Mathew D. McCubbins, *Legislative Leviathan: Party Government in the House* (Berkeley: University of California Press, 1993).

we adequately ascertain whether this interest is promoted in Congress and specifically by the Democratic party? Once we gather such data, how are we to judge what constitutes satisfactory representation? I begin, then, by answering these questions in some detail. I spend the rest of the chapter discussing how to interpret my findings and examine what they mean for the broader theoretical claims of the book.

A study that attempts to determine whether the Democratic party has actively represented the interests of African Americans is necessarily premised on a controversial point — that a "black" interest, at least one among those African Americans who identify themselves as Democrats, does indeed exist. Prior to the 1960s, race was the decisive influence in determining life opportunities and shaping the identity of the vast majority of African American citizens. The passage of significant civil rights laws, however, has made this claim considerably more complicated. With the passage of the Civil Rights Act of 1964, African Americans were expected to develop multiple, conflicting interests as had other immigrant groups already given the opportunity to legally pursue identities not based solely on their racial background.[19] Scholars have pointed to diversity among African Americans — for instance, a growing middle class and occupational, intellectual, and cultural heterogeneity — and they claim that the more important determinant of individual identity among African Americans is economic background.[20] When scholars do attempt to analyze the representation of African American interests, they tend to focus specifically on how often civil rights legislation is passed or whether the election of black individuals to Congress is necessary to represent black voters.[21]

Race, nonetheless, remains an overriding issue for African Americans in ways not comparable to most other Americans' ethnicity or occupational group. Racial discrimination and residential segregation continue to plague African Americans regardless of social and economic class, severely affecting the quality of education and social services available

[19] See Robert A. Dahl, *Who Governs?* (New Haven: Yale University Press, 1961); and Nathan Glazer and Daniel Patrick Moynihan, *Beyond the Melting Pot* (Cambridge: MIT Press, 1963).

[20] See William Julius Wilson, *The Declining Significance of Race* (Chicago: University of Chicago Press, 1978).

[21] On civil rights legislation, see Mary Alice Nye, "Changing Support for Civil Rights: House and Senate Voting, 1963–1988," *Political Research Quarterly* 46 (December 1993): 799–822. On the debate over the importance of descriptive representation, see Kenny J. Whitby, *The Color of Representation: Congressional Behavior and Black Interests* (Ann Arbor: University of Michigan Press, 1997); Kenny J. Whitby and Franklin D. Gilliam, Jr., "Representation in Congress: Line Drawing and Minorities," in Herbert Weisberg and Samuel C. Patterson, eds., *Great Theater: American Congress in the 1990s* (Cambridge: Cambridge University Press, 1997); and Swain, *Black Faces, Black Interests.*

to the black community.[22] As Michael Dawson claims, "Exiting from their community is much harder for black Americans than it was for European ethnic groups earlier in the nation's history or for Asian and Latinos today. In addition, to the degree to which the political and social climate is still perceived to be racially hostile, economic information is counteracted, with the result that racial group politics remains salient for African Americans."[23] African American public opinion and electoral behavior reflect the continuing importance, and indeed the dominance, of racial identity. Despite the increasing economic heterogeneity and the prominence of conservative black intellectuals and politicians in the media, relatively few in the black voting population have crossed over from the Democratic to the Republican party. As both Dawson and Katherine Tate have found, African Americans regardless of class and education remain strikingly more liberal than whites on many national policy issues, particularly those germane to race politics. Two to five times as many blacks as whites provide the liberal response to questions regarding their support for federal aid to minorities, jobs programs, social services and food stamps, as well as for spending on public schools and health care.[24] Moreover, African Americans suffer from high rates of unemployment, which have consistently been at two to three times the rate of that for whites. The infant mortality rate is more than double among blacks than whites, and similarly stark differences still exist between the races in educational achievement, health care benefits and coverage, and suffering wrought by crime, violence, and environmental pollution.[25]

In exploring the representation of African American interests in Congress, however, it is important to take a step beyond general and often latent concerns, and to look more specifically at what issues are perceived as most urgent by the black community and its leaders. To what degree has the Democratic party promoted the publicized and prioritized concerns of one of its largest and most loyal constituencies in legislative battles? To answer this question, I focus on the most visible force representing African American concerns in Congress and in the Democratic party, the Congressional Black Caucus.

---

[22] See Douglas S. Massey and Nancy A. Denton, *American Apartheid: Segregation and the Making of the Underclass* (Cambridge: Harvard University Press, 1993); and Joe Feagin, "The Continuing Significance of Race: Anti-Black Discrimination in Public Places," *American Sociological Review* 56 (1991): 101–23.

[23] Dawson, *Behind the Mule*, 11.

[24] Ibid.; and Katherine Tate, *From Protest to Politics* (Cambridge: Harvard University Press, 1993), 34–37.

[25] Swain, *Black Faces, Black Interests*, 7–11. Also see Dawson, *Behind the Mule*, chap. 2.

While by no means the only members of Congress who attempt to directly represent the interests of a large black constituency,[26] Black Caucus members have become, at least symbolically, the most prominent voice of black Democrats in the legislative process. Founded officially with thirteen members in 1970 when black members in the House declared themselves a "shadow cabinet" in protest of Republican President Nixon's policies, the Caucus initially attempted to fill a leadership vacuum in the black community created by the deaths of Martin Luther King and Malcolm X. On quite a few occasions, the Caucus put forth legislative agendas on behalf of their black constituents and other underrepresented groups. In 1971, they presented a list of sixty-one recommendations to President Nixon. In 1972, they participated in drawing up a Black Bill of Rights for the Democratic National Convention, and the following year, Chairman Louis Stokes presented a list of recommendations in response to Nixon's State of the Union Address. Since the election of Jimmy Carter, the Caucus has issued specific policy platforms less often, but nonetheless continues to claim to represent the interests of the black community through both symbolic proclamations and leadership on various legislative issues.

There are, of course, a number of caveats with using this group of legislators as a proxy for black interests. For one, there have been many instances in which the Caucus has been divided over policy positions and strategies or has disagreed with other black political organizations and leaders. The Caucus has had notable internal conflicts, as well as disagreements with presidential candidates Shirley Chisolm and Jesse Jackson, black Republican members of Congress such as Gary Franks and J. C. Watts, and black organizations such as the Urban League and the NAACP. Moreover, a number of scholars have criticized the Caucus for failing to represent national black public opinion or failing to be as effective as possible in influencing the legislative process.[27] As Swain and others have pointed out, the Caucus has taken positions and promoted agendas that differ considerably from black public opinion. The Caucus has tended to oppose the death penalty while the majority of African Americans tend to support it. In 1991, the Caucus came out strongly against Supreme Court nominee Clarence Thomas, while a majority of

[26] Swain, for instance, points out in chapter 8 the ability of a number of white Democratic House members to zealously promote African American interests in the House of Representatives. *Black Faces, Black Interests.*

[27] Ibid., 11–13; Marguerite Ross Barnett, "The Congressional Black Caucus," in Michael Preston, Lenneal Henderson, Jr., and Paul Puryear, eds., *The New Black Politics: The Search for Political Power* (New York: Longman, 1981); and Robert Singh, *The Congressional Black Caucus: Racial Politics in the U.S. Congress* (Thousand Oaks, Calif.: Sage Publications, 1998).

African Americans supported him. And throughout the years the Caucus has remained much more supportive of affirmative action, gay and lesbian civil rights, and abortion rights than has the broader African American public.

Still, within the Democratic party legislative arena, the Caucus has remained the most visible and vocal organization attempting to represent black interests. Perhaps most importantly, members are also the elected representatives of a significant portion of the African American voting community. In the 103d Congress, for instance, twenty-eight of the thirty-nine House districts represented by members of the Caucus had more than a 50 percent black voting-age majority, and the average black voting-age population for Caucus member districts overall has been 53 percent, as compared to just 7 percent for other U.S. House districts.[28] Whether or not the interests they represent are in actuality "African American" Democratic interests, they do offer as good of a proxy as we are likely to find.

A final problem is determining the overall success of the Caucus. To focus on all of the legislative measures promoted or endorsed by the Caucus and its members would blunt the significance of specific CBC priorities. In the 103d Congress alone, Caucus members sponsored a total of 506 bills and cosponsored 2,089 different pieces of legislation (see table 6.1).[29] This list does not even include a comprehensive alternative budget proposed by the Caucus. Moreover, like other members of Congress, CBC members spend much of their time on symbolic and noncontroversial legislation. Most members are not only preoccupied with representing their constituents, they are preoccupied with staying in office, and that means keeping their constituents happy with case work and particularized benefits.[30] Even on substantive legislation, as David Mayhew has argued, members will at times care less about whether the bill passes on the floor than whether they are able to "position take" correctly for their constituents back home.[31] Thus, having been provided the opportunity to display to their voters that they are on the right side of the issue, CBC members may be pleased with the Democratic party leadership even when the legislation goes down to defeat.[32]

---

[28] David A. Bositis, *The Congressional Black Caucus in the 103rd Congress* (Washington, D.C.: Joint Center for Political and Economic Studies, 1994), 23–24.

[29] Congressional Black Caucus, *Congressional Black Caucus Legislative Synopsis* (Washington, D.C., 1994), 3.

[30] See Mayhew, *Congress*; Swain, *Black Faces, Black Interests*.

[31] Mayhew, *Congress*.

[32] A potential example of this, as we will see later in the chapter, is the period during the 1980s when the Democratic leadership in the House created special rules that allowed for CBC members to position take on the budget. The CBC did not win any of these budget

TABLE 6.1
Legislative Agenda of the Black Caucus by Issue, 103rd Congress
(Number of Bills Proposed)

Domestic Policy	Foreign Policy
age discrimination 2	relations and trade 14
banking 12	Algeria 1
budget 5	Cuba 1
civil rights 10	Haiti 9
college athletics 2	Nigeria 1
consumer protection 13	Rwanda 1
crime and gun control 36	Somalia 2
defense and defense conversion 10	Zaire 1
District of Columbia 18	health care 30
drug enforcement 8	historically black colleges 3
economic and community development 23	housing 16
education 21	jobs 6
election reform 7	labor 11
environment and energy 16	law enforcement 4
equal employment 2	memorials and commemoratives 76
federal employment 21	minority and small business 7
food and disaster relief 7	prayer 1
government operations 31	reparations 1
	social security 15
	special federal programs 7
	taxation 24
	unemployment 5
	veterans 7
	voting 2
	youth 11

To determine the success of the CBC, I have examined the issues that have brought the Caucus to the public eye over the first twenty-five years of its existence. Through a study of three prominent indexes, I have been able to determine the issues the Caucus has most visibly championed and what successes they have had.[33] The indexes are from

votes, but some would attribute just having the opportunity to vote on such bills as a victory for Caucus members.

[33] To back up some of this research, I've also conducted interviews with eight members of the Congressional Black Caucus. They were asked, among other questions, what have been their main legislative priorities since they took office, and what have been their greatest legislative victories and defeats. Interviews focused on members with longevity in the House (i.e., John Conyers, Ron Dellums, Julian Dixon, and Charles Rangel). Results of the interviews are included throughout the chapter.

Congressional Quarterly Weekly, the *New York Times*, and the *Washington Post*. From these three journals, I have compiled a list of issues either promoted or challenged by the Caucus. I have excluded references to stories about side issues such as fighting among members, internal fighting over the choice of a presidential candidate, ethical investigations of both the Caucus as an organization and specific Caucus members, the retirements or deaths of Caucus members, and social occasions such as the annual Congressional Black Caucus dinner and fashion show (unless policy announcements are made at the social occasion).

This list is by no means a perfect tool. Action quite often takes place in the legislative process outside the view of the media. Members of the media, moreover, have their own criteria in determining what stories to run. That Caucus activity is not reported in one or all of the three journals does not mean that it is not active in the legislative process and having an impact.[34] Such a list also downplays the impact Caucus members have in the committee process. This is not a trivial point (and one that I will deal with later in the chapter), given the dominant role of committees and subcommittees in the congressional legislative process, and given that one of the main goals of Caucus organizers in 1971 was to secure key committee assignments for their members as a way to gain influence over important pieces of legislation.[35] The CBC has since placed members on most important committees. By 1973 members sat on the three primary "power" committees (Appropriations, Rules, and Ways and Means), and in the mid-1980s a representative chaired the powerful House Budget Committee (William Gray from Pennsylvania).

Finally, the tables do not provide any type of baseline by which we can compare the publicity of the CBC to other similarly sized interests. As such, how are we to interpret the findings? In an attempt to provide such a baseline, figure 6.4 provides a comparison of the *Congressional Quarterly Weekly* index with a similarly sized interest (in terms of numbers of voters) in the Democratic party coalition, the AFL-CIO. The comparison, however, is purely for descriptive purposes. Such a comparison is problematic and most likely biased, since the AFL-CIO is an interest group external to Congress. Its leaders, as a result, may be more likely to turn to the media and publicize their concerns than might the CBC, which is often working internally in the party structure. Unfor-

---

[34] However, the use of *Congressional Quarterly Weekly*, a journal with a small and select audience who have a special interest in legislative affairs, should help minimize the impact of media bias on the coverage.

[35] Robert C. Smith, "The Black Caucus Delegation," *Western Political Quarterly* 34 (1981): 203–21.

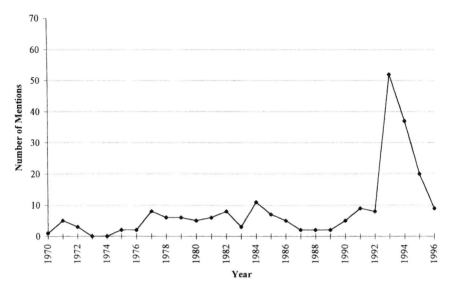

6.1   Mentions of Congressional Black Caucus (*Congressional Quarterly Weekly*)

tunately, there is no potentially comparable group to provide a meaningful baseline. Would an interest group like the NAACP provide more mentions than the CBC? (The answer is no.)[36] Does another congressional caucus represent a large and relatively homogeneous demographic group in the same way as blacks do during this period? (Again, the answer is no.) Recognizing this, the numbers must be taken as descriptive and the interpretations of the numbers maintained in context. All of these qualifications aside, the list still presents a quite powerful description of the role the Caucus has had in Congress over the last twenty-five years. Both the Democratic party and the Black Caucus are motivated to publicize their accomplishments. If the Caucus or the party believes that it has accomplished an important piece of legislation on behalf of its black constituents, it seems probable that at least one of these three media outlets would cover it. Figures 6.1–6.3, then, present the total number of references to Caucus legislative activity or stated policy positions in each of the three journals over the twenty-five-year period. The figures are presented to illuminate the significance and centrality of the Caucus in the national legislative debates. Table 6.2 offers a comprehensive list of the issues discussed in these journal articles. The intent of this table is to provide an overall sense of the Caucus's agenda and the

---

[36] I conducted the same search with the NAACP and found only a few to a half-dozen mentions a year.

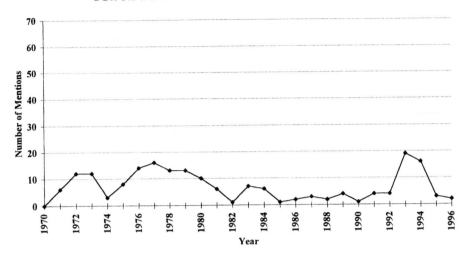

6.2   Mentions of Congressional Black Caucus (*New York Times*)

degree of success they have had. Included in the table are a few key words to offer a brief description and general tenor to the stories. Is the Caucus satisfied or angry? Are they pushing issues onto the legislative agenda or merely reacting to others?

To better decipher the long list in table 6.2, and to provide further analytical detail about the Caucus agenda, I coded table 6.2 into some important categories, subsequently presented in table 6.3. The intent of this coding is, as with the other tables, primarily descriptive. Some is-

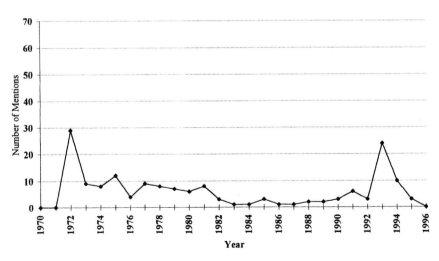

6.3   Mentions of Congressional Black Caucus (*Washington Post*)

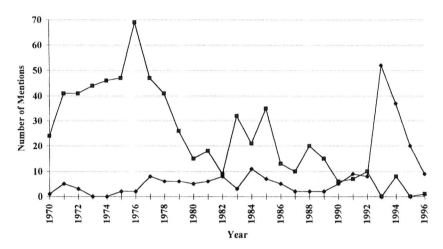

6.4 Mentions of Congressional Black Caucus and AFL-CIO (*Congressional Quarterly Weekly*)

sues on the list fit multiple categories, others do not fit clearly into any of the categories. Nonetheless, the coding summarizes the types of issues presented in table 6.2 and offers a general sense of the direction of the Caucus's actions and efforts. First of all, what type of news is the Caucus making? Is it attempting to place an issue on to the agenda or is it reacting to an issue already placed on the agenda? If it is reacting, is it supportive of the action or critical? If the story refers to a congressional vote, is the Caucus on the winning or losing side? Second, who or what is the object of the Caucus's attention? In this regard, I code the list presented in table 6.2 into six possible categories: Committee or House rules, congressional legislation, a congressional investigation or hearing, a president or member(s) of the executive branch, a decision by the Supreme Court, or, finally, a statement made by a foreign nation. Third, I code the journals' mentions of the Caucus according to subject matter, of which I provide eight broad areas: domestic civil rights issues (which includes a wide range of issues from affirmative action and busing to discrimination in the government and media), reaction to nominees to the Supreme Court or the executive branch, symbolic-commemorative issues (i.e., the Martin Luther King national holiday), socioeconomic concerns (i.e., welfare, health care, employment, and education),[37]

---

[37] Defense spending is also included in this category since it is commonly juxtaposed with domestic spending for social programs.

TABLE 6.2
Public Activities of and Stances by the Congressional Black Caucus as
Reported by Three Major Journals, 1970–1996

1970

1. Announce the formation of a "Shadow Cabinet" to oversee the enforcement of civil rights laws by the Nixon administration.
2. Propose a national holiday commemorating Martin Luther King.

1971

1. Present sixty-one recommendations to President Nixon—among them to guarantee each citizen an adequate income, to expand the Equal Employment Opportunity Commission, to keep funding for the Office of Economic Opportunity, to increase education spending, to integrate education, to increase aid for public housing, to declare war on drugs, to appoint black federal judges, and to create a permanent jobs program.
2. Critical of their meeting with President Nixon.
3. Hold hearings on discrimination in the military.
4. Criticize an EEOC bill that was passed by the House.
5. Senator Mansfield refuses to meet with Caucus.
6. Fight welfare bill.
7. Assail aid to Portugal.
8. Want more aid to Africa.
9. Want illegal drugs kept out of the United States.
10. Conduct hearings on health problems in the black community.

1972

1. Hold hearings on racism in the media.
2. Criticize Nixon's proposed budget.
3. Criticize the passage of an antibusing bill.
4. Pressure U.S. firms in Namibia.
5. Demand the expulsion of Representative Wayne Dowdy.
6. Upset with Youth Jobs Corps plans.
7. Exhort Democrats to oppose any welfare plan without minimum income limits.
8. Demand more education, jobs, and housing in a "Black Bill of Rights." Also ask for war on illegal drugs, new Homestead Act to rebuild inner cities, prison reform, Home rule for the District of Columbia, and national health insurance.
9. Want a boycott of Rhodesia.
10. Criticize racial tension in the military.
11. Criticize Nixon's antibusing comments.
12. Criticize Nixon's State of the Union speech.
13. Criticize the absence of black aides on Nixon's trip to China.
14. Begin hearings on "government lawlessness."
15. Want increased aid to Africa, decreased to Portugal.
16. Upset with situation in South Africa.

TABLE 6.2 (*cont.*)

1973

1. Attack Nixon budget for cutting domestic programs.
2. Oppose easing of radio station licensing law.
3. Criticize Nixon for not meeting with Nigerian president.
4. Push minority capitalism program.
5. Oppose Senate confirmation of P.J. Brennan as Labor Secretary.
6. Lose demand to FCC for free time after State of the Union speech.
7. Propose legislation to help elderly blacks.
8. Criticize as inadequate government programs to prevent discrimination.
9. Criticize court decision on Rhodesian imports.

1974

1. Attack coal contracts with South Africa.
2. Seek to reply to State of the Union Address.
3. Meet with President Ford.
4. Hold workshop on legislative priorities.
5. Commend Ford for opposing importation of chrome from Rhodesia.
6. Want decrease in military budget.

1975

1. Seek Martin Luther King assassination hearings.
2. Urge tighter arms embargo on South Africa.
3. Help defeat Georgia House member Ben Blackburn's nomination to the Federal Home Loan Bank Board.
4. Endorse full employment Hawkins-Reuss bill.
5. Criticize Ford's economic programs.
6. Outline legislative goals: stricter gun control, changes in economic policy and spending.
7. Oppose Daniel Boorstin's appointment to Library of Congress.
8. Want increased aid for U.S. poor.
9. Hold conference on unemployment.
10. Discuss African policy with Kissinger.
11. Urge tighter arms embargo on South Africa.
12. Oppose nomination of John Bell Williams to Federal Energy Commission.

1976

1. Seek to reopen Martin Luther King assassination hearings.
2. Endorse Humphrey-Hawkins Bill.
3. House agrees to hold Martin Luther King assassination hearings.
4. Investigate discrimination in the media.
5. Support busing for integration.
6. Criticize U.S. Rhodesian policy.
7. Want energy stamps to assist poor with bills.
8. Criticize South African apartheid.

TABLE 6.2 (*cont.*)

9. Criticize pre-inaugural moves by Carter.
10. Criticize Carter's cabinet nominees.
11. Are pleased with appointment of Andrew Young as ambassador to the United Nations.
12. Meet with Kissinger about Africa.

1977

1. Warn Carter about racial quotas stance.
2. React to Carter's stance on South Africa.
3. Oppose abortion ban.
4. Oppose confirmation of Griffin Bell as U.S. attorney general.
5. Support affirmative action programs.
6. Upset with being neglected on energy bill.
7. Oppose hearings on Public Broadcasting System nominee, Irby Turner.
8. Criticize delay in Martin Luther King assassination hearings.
9. Upset with lack of black appointments by Carter.
10. Remain far apart from Carter on top priority Humphrey-Hawkins Bill. Also upset with his avoidance on welfare reform and national health insurance. Support his proposed voter registration bill.
11. Criticize Carter on jobless rate.
12. Carter pledges support to Humphrey-Hawkins.
13. Criticize discrimination in media. Want more black owners.
14. Upset with direction of Carter administration.
15. Support Vernon Jordan's criticism of Carter's urban policy.
16. Criticize Carter's welfare policy.

1978

1. Support Humphrey-Hawkins Bill.
2. Oppose aid to Angolan guerrillas.
3. Oppose Hyde amendment on abortion.
4. Oppose Carter's public service jobs program and intent to increase spending for defense instead of for jobs.
5. Criticize Carter's job proposal.
6. React to Bakke decision. Support constitutionality of affirmative action.
7. Lukewarm support for embargo against Uganda. Want it tied to sanctions against South Africa.
8. Increase pressure for Humphrey-Hawkins Bill.
9. Criticize Rhodesian peace plan.

1979

1. Support Martin Luther King holiday. Upset with House refusal.
2. Upset with Education Department bill's amendments on quotas and busing. Succeed in defeating amendments.
3. Oppose Budget Committee recommendations on Humphrey-Hawkins Bill.
4. Vote against 1980 Budget Resolution.

TABLE 6.2 (*cont.*)

5. Meet with President Carter.
6. Succeed in withdrawal of Marshall Smith from Education Commission.

1980

1. Support job programs.
2. Lose proposed alternative budget 74 to 313. Would have increased domestic spending, cut defense.
3. Protest 1981 Budget Resolution.
4. Fair Housing Bill loses by filibuster in Senate.
5. Criticize Carter for lack of urban policy.
6. Criticize policy on Haitian refugees.
7. Meet with Carter.
8. Support enterprise zones.

1981

1. Oppose congressional caucus financial reforms.
2. Support Voting Rights Act extension.
3. Support enterprise zones.
4. Oppose budget cuts.
5. Oppose anti–affirmative action bill.
6. Lose alternative budget 69 to 356. Would have restored social spending, cut defense.
7. Succeed in blocking Dan Mica from subcommittee chair of Africa.
8. Harold Washington loses attempt to get on Budget Committee.

1982

1. Oppose immigration bill.
2. Oppose loans to South Africa.
3. Lose alternative budget 86 to 322. Would have increased social spending.
4. Oppose House finance rules.
5. Lose bill to cut defense spending 55 to 348.
6. Vote against House passed tax bill.
7. Support Voting Rights Act extension.
8. Criticize Reagan Caribbean bill for ignoring black nations.
9. Oppose G-5B plane.
10. Criticize Reagan budget cuts.

1983

1. Oppose House finance rules for caucuses.
2. Complain that their budget proposals are being ignored.
3. Upset about absence of job bill.
4. Oppose Reagan desire to extend Civil Rights Commission rather than to make it permanent.
5. Oppose firing of three Civil Rights Commission members.
6. Succeed in stopping cuts in aid to Zimbabwe.

TABLE 6.2 (*cont.*)

7. Sponsor gay and lesbian civil rights legislation.
8. Sponsor Fair Housing Bill.
9. Martin Luther King holiday bill passes Senate 78 to 22.
10. Alternative budget refused by Rules Committee.

1984

1. Support protests for divestment from South Africa.
2. Vote "present" on South African Sanction Bill, which passes House 269 to 62.
3. Support bipartisan bill extending prohibition on discrimination.
4. Lose budget alternative 76 to 333. Would have increased domestic spending, decreased defense.
5. Support bill to make Haitian immigrants U.S. citizens.
6. Criticize youth summer wage bill.

1985

1. Oppose aid to Angola.
2. Support sanctions against South Africa. House passes bill supporting sanctions 295 to 127.
3. Oppose lower minimum wage.
4. Grudgingly support Democratic party budget.
5. Fight for African hunger relief.
6. William Gray elected chair of Budget Committee.
7. Support Civil Rights Restoration Act.
8. Lose alternative budget, 54 to 361. Would have raised taxes, cut defense.
9. Oppose nomination of William Reynolds for associate attorney general.
10. Push for passage of South Africa sanctions in Senate.

1986

1. Win South Africa sanctions vote: House 313 to 83, Senate 78 to 21.
2. Lose alternative budget 61 to 359.
3. Push for funding from Pentagon for minority firms.
4. Vote against death penalty provisions in antidrug bill.
5. Oppose military use to fight drugs; lose 392 to 16.
6. Support farm bill.
7. Lose Aid to Families with Dependent Children provision on one-parent eligibility.

1987

1. Support census bill to readjust figures of missed groups.
2. Support ousting of Les Aspin as Armed Services Committee chairman.
3. Lose alternative budget. Would have increased spending for social services, decreased defense spending.
4. Oppose nomination of Robert Bork for justice of the Supreme Court.
5. Examine human rights abuses in Haiti.

TABLE 6.2 (*cont.*)

1988

1. Examine Anti-Apartheid Act because of infractions.
2. Oppose Contra aid.

1989

1. Oppose court decisions on affirmative action.
2. Criticize Zaire president on civil rights.
3. Support passage of community reinvestment act making banks and savings and loans disclose rejections of mortgages based on race.
4. Lose alternative budget. Would have further cut defense spending and raised taxes on the wealthy.
5. Approve bill to reform school lunch aid.
6. Meet with and criticize President Bush for inattention to the problems of the inner city.

1990

1. Lose alternative budget 90 to 334.
2. Oppose president's budget proposal.
3. Support motor-voter bill.
4. Support increased spending on AIDS research.
5. Promote economic conversion of Pentagon bases.
6. Win increased aid for Africa.

1991

1. Oppose president's efforts to undermine Civil Rights Act of 1991.
2. Oppose Clarence Thomas nomination to Supreme Court.
3. Oppose lifting of sanctions against South Africa.
4. Lose their own bill on Civil Rights Act.
5. Oppose Gulf War.
6. Seek increased aid to Africa.
7. Establish national commission on education.

1992

1. Oppose aid to Russia.
2. Protest cut of $14 million for inner-city AIDS project.
3. Oppose Bush's handling of Haiti.
4. Promote safe haven for Haitian exiles.
5. Lose alternative budget, 77 to 342.
6. Promote urban relief in response to Los Angeles riots.
7. Oppose nomination of Edward Carnes to Court of Appeals because of his stance on death penalty.
8. Support military intervention in Somalia.

1993

1. Oppose Senate bill that would disallow AIDS victims to immigrate to U.S.
2. Lose alternative budget 87 to 335.

TABLE 6.2 (*cont.*)

3. Oppose line-item veto.
4. Complain about lack of domestic spending.
5. Lose job bill.
6. Upset about Lani Guinier nomination.
7. Threaten to defeat Foreign Aid Bill before increase of $100 million in aid to Africa.
8. Oppose budget cuts and scaling back of stimulus plan.
9. Support cleanup of savings and loan that gives preference to minority investors.
10. Support efforts to diversify Federal Reserve System.
11. Oppose NAFTA.
12. Push for crime bill.
13. Oppose defense spending.
14. Promote increased aid to poor nations.
15. Decline meeting with President Clinton.
16. Attempt to block further cuts in entitlements and programs benefiting poor.
17. Support deficit-reduction bill.
18. Criticize Medicare cuts, lack of summer jobs for youths, and cuts in child nutrition.
19. Tell Clinton that antihunger provisions are not negotiable.
20. Support empowerment zones.
21. Criticize Haitian refugee policy.
22. Upset with crime bill's emphasis on punishment and death penalty.
23. Support aid to Africa.
24. Want expansion of EITC (program for working families).
25. Support energy tax for poor and urban areas.
26. Support nomination of Jocelyn Elders to the post of surgeon general.
27. Insist that reconciliation bill include more social spending.
28. Trade Medicare cuts for immunization program.
29. Support final budget reconciliation.
30. Support bill for student loans.
31. Introduce alternative crime bill focusing on prevention.
32. Lose vote on Distirct of Columbia statehood, 153 to 277.
33. Support intervention in Haiti.
34. Support job training bill.
35. Push for settlement in Somalia.
36. Investigate National Collegiate Athletic Association.
37. Oppose nomination of John Payton to Justice Department.

1994

1. Support empowerment zones.
2. Oppose crime bill and promote alternative.
3. Criticize three-strikes policy proposal.
4. Oppose Haitian policy.
5. Push for racial justice part of crime bill (passed by House).

TABLE 6.2 *(cont.)*

6. Support assault weapon ban.
7. Support majority-minority redistricting.
8. Lose racial justice part of crime bill.
9. Speaker Tom Foley supports Caucus on racial justice in crime bill.
10. Oppose Clinton welfare proposals.
11. Applaud decision to send diplomats to Haiti.
12. Promote use of force in Haiti.
13. Oppose cuts in aid to Africa.
14. Comment on proposed health care reform.
15. Support seniority system over majority vote in House.
16. Split in support of crime bill.
17. Oppose freeze in aid to South Africa, lose 103 to 321.
18. Lose funding for Caucus.
19. Vote against lobbying bill — done with intent to remind leadership not to take them for granted.
20. Criticize plans for welfare reform.

1995

1. Charge GOP majority as racist.
2. Oppose tax break issue.
3. Oppose bill to curtail death row appeals.
4. Oppose HR 831 as anti–affirmative action.
5. Oppose welfare overhaul bill.
6. Present budget substitute.
7. Oppose cuts in Africa funding.
8. Alternative budget proposal loses, 56 to 367.
9. Lose economic aid to Africa amendment
10. Talk with Clinton about affirmative action.
11. Angry at the ending of a minority tax break.

1996

1. Oppose decision to end minority tax break.
2. Question encouragement of interracial adoptions.
3. Push for greater voter-registration efforts.

crime, human rights concerns in foreign nations such as South Africa, aid to foreign nations, and institutional maintenance of the Caucus (i.e., the placement of Caucus members on congressional committees).

The rest of this chapter will look behind the numbers and brief descriptions of the tables. First, I look at the success the Caucus has as a subpart of the Democratic party's legislative agenda. How has the Caucus fared on issues that rely on party majorities for their passage? Second, I look at what the Caucus has achieved through nonmajori-

TABLE 6.3

Public Stances by the Congressional Black Caucus,
by Subject Matter

Public Stance	Number of Mentions
Proposals	63
Reactions (total)	160
Positive	25
Negative	135
Votes	40
Win	12
Lose	28
Directed At	
Congressional legislation	141
Executive action	81
Supreme Court	4
Foreign leaders	4
Investigations	16
Committee/House Rules	13
Subject Matter	
Civil rights	41
Socioeconomic issues	106
Crime	9
Federal nominees	22
Commemoratives	4
Human rights	40
Foreign aid	23
Committee/House Rules	13

tarian means. How many of the Caucus's achievements are a result of rules that advantage minority interests in the House? In the end, just as organizational protections in the national party (such as the McGovern-Fraser reforms) were vulnerable to counter reforms as a result of electoral pressures, these congressional victories remain vulnerable to the electoral pressures of the national party. Majority-minority districts, for instance, grew vulnerable to a backlash by the Democratic party after their electoral defeats in 1994, as well as to a change by the Supreme Court in interpretation of the Civil Rights Act and its amendments. Seniority on committees presents a second possibility for backlash, if and when the Democrats regain control of the House. Electoral pressures to maintain a moderate national image could force the Democratic leadership to limit the ability of senior Caucus members to promote liberal policies aimed at helping African American constituents. Just as liberal Democrats took power away from the Conservative Coalition when southern Democrats were harmful to their interests, so may more moderate Democrats take that power away from the Black Caucus.

RESULTS, PART 1: RELYING ON THE MAJORITY PARTY
FOR LEGISLATIVE INITIATIVES

When scholars and pundits discuss the Black Caucus's current predicament over majority-minority districts, they generally raise the question of whether African American interests are better off in Congress as a small minority within a majority party or whether their interests are represented best as a larger minority within a minority party. While few disagree that the current status of the Congressional Black Caucus as a minority within a minority party is undesirable, the legislative history of the period prior to 1992 suggests that the alternative was not particularly successful either. Only the two-year period between 1993 and 1994, when the Caucus was a sizable minority in a majority party—a direct result of Court-ordered racial gerrymandering—did the Caucus notably influence the party's legislative agenda (see figures 6.1–6.3). Relying on the Democratic party to publicly promote the CBC's agenda in Congress, then, they met many pitfalls similar to those created by the captured status of blacks in presidential politics.

A number of points are striking about the success of the CBC as a minority within a congressional majority party. First of all, the main tenets of the Caucus agenda have been quite consistent over the years. One issue dominates all others: increased spending on domestic services such as education, welfare, health care, and employment opportunities. In fact, almost half of the issues (43 percent) listed in table 6.2 relate specifically to socioeconomic concerns. In addition, the Caucus consistently denounces the U.S. government's association with human rights violators in Africa and Latin America (which account for 17 percent of the listings) and consistently announces support for three of the main tenets of the post-civil rights movement—busing, voting rights, and affirmative action (16 percent of the list deals with civil rights concerns).

In 1971, for instance, the Caucus presented President Richard Nixon with sixty-one recommendations. Among the most prominent were a national program creating one million public service jobs and a government guaranteed income, increased support for a national welfare program, increased federal aid for education and further integration of education facilities, increased funding for public housing, increased attention to drug abuse, home rule for the people living in Washington, D.C., increased aid to Africa, and an end to the Vietnam War. Except for the call to end the war in Vietnam, each of these issues has remained prominent on the Caucus agenda throughout most of the twenty-five years examined. Little more than the phrasing and emphasis has changed. In 1972, for instance, the Caucus issued a Black Bill of Rights at the Democratic Convention, demanding a new Homestead Act for poor urban areas. In the mid-1970s, they concentrated much of their interest on the Humphrey-Hawkins Full Employment Bill. Throughout the 1980s and 1990s, these demands came in the form of alternative budgets offered each year to the House floor. These budgets consistently proposed large cuts in defense spending and higher taxes for the wealthy in exchange for increased spending on social services that would target the black urban poor.

On occasion, new issues have entered the agenda, and in two instances took the center of the political stage. In the mid-1970s, the Caucus conducted a series of committee hearings (accounting for 12 percent of the list between 1970 and 1980) on discrimination in the military, discrimination in the media, and the Martin Luther King assassination. Although the Caucus received some publicity surrounding these investigations, they resulted in little more than a series of recommendations. The Caucus was more successful during this time when it increasingly raised the issues of apartheid in South Africa and of a national holiday commemorating the birthday of Martin Luther King. Both of these issues would receive a great deal of public attention in the early and mid-1980s, providing the Caucus with two of its most notable victories. In the late 1980s and early 1990s, as the Caucus expanded in size and influence, they began to speak out on issues such as the environment, AIDS, abortion rights, as well as to respond to specific events such as the Civil Rights Act of 1991 and the invasion of Haiti in 1994.

The second notable point is the overall lack of prominence accorded to Caucus issues. In figures 6.1–6.3, for instance, we see how infrequently the Caucus makes news throughout the 1970s and 1980s. Except for occasional moments, such as the two mentioned above, the Caucus has remained on the margins of the legislative debate, spending as much of their energy reacting and holding on to gains of the 1960s rather than actively promoting new legislation of their own. Tables 6.2 and 6.3 illustrate how often the Caucus has reacted to, and criticized, already determined agendas. This began during the Nixon administration as the Caucus tried to hold on to gains in school integration and various government agencies designed to protect civil rights. It continued up to the 104th Congress as the members of the Caucus voiced their displeasure at the Republican majority's attempts to overhaul government welfare programs and to add punitive measures to anticrime legislation.

Placing their own issues on the agenda has necessitated a great deal of fortitude, pressure, and external circumstance. Representative John Conyers of Michigan first proposed the Martin Luther King holiday in 1968. Violations against human rights in South Africa were raised initially in the early 1970s. Although the final legislative results differed from their initial proposal, the Caucus was pushing for an anticrime bill, welfare reform, and a crackdown on illegal drugs roughly two decades before the three issues would reach the top of the congressional agenda. The mere existence of members of Congress representing blacks meant that these issues were being raised in at least some form. The institutional design of the House provided such opportunities to any minority interest. While it was not enough to turn the issues into policy, it did mark a distinct difference from presidential politics during this time period.

As an example, let us take the Caucus's efforts to pass a full employment bill. Full employment was first promoted as the Caucus's number one issue in 1971 and later officially proposed as a piece of legislation, the Equal Opportunity and Full Employment Act, in 1974. Pushed through a subcommittee chaired by a leading Caucus member, Augustus Hawkins, the Caucus eventually brought the bill to the floor for a vote during the Carter administration. The bill initially had the support of the House and Senate Democratic leadership, as well, enabling further opportunities to keep the issue on the agenda. Hearings were halted in 1976, however, and members of Congress persuaded the leadership not to bring the bill to the floor for a vote.[38] In the presidential election of that year, Democratic candidate Jimmy Carter did not make the employment act a central issue. He made only passing references to his support for the bill, and then only after he made a comment supporting the notion of "ethnic purity," which placed him under the scrutiny of civil rights leaders and black Democrats.[39] Black voters still gave strong support to Carter, votes that arguably provided the difference for Carter to win seven different states in the 1976 election, and the Caucus and other black political organizations held high expectations of his administration. Once in office, however, the Caucus felt that it had to persistently badger the president to give any attention to the bill and to the broader concerns of inner-city poverty, joblessness, and violence.[40] Car-

[38] Margaret Weir, *Politics and Jobs: The Boundaries of Employment Policy in the United States* (Princeton: Princeton University Press, 1992), 138.

[39] See James W. Singer, "Humphrey-Hawkins Bill: Boondoggle or Economic Blessing?" *National Journal* 8 (June 12, 1976): 815.

[40] See William L. Clay, *Just Permanent Interests: Black Americans in Congress, 1870–1991* (New York: Amistad, 1992), esp. 98–102 and 302–11.

ter's primary concerns were deficit reduction, energy reform, and downsizing the federal bureaucracy, concerns that conflicted with the priorities of black legislators and interest groups.[41]

After the failure of Carter's welfare reform plan, which would have provided jobs to welfare recipients, black leaders turned up the volume of their attacks on the president.[42] National Urban League president Vernon Jordan publicly accused the president of being "recalcitrant" and "insensitive." John Conyers denounced Carter and the Democratic version of the Full Employment Bill as "decisively harmful," and Representative Parren Mitchell claimed that Carter's job program amounted to "abandoning a whole group of people who are out of work." Caucus denunciations of Carter helped put the bill back on the legislative agenda, leading to a floor vote and passage of the bill in 1978. By late 1977, however, the full employment legislation had come to be identified primarily as a race-specific measure at odds with Carter's anti-inflation measures, and as a result, it received little support from non-Caucus congressional members of either party.[43] The final form of the Humphrey-Hawkins legislation was primarily a symbolic measure, since it included a number of crippling amendments that made it more or less irrelevant. Most important was an amendment calling for the rate of inflation to drop to 3 percent by 1983 and 0 percent by 1988 before the provisions of the bill could go into effect. The bill was thus set up so that no one ever had to act on it. Despite its largely symbolic nature, Carter chose not to participate in the public celebration surrounding the signing of the bill into law.

The Caucus also criticized Carter for his neutral stance on legislation to declare Martin Luther King's birthday a national holiday. When the bill came up for a vote in Congress in 1979, it lost to a substitute measure celebrating the birthday on a Sunday, making it a nonpaid federal

---

[41] In fact, in two of the primary scholarly discussions of the Carter legislative years, neither the Congressional Black Caucus nor specific racial concerns are present in either scholar's list of Carter's legislative priorities in the 95th and 96th Congresses. The two studies are Charles O. Jones, *The Trusteeship Presidency: Jimmy Carter and the United States Congress* (Baton Rouge: Louisiana State University Press, 1988), chaps. 6–7; and Garland A. Haas, *Jimmy Carter and the Politics of Frustration* (Jefferson, N.C.: McFarland, 1992). Burton I. Kaufman argues that while Carter had few legislative initiatives to assist blacks, he did undertake a number of personal executive actions, such as appointing more black federal judges, channeling more government contracts to minority firms, and strengthening the effectiveness of both the Justice Department and the Equal Employment Opportunity Commission. *The Presidency of James Earl Carter, Jr.* (Lawrence: University of Kansas Press, 1993), 110–11.

[42] On the welfare reform plan, see Laurence E. Lynn and David deF. Whitman, *The President as Policymaker: Jimmy Carter and Welfare Reform* (Philadelphia: Temple University Press, 1981).

[43] Weir, *Politics and Jobs*, 140.

holiday. The CBC criticized Carter's nominee to head the Justice Department, Griffin Bell, as a supporter of segregation (he passed in the Senate 75 to 21), denounced Carter and the Democratic Congress for supporting federal funding to schools that refused to integrate, and spoke at length against the president's attempt to balance the budget while simultaneously increasing spending on a military buildup. In 1980, the Caucus offered an alternative budget that would have cut spending for defense and energy programs on behalf of increased spending on welfare reform, food stamps, and job programs. The amendment was defeated on the floor of the House 74 to 313.

A notable achievement of the Caucus during these years was an amendment offered by Parren Mitchell to the Public Works Employment Act. While receiving little public attention, the amendment offered a set-aside provision for minority enterprises in a bill otherwise designed to boost employment during the recession. The legislation at the time passed through Congress with little fanfare from the press and with only minor opposition from members of either party. It passed "without committee hearings or a report offering findings about discrimination in the construction industry or elsewhere, and without attempting to offer a rationale for selecting a 10 percent figure."[44] The use of minority set-asides, first initiated during the Johnson administration, remained popular with legislators throughout the 1980s, not just with the Congressional Black Caucus and liberal Democrats, but with Republican presidents Ronald Reagan and George Bush. Together, the national government passed the Surface Transportation Assistance Act of 1982 and the National Defense Authorization Act of 1987. By 1990, federal agencies were awarding $8.65 billion in minority set-aside contracts.[45] While publicly in opposition to any bills explicitly mentioning the use of quotas, Republicans and Democrats alike agreed to give roughly 10 percent of federal contracts to minority businesses.

The civil rights issue attracting the greater attention during the 1970s was busing. The Caucus did not play a prominent role in this debate. It supported busing, but it was not treated by the media as a major protagonist. Congress and President Nixon began moving against court-ordered desegregation plans by the late 1960s, led by a series of anti-busing amendments proposed by southern Democratic representatives Jamie Whitten and John Stennis. By 1971, northern Democrats responding to fierce constituent opposition to busing led the charge

[44] Hugh Davis Graham, "Race, History, and Policy: African Americans and Civil Rights since 1964," in *Civil Rights in the United States* (University Park: Pennsylvania State University Press, 1994), 24.

[45] Ibid., 25.

against the policy. On the Higher Education Act of 1971, fifty-six northern Democrats voted to restrict busing, combining with Republicans and southern Democrats to pass the bill. In 1972, the House voted 283 to 102 on a stronger antibusing bill. This bill was blocked in the Senate by a minority filibuster that survived cloture by nine votes. Also in that year, the House Rules Committee voted to discharge an antibusing constitutional amendment being held up in the liberal Judiciary Committee. In 1975, Senator Joseph Biden of Delaware proposed and helped pass an amendment to end the power of the Department of Health, Education, and Welfare to enforce school integration through busing. The Black Caucus, together with black Republican Senator Edward Brooke, opposed the antibusing measures quite strongly throughout this time. Clarence Mitchell of the NAACP called the antibusing legislation "the most blatant products of racism that I have seen in the federal government since I came to Washington during the administration of President Franklin Delano Roosevelt in 1941."[46] Consistent efforts by Caucus members to amend the legislation by providing additional money for schools failed. Both northern and southern Democrats whose constituents passionately opposed busing voted to weaken Court orders. Through various antimajoritarian rules utilized by Democratic Senate members, the antibusing tide was at least slowed.[47]

Overall, then, the Caucus had few highly public legislative accomplishments in the 1970s, despite being members of the congressional majority party. Perhaps reflective of this, most studies of the Caucus at this time criticized its ineffectiveness.[48] A great deal of its energy was placed in the disappointing Humphrey-Hawkins Bill, as it was in averting attempts by Nixon and Carter to cut federal spending for the poor and unemployed and in efforts to curtail busing programs. In the 1980s, the Caucus would have a few more victories and would also find greater representation through a different legislative approach.

The 1980s were particularly notable for three dramatic legislative achievements. In 1982, the Voting Rights Act was extended and provisions were added without a great deal of fanfare. These provisions would eventually lead (with the assistance of the Supreme Court in *Thornburg v. Gingles*) to the creation of "majority-minority" congressional districts, or legalized racial gerrymandering.[49] While racial gerry-

---

[46] Congressional Quarterly Almanac (Washington, D.C.: Congressional Quarterly, 1972), 680.

[47] See Gary Orfield, *Must We Bus? Segregated Schools and National Policy* (Washington, D.C.: Brookings Institution, 1978), chap. 8.

[48] See Swain, *Black Faces, Black Interests*, 37–39, for a review of this literature.

[49] See Abigail M. Thernstrom, *Whose Votes Count? Affirmative Action and Minority*

mandering became a controversial issue in the 1990s, there was little discussion of the issue in 1982. Section 2 of the amended Voting Rights Act, the section that would be used to justify racial gerrymandering, was generally ignored during House debate. The bill emerged from the House's liberal Judiciary Committee and passed on the floor 385 to 24. Abigail Thernstrom contends that "potential opponents were asleep at the switch, and enthusiasts had nothing to gain from rousing them." In the Senate, sixty-one members immediately proclaimed their support for the bill, including eight southern Democrats and twenty-one Republicans. Orrin Hatch raised objections to section 2 on the grounds that it would lead to racial gerrymandering, but he had a great deal of difficulty in getting anyone to listen to him or to believe him, and the bill eventually passed on the Senate floor 85 to 8. Civil rights groups were unified and aggressive in passing the bill, and few Democrats or Republicans wanted to appear in any way opposed to legislation that was framed as an extension of the most symbolic gain of the 1960s, access to the voting booth.[50]

In 1983, the Caucus-initiated Martin Luther King holiday passed through Congress, followed three years later by the passage of the Caucus's proposed sanctions against South African apartheid. All three of these bills, however, were unique in their degree of bipartisan support (the Voting Rights Act extension passed the House 389 to 24 and the Senate 86 to 8; the Martin Luther King holiday bill passed 338 to 90 and 78 to 22; and the apartheid sanctions passed the House over a Reagan veto 313 to 83 and 78 to 21) and their focus on broad civil rights issues. All dealt with issues still supported by most whites, the basic necessity for legal equality, and the notions of liberal individualism and equal opportunity implicit in them. But while civil rights issues in Congress remained, as Abigail Thernstrom notes, "an almost protected status," less celebratory aspects of the black agenda had a much more difficult time gaining interest and support.[51]

The Caucus kept an otherwise very low profile throughout the 1980s (notice the dearth of mentions of the Caucus throughout the decade in figures 6.1–6.3). In part, this was due to a shift in tactics during the decade as the Caucus attempted to work within the party's committee structure more often, rather than to push their stance as outsider. The influence of William Gray as chair of the Budget Committee, in particular, was promoted by the Caucus as a reflection of their influence in the

Voting Rights (Cambridge: Harvard University Press, 1987), chaps. 5–6. The quote is from page 83.

[50] Ibid.

[51] Ibid., 233.

House. Caucus officials took credit as well for the 1983 budget, which included increased funding for social programs due to Gray's involvement. For most of the 1980s, however, the Caucus focused their energy on reacting critically to threats from the Reagan and Bush administration. This is illustrated by table 6.2; 73 percent of the mentions of the Caucus in the list during the 1980s are as reactions to other political actors. More than 80 percent of these reactions were critical, responses primarily to cutbacks in social welfare programs and rollbacks of the civil rights agenda. On the rare occasions that the Caucus promoted legislative alternatives that were recognized in the media, they lost quite decisively. Their alternative budgets, which aimed to increase aid to education, job training, health care, and welfare programs while dramatically decreasing funding toward defense, lost year after year with fewer than one hundred votes in their favor (although some Caucus members believed it to be a measure of success that their budget alternatives were allowed roll call votes at all). Not until the fight over the Civil Rights Act in 1990 and 1991 did the Caucus again gain a measure of public prominence in the legislative process.

The passage of the Civil Rights Act of 1991, designed to strengthen laws against discrimination in the workplace, fits with the success of previous civil rights legislation in that it eventually won with widespread congressional support. In contrast to the passage of the civil rights legislation in the 1960s or 1980s, the 1991 act faced fierce opposition not only from the president, but from members of Congress as the bill became a battleground over the issue of affirmative action. President George Bush labeled the legislation a "quota bill" and vetoed it in 1990. Congressional efforts to override the veto came up one vote short in the Senate. Trying to deflect such criticism and defuse the race issue in 1991, one Democrat tried to rename the bill the Women's Equity in Employment and Civil Rights Act.[52] Democrats and Republicans were well aware of national polls that showed sharp divides between blacks and whites over both employment discrimination laws and affirmative action. Nonetheless, Democrats held together on the legislation. While the CBC substitute legislation failed in the House with Democrats split roughly in half, the party remained unified on the final legislation, voting 250 to 15 in the House compared to the Republicans, who voted 22 to 143. The House Rules Committee assured the success of the compromise bill with a "king of the hill" order that limited the ability of conservatives to embarrass and split the Democrats over affirmative action.[53]

[52] See Joan Bikupic, "Behind the Fight over Quotas Lie Divisive Racial Issues," *Congressional Quarterly Weekly* (June 1, 1991): 1442–45.

[53] See Nicole L. Gueron, "An Idea Whose Time Has Come: A Comparative Procedural

The final version of the bill passed the Senate 93 to 5 and eventually passed overwhelmingly in the House as well (381 to 38).

RESULTS, PART 2: RELYING ON NONMAJORITARIAN RULES AND PROCEDURES

Throughout the 1970s and 1980s, the CBC and other leading supporters of black political interests often relied on a number of procedures that protected minority rights. In the 1970s, they used these protections in both the House and the Senate to stop antibusing measures from passing despite majority floor support. In the 1980s, as mentioned above, this meant switching tactics from outspoken advocacy to quiet moves up the ranks of the committee system, and in the process gaining power to advocate specific constituency concerns. This tactic paid off initially with William Gray, who became chair of the House Budget Committee between 1985 and 1990, Augustus Hawkins, who chaired the Education and Labor Committee between 1985 and 1992, and Parren Mitchell, who chaired the Select Committee on Small Business between 1983 to 1988. A number of the members interviewed for this book mentioned specifically that a primary success of the CBC was Gray's ability to maintain spending for social and economic programs in the congressional budgets of the late 1980s. With both parties in Congress increasingly conscious of a rising deficit, Gray's position as chair of the Budget Committee granted him enormous power to raise the interests of the Caucus and keep some type of compromise written into the budget reconciliation process. CBC members attributed the protection of a number of social spending programs to Gray's position.

Today, while the CBC is part of a minority party in the House, it is nonetheless poised to benefit from committee chairmanships if and when the Democratic party returns to majority status. Charles Rangel of New York, for instance, would chair the powerful Ways and Means committee; John Conyers of Michigan is in line to chair Judiciary; and William Clay of Missouri is in line to chair Education and Educational Opportunities. Congressmen Julian Dixon and Louis Stokes, meanwhile, have moved up the ladder on the Appropriations Committee, and Harold Ford of Tennessee and John Lewis of Georgia have similarly done so on Ways and Means. Before retiring recently, Ron Dellums of California had chaired and was in line to chair again National Security, formerly known as Armed Services. In their actions and in interviews,

History of the Civil Rights Acts of 1960, 1964, and 1991," *Yale Law Journal* 104 (March 1995): 1201–34.

CBC members have strongly endorsed the seniority system. In 1985, for instance, most black caucus members supported the conservative House Armed Service Committee chair, Melvin Price, over the more liberal Les Aspin.[54] In 1994 higher-ranking Caucus member Charles Rangel endorsed conservative Democrat Sam Gibbons for chair of the Ways and Means Committee despite protests from liberal Democrats and despite the fact that he could have directly benefited on the seniority ladder from Gibbons's departure. That same year the Caucus, because of its support of the seniority system, endorsed a moderate member for the chairmanship of Appropriations, Neal Smith (Iowa), over a more liberal party member. When two Caucus members endorsed the liberal candidate, David Obey, William Clay wrote a terse memo to them, pointing out that "the cavalier manner" in which these Caucus members endorsed Obey "is appalling. The willy-nilly excuses offered for promising to support a candidate in violation of the rule of seniority is not in the permanent interest of black legislators or the broader black community."[55] For Caucus members, committee chairmanships represent autonomy and an opportunity to entrench power that can function outside of the wishes of the larger party and House. This strategy of entrenchment, a strategy successfully used many years ago by conservative southern Democrats, reflects the policy of a group that has come into conflict on a number of occasions with its party's leadership over agenda and substantive matters.

The Impact of the Courts and Racial Redistricting for Caucus Influence

Although relatively uncontroversial at the time, the passage of the Voting Rights Act extension in 1982 has had perhaps the biggest impact on the Caucus during the 1990s. Section 2 of the VRA extension stated that "No voting qualification or prerequisite to voting or standard, practice, or procedure shall be imposed or applied by any State or political subdivision in a manner which results in a denial or abridgment of the right of any citizen of the United States to vote on account of race or color." This led the Supreme Court in the 1986 decision *Thornburg v. Gingles* to examine whether congressional districts were drawn in a manner that had a discriminatory result. The Court devised a three-part test to force legislators to draw congressional districts in such a way

---

[54] See Michael R. Gordon, "MX Foes Say Aspin Wooed Them to Win Post," *National Journal* 17 (January 12, 1985): 128.

[55] Quoted in Janet Hook, "Seniority System Tested by Smith-Obey Face-Off," *Congressional Quarterly Weekly* (March 5, 1994): 520.

that African Americans would form a majority in the district. Majority-minority redistricting took place after the 1990 census, and African American voters became majorities in thirteen new districts. All thirteen districts elected African American representatives to Congress in 1992, pushing the total number of Democratic party CBC voting members to thirty-eight, and increasing considerably the leverage of the Caucus over their party's legislative effort. The gain in attention and influence for the Caucus is demonstrated by the dramatic increase in mentions by the journals in figures 6.1–6.3. After standing for years along the margins of the congressional party, the Caucus suddenly was in a position to influence large portions of Clinton's agenda. As a result, the Caucus received "more attention in the [first] five months [of the 103d session] than it had in the previous 20 years."[56] David Canon, in fact, finds that the CBC provided the margin of victory on nine of the sixteen "key votes" identified by *Congressional Quarterly* in the first year of the 103d Congress.[57]

The Caucus made news often during the 103d legislative session. The media publicized their decision not to meet with President Clinton because of their disapproval with his budget proposal and his handling of the nomination of Lani Guinier to head the Justice Department's Civil Rights Division; their ability to help initially defeat Clinton's prized crime bill because of their insistence on a racial justice provision; their anger at Clinton's initial handling of the Haitian situation; and their ultimate influence in leading the president to take action in Haiti. They also had some notable legislative disagreements with the rest of their party in the House, namely over defense authorizations, an appropriations report regarding the question of statehood for the District of Columbia, the crime bill, the North American Free Trade Agreement, and the spending bill they criticized for its lack of funding for urban youth summer jobs programs.[58] The Caucus forced Democratic leaders to pull back a vote on the line-item veto and, in an exchange for Medicare cuts in the budget, received funding increases for food stamps and for a program that provided for immunizations to poor and uninsured children.[59] Perhaps the most remarkable success of the Caucus was its ability to pressure President Clinton to intervene in Haiti. What is so noteworthy about this involvement is that majorities of both parties in Congress were reluctant to get involved in the affairs the Caribbean

[56] Quoted in Kitty Cunningham, "Black Caucus Flexes Muscle on Budget — And More," *Congressional Quarterly Weekly* 51 (July 3, 1993): 1711.

[57] David T. Canon, "Redistricting and the Congressional Black Caucus," *American Politics Quarterly* 23 (1995): 166.

[58] See Bositis, *Congressional Black Caucus*, 133

[59] Cunningham, "Black Caucus Flexes Muscle."

nation, as was the American public.[60] Even when the Caucus was defeated during these years, such as in its nearly annual attempt to pass an alternative budget, it received more than $10 billion for a priority project, the Earned Income Tax Credit.[61]

Nonetheless, the Caucus also had a number of significant failures in this period, illustrating the often complicated position of African American interests in party politics. Perhaps most notable in this regard was the 1994 Crime Bill. In early August of 1994, President Clinton suffered one of the bigger embarrassments of his first term when the Democrat-controlled House failed to pass a rule that would have allowed one of his central agenda items, the Crime Bill, to move to the House floor for debate and a vote. A number of Democratic party factions were crucial in leading the vote to defer the rule change. Many southern Democrats, for instance, with strong backing from the National Rifle Association, opposed the bill because of its stiff gun control regulations. Ten Black Caucus members also voted against the rule, which was significant if the bill was to pass with strong gun control language. The CBC members supported the gun control language but opposed the overall legislation because the bill increased the opportunities for states to use the death penalty. In particular, they were upset that the legislation failed to include language aimed at combating racial bias in the sentencing of criminals for the death penalty.

By voting against the party leadership's position these ten members exerted a great deal of leverage. Their votes provided the difference for the passage of the rule. Yet unlike previous efforts to create leverage for the Caucus, this veto by Caucus members backfired. Faced with either making the bill more liberal to gain the votes of the ten Caucus members or making the bill more conservative to gain the votes of southern Democrats and moderate Republicans, Clinton and the Democratic leadership in Congress opted for the latter. The revised legislation that reached the floor two weeks after the initial embarrassing loss contained a cut of over $3 billion in spending for social programs that the Caucus had enthusiastically endorsed. Three of the ten CBC members who initially voted against the rule changed their vote for the latter rule. This change was based in part on pressure by the party to remain unified and in part on assurances by the Clinton administration to work for racial justice in the implementation of the federal death penalty. At the same time, Clinton received thirty-one new Republicans on the rule vote who were responding to additions to the bill that cut social spending and increased punitive measures. On the final floor vote, a majority of the

[60] See Peter J. Boyer, "The Rise of Kweisi Mfume," *New Yorker* (August 1, 1994).
[61] Ibid., 26.

Caucus members voted against a piece of legislation that was more conservative than the original.

INTERPRETATION

A number of points are important here. First, the Caucus has been more successful in advocating issues specifically related to civil rights rather than economic and urban concerns. The Caucus's significant victories during this time period — the Martin Luther King Holiday, sanctions against South Africa, the 1982 Voting Rights Act extension, the 1991 Civil Rights bill, and the Clinton intervention into Haiti–have little to do with economics. All except the Haitian intervention dealt specifically with civil rights issues and were in essence extensions of legislation passed during the civil rights era. While certainly few in number, all of these civil rights measures received strong bipartisan support when they reached the floors of Congress. Only on the issue of busing did the Caucus fail to exert significant influence on a goal originating from the civil rights movement. The Caucus has had much less influence over socioeconomic concerns, especially with regard to programs concentrating primarily on African American citizens. Few of their legislative proposals were on the agenda, and thus they primarily played the role of trying to slow down cuts to social services. Attempts to get Congress and the president to look at urban and inner-city concerns generally failed, as did attempts to get the legislative branch to deal with crime and drugs in urban and predominantly black neighborhoods.

Second, the Caucus's influence increased dramatically in the 103d Congress, when its membership increased to thirty-eight Democratic party members. Not only is the Caucus featured much more prominently in the print media, but their proportion of proposals and positive reactions rises considerably, as can be seen in table 6.3 (55 percent of their statements during these two years were either proposals or positive reactions in the 103d Congress, compared to 36 percent in the previous years). This has relevance for the considerable debate that has taken place over the value of "descriptive representation," that is, black members of Congress representing black voters. Carol Swain, for instance, has criticized descriptive representation on the grounds that black faces do not necessarily promote black interests. Swain argues that since Democrats of any race represent black interests better than Republicans, and since racial redistricting has been implicated in the 1994 loss of Democratic House seats in the South, the emphasis on descriptive representation has had negative consequences for the "substantive representation" of African American voters.[62] As mentioned earlier, other scholars have argued that the implementation of majority-minority redistricting has led to the defeat of some white moderate Democrats, and to their replacement by more conservative white Republicans.[63]

Clearly, however, increased numbers of African Americans in the Democratic party's legislative branch made a difference. The institutional presence of the Caucus transcends changes in party voting scores. This visibility corresponds to a powerful role in setting the legislative agenda and a much more powerful veto voice. President Clinton and the Democratic leaders in Congress certainly took their presence seriously.[64] Although Clinton and other Democrats still had opportunities to ignore the Caucus by pursuing moderate Republicans, they ultimately listened more often to the Caucus than Democrats had at any time in the past.

Also consequential, however, is the Caucus's complete forfeiture of power only two years after the peak of its influence. The 1994 midterm elections produced landslide victories for the Republican party in both houses of Congress. While no member of the CBC was defeated in a bid for reelection, the newly formed Republican majority in the House took immediate steps to eliminate the institutional legitimacy of the Caucus. Shortly after the 1994 election, David Bositis commented that "the Black Caucus is weaker and more diminished than at any time since founded in 1971. The black agenda will be nonexistent."[65] Juan Williams of the *Washington Post* commented, "black liberal demands for more seats in Congress, more special programs for minorities, and more support for a black separatist movement have pushed black America out of the mainstream of the national political dialogue."[66] Although the prominence of the Caucus's agenda for the party's electoral downfall has been debated,[67] it nonetheless exemplifies the degree to which black

[62] Swain, *Black Faces, Black Interests*, esp. chaps. 9–11.

[63] See David Ian Lublin, "Race, Representation, and Redistricting," in Paul Peterson, ed., *Classifying by Race* (Princeton: Princeton University Press, 1995); Kevin A. Hill, "Does the Creation of Majority Black Districts Aid Republicans? An Analysis of 1992 Congressional Elections in Eight Southern States," *Journal of Politics* 57 (1995): 384–401; Charles S. Bullock III, "The Impact of Changing the Racial Composition of Congressional Districts on Legislator's Roll Call Behavior," *American Politics Quarterly* 23 (1995): 141–58.

[64] See Boyer, "Rise of Kweisi Mfume"; and Cunningham, "Black Caucus Flexes Muscle."

[65] Quoted in Isabel Wilkerson, "The 1994 Elections: Voters, Minorities," *New York Times* (November 10, 1994), B4.

[66] Juan Williams, "Blacked Out in the Newt Congress," *Washington Post* (November 20, 1994), C1.

[67] See Paul Frymer, "The 1994 Electoral Aftershock: Dealignment or Realignment in the

political representation can remain directly at odds with the national Democratic party's overall electoral interests.

Finally, the Caucus has increasingly made attempts to exert its influence in Congress through means not tied to a strong, centralized, and "responsible" majority party. During the busing battles, the Caucus relied on rule decisions to defeat the efforts of the majority of the members. During the 1980s, a time of little majoritarian interest in advancing the concerns of black Americans, the Caucus focused on increasing its role on important committees, gaining more influence through William Gray's position on the Budget Committee than through the majoritarian party. By the 103d congressional session, the Caucus had become one of the most ardent defenders of the seniority system. What once benefited southern whites in keeping black issues off the legislative agenda now benefits African American members hoping to keep their issues on the agenda while simultaneously keeping veto power over issues they deem threatening.

Given the tendency of public support for civil rights and related issues to be somewhat shallow and short-lived, African Americans have found minority protections, rather than a strong majority party leadership, to be more helpful. When the public has turned against issues of importance to blacks — for example, when large majorities of whites opposed busing during the 1970s — many Democratic representatives sided just as quickly as their Republican counterparts with the white majority, despite the protests of black leaders. When the public mood turned against social spending and welfare, so did large numbers within both of the national political parties. Only when the public became aroused to the apartheid situation in South Africa did Congress finally act, years after the Caucus had made their initial proposals for sanctions.

The Democratic party's relationship, then, to black interests is not as simple as scholars such as Carmines and Stimson, Swain, and Rohde have claimed. As long as black issues remain divisive and programs to redress racial inequality remain unpopular, antimajoritarian instruments will remain vital to protecting African American interests. A strong and responsible political party in a racially divided society can hinder racial equality just as much as it can champion it.

South," in Philip A. Klinkner, ed., *Midterm: The Elections of 1994 in Context* (Boulder, Colo.: Westview Press, 1996).

CHAPTER 7

Is the Concept of Electoral Capture Applicable to Other Groups? The Case of Gay and Lesbian Voters in the Democratic Party and the Christian Right in the Republican Party

[The Defense of Marriage Act is] this year's
Sister Souljah — a way to show [Bill Clinton]
isn't beholden to gay people.
(David Mixner)

Robert J. Dole appears to have stolen a page
from Bill Clinton's Sister Souljah playbook. . . .
This past week, Dole has similarly sought to
draw a line separating himself from the
religious-conservative wing of his own party . . .
a stand that has infuriated the Christian right.
(Thomas Edsall)

And it is this which frightens me: Who knows
but that, on the lower frequencies,
I speak for you?
(Ralph Ellison)

I HAVE ARGUED throughout this book that racial cleavage, in conjunction with majority-based electoral laws, has created a set of incentives for party leaders to capture black interests and, in the process, make their concerns largely invisible in electoral competition. Envisioned by elites in the late 1820s as an institution to prevent racial issues from dominating the national political agenda, the two-party system continues to marginalize black interests in a way that is unique in American society.

While this argument is relevant for mainstream public debates about the relationship between African Americans and the Democratic party, my intent in this book is not to argue that the Democrats could do more to help their African American constituents. There is little question that this is true — yet it misses a deeper point. As institutions founded in part to remove race from the national agenda, our national parties are bound by important structural incentives that ensure their ultimate failure as vehicles for racial progress. To implore the Democrats to do better is to ignore the incentives that lead them to do worse. The marginalization of black political interests in the party system endures in part because the institution was designed to create and maintain this marginalization. As long as racial cleavage remains ingrained in the underlying social fabric, party leaders will have incentives to avoid black interests in their quest for the median voter.

The same point can be made with regards to the potential claim that party officials are in some way "racist." Again, there is little doubt that many party officials are personally prejudiced against African American citizens. Yet what is interesting is how many individual party actors who are initially progressive on racial issues nonetheless succumb to behavior that marginalizes black interests. From Martin Van Buren to Tom Watson to George Wallace to Bill Clinton, these individuals, primarily motivated by electoral incentives, distanced themselves from black interests. Watson, for instance, initially supported black voting rights when his Populist party entered electoral competition in the South around the turn of the twentieth century. When he realized that more votes could be won for his cause by distancing himself from black voters, he became a leader of black disenfranchisement.[1] George Wallace ran for governor in Alabama in 1958 as a racial moderate. While by no means a civil rights supporter, Wallace emphasized economic programs and attacked his opponent for "rolling with the new wave of the Klan and its terrible tradition of lawlessness." His opponent, Attorney General John Patterson, claimed after the election that the "primary reason I beat him was because he was considered soft on the race question at the time." Wallace did well in the election with black voters, lost large portions of the state's white voters, and reportedly announced after the defeat that "no other son-of-a-bitch will ever out-nigger me again."[2]

Finally, compare the campaign stories of Walter Mondale and Bill Clinton, two pro-civil rights Democrats who have run for president in the last couple of decades. In chapter 4, I mentioned Mondale's unwillingness to take a stand against Jesse Jackson, even though his aides were pushing him to make a break with his opponent. According to Steve Gillon, a group of Mondale's advisers drafted a speech "charging that Jackson had not renounced anti-Semitism, refused to repudiate Far-

---

[1]   See Russell Korobkin, "The Politics of Disfranchisement in Georgia," *Georgia Historical Quarterly* 74 (1990).

[2]   Both Wallace and Patterson are quoted in Dan T. Carter, *The Politics of Rage: George Wallace, the Origins of the New Conservativism, and the Transformation of American Politics* (New York: Simon and Schuster, 1995), 95.

rakhan, and stood outside the Democratic mainstream." Mondale refused to give the speech: "Not because I had much affection for Jesse," Mondale told Gillon, "but I knew of the tremendous emotional significance of this event on blacks and other Americans."[3] Few would argue that Bill Clinton's early support for civil rights was far different from Mondale's. And, according to behind-the-scenes accounts, he also expressed trepidation about attacking Jackson in order to gain political capital. Yet, when Clinton advisers George Stephanopoulos and Paul Begala saw an opportunity for Clinton to distance himself from Jackson, the presidential candidate agreed, making the subsequent reference to Sister Soulja in a speech before the NAACP. Clinton snapped at Begala and Stephanopoulos afterward, "Well, you got your story."[4] What is instructive about these examples, then, is how party members who behave strategically are rewarded; "good" people often find it in their interest to behave "badly."

IS "ELECTORAL CAPTURE" APPLICABLE TO OTHER GROUPS?

For a number of reasons, I do not believe that equating the experience of African Americans as a captured group to the situations of other political groups in the electoral system is appropriate. To do so is to minimize the longevity and power of racism, as well as its long-standing political consequences. Discrimination against blacks, for instance, has consistently forced them to turn to national government agencies to intervene on their behalf. As a minority group in the United States, blacks have often needed federal protection from those who willingly break laws to discriminate, especially when the lawbreakers are protected by local law enforcers. Not only has social prejudice forced black Americans to seek assistance from the federal government to enforce equal rights before the law, but historical discrimination has created inequalities that require government involvement to provide equal opportunity. This relationship between black Americans and the federal government has made the lack of national party response to their interests all the more consequential.[5]

---

[3] Mondale is quoted in Steven M. Gillon, *The Democrats' Dilemma: Walter F. Mondale and the Liberal Legacy* (New York: Columbia University Press, 1992), 350.

[4] Bob Woodward, *The Agenda: Inside the Clinton White House* (New York: Simon and Schuster, 1994), 40–41.

[5] Steven Erie makes a strong case for why African Americans have not succeeded in insulating themselves from national prejudice in the same way that immigrants like the Irish Catholics have. Irish Catholics benefited from an historical opportunity to incorporate themselves (and indeed dominate) urban machines during their initial formation. By

White racism and the fears of party leaders make it much more difficult for blacks to escape their captured electoral status. Black leaders
face formidable obstacles to building coalitions with groups that share
similar social and economic issues. Other groups in society have been
the subject of prejudice and discrimination. Yet no other demographic
group has had the same difficulty forming enduring coalitions. Short-
term efforts by black organizers to form coalitions with the Populist
movement, northern urban machines, Jewish groups, white labor union
movements, and most recently nonwhite immigrants have all sustained
significant damage deriving from racial tensions between the groups.

Moreover, white racism has also stigmatized black voters and their
interests to a degree unseen by other groups in national politics. That
nonracial issues such as welfare and unemployment assistance, crime,
and general government spending have come to connote "black" issues
in the eyes of many Americans is indicative of the enormous power that
racial prejudice continues to have in the political process.[6] Party leaders
recognize the long-term divisive power of this prejudice and, as a consequence, are often hesitant to make public appeals to black interests. Just
as often, leaders of both the opposition party and the party closest to
black voters will attempt to use black political interests as a wedge to
increase their support among white voters. For every Republican "Willy
Horton" there is a Democratic "Sister Soulja."[7]

Nonetheless, a constant question that arises when I discuss with
friends and colleagues the idea of an electorally captured group is
whether other groups in the United States or other countries have been
faced with similar circumstances and, hence, fit the profile of electoral
capture. In the international context, one can point to the position of
"blacks" in Great Britain,[8] Tamils in Sri Lanka, or even labor and busi-

---

the time African Americans were in a position to receive similar benefits from urban
governments, the machines had lost a great deal of power and ability to provide benefits
to their constituents. See "The Two Faces of Ethnic Power: Comparing the Irish and Black
Experiences," *Polity* 13 (Winter 1980): 261–84.

[6] See Donald R. Kinder and Lynn M. Sanders, *Divided by Color: Racial Politics and
Democratic Ideals* (Chicago: University of Chicago Press, 1996); and Martin Gilens,
" 'Race Coding' and White Opposition to Welfare," *American Political Science Review* 90
(September 1996): 593–604.

[7] Not to mention their own Willy Horton. As I mentioned in chapter 5, few remember
that the Willy Horton issue was first raised against Democratic presidential candidate
Michael Dukakis during the Democratic primaries of 1988 by fellow party candidate Al
Gore.

[8] "Blacks" is placed in quotations because the word in British politics is not used exclusively for those groups of African descent. See Paul Gilroy, *There Ain't No Black in the
Union Jack*. More specific to the role that race plays in British party politics, see Anthony
M. Messina, *Race and Party Competition in Britain* (New York: Oxford University Press,
1989); and Robert C. Lieberman, "Race and Political Institutions: The United States in

ness interests in South Korea.[9] In the United States, many poor whites were disenfranchised by party politics in the South during the post-Reconstruction period. Irish-Catholic immigrants were subjected to widespread discrimination in the 1800s and found the Republican party making few appeals for their vote, at least at the national level. Studies of Irish-Catholic voters in New York, Massachusetts, and Michigan during this time have found their support to be as high as 95 percent for the Democratic party.[10] In part, this is because the Republican party absorbed at least some of the goals of the "Know-Nothings" — a movement based significantly on anti-immigrant sentiments. The Know-Nothings, in turn, were rarely appealed to by the Democratic party for votes.

In the 1900s, both labor and agrarian interests have at times found themselves marginalized by electoral politics, and labor union interests continue to face the potential of electoral capture within the Democratic party. Over almost seven decades, Jewish voters have proven quite loyal to the Democratic party, at levels close those of African Americans. During this period, generally two-thirds of the Jewish voting population has maintained supported the Democratic party, ranging from as high as 95 percent for Franklin Roosevelt in 1940 and 90 percent for Lyndon Johnson in 1964, to only 45 percent for Jimmy Carter in 1980, a year in which roughly 20 percent of the Jewish vote went to third-party candidate John Anderson.[11] More recently, Mexican Americans have voted in large numbers for the Democratic party in key electoral states such as Texas and California. In 1996, for instance, more than 80 percent of Mexican Americans voted for Bill Clinton and the Democratic party.

Although it is beyond the scope of this book to deal adequately with

Comparative-Historical Perspective," (paper read at American Political Science Association Conference, Washington, D.C., 1997).

[9] See Jeeyang Rhee Baum, "Korea's Democratic Paradox: How Labor Politics Moved from Reform to Repression" (manuscript, UCLA, 1997).

[10] See Ronald P. Formisano, *The Birth of Mass Political Parties: Michigan, 1827–1861* (Princeton: Princeton University Press, 1971), particularly chaps. 5, 9, and 14. "Republicans deliberately played off Germans and Irish against one another, frequently using the German Protestants as examples of the 'good immigrants' who favored 'American interests' while the Irish of course served always to define the bad foreigners. Republican rhetoric portrayed Germans as true to the principles of freedom for which they immigrated, while the Irish obeyed the slavery of 'party'" (302). Also see Paul Kleppner, *Continuity and Change in Electoral Politics, 1893–1928* (New York: Greenwood Press, 1987); and Lee Benson, *The Concept of Jacksonian Democracy: New York as a Test Case* (Princeton: Princeton University Press, 1961).

[11] See Lee Sigelman, "Jews and the 1988 Election: More of the Same?" in James L. Guth and John C. Green, eds. *The Bible and the Ballot Box: Religion and Politics in the 1988 Election* (Boulder, Colo.: Westview Press, 1991), 190; and Marjorie Connelly, "Portrait of the Electorate: Who Voted for Whom in the House," *New York Times* (March 1, 1995).

the complexities of each group, at the surface level all of these political groups lack critical aspects of electoral capture. For groups such as Irish Catholic voters, the historical period in which they were marginalized in national politics coincided with the high point of political power for urban machines. The large and concentrated numbers of Irish Catholic voters in cities ensured that their political interests were met at local levels. Most of their chief political interests were not dependent on national party or government support.[12] The Know-Nothings found opportunities in the Republican party's coalition because their position on ridding the nation of immigrant voter fraud overlapped nicely with Republican party electoral strategy.[13] Know-Nothings and Radical Republicans agreed on the passage of federal election legislation: Know-Nothings wanted tighter federal enforcement of voting laws in order to keep immigrants from voting in northern cities, while the Radical Republicans wanted tighter federal enforcement laws in order to protect African American voting rights in the South. Farmworkers, meanwhile, constituted a majority of the population in the United States until the 1920s and were almost never a unified voting bloc in any one political party.[14] The power of labor unions in electoral politics has varied significantly over time, at times dominating many important electoral arenas, at times remaining somewhat "nonpartisan" in national politics.[15] When the labor vote has attached itself to one political party, it has rarely had much difficulty building coalitions within that party with groups of similar political interests. In recent years, as the union vote has declined in force and number in national elections, its voting bloc has split much more between the two national parties. Since the 1960s, significant portions of its voting bloc have been successfully wooed by largely noneconomic appeals from the opposition party.[16]

---

[12] See Erie, "Two Faces of Ethnic Power."

[13] See Scott C. James and Brian L. Lawson, "The Political Economy of Voting Rights in America's Gilded Age," *American Political Science Review* (forthcoming). For earlier examples of Republican party strategy and their appeals to the Know-Nothings with anti–voting fraud legislation, see Formisano, *Birth of Mass Parties,* chap. 13.

[14] See John Mark Hansen, *Gaining Access: Congress and the Farm Lobby, 1919–1981* (Chicago: University of Chicago Press, 1991).

[15] See J. David Greenstone, *Labor in American Politics* (New York: Knopf, 1969); Karen Orren, "Union Politics and Postwar Liberalism in the United States, 1946–1979," *Studies in American Political Development* (1986): 215–52; Michael Rogin, "Nonpartisanship and the Group Interest," in *Ronald Reagan, the Movie: and Other Episodes of Political Demonology* (Berkeley: University of California Press, 1987); and David Plotke, *Building a Democratic Political Order: Reshaping American Liberalism in the 1930s and 1940s* (New York: Cambridge University Press, 1996).

[16] See Thomas Byrne Edsall and Mary D. Edsall, *Chain Reaction: The Impact of Race,*

While to some degree the presence of Jewish voters does attach a stigma to a political party, there is little evidence to suggest that adding Jewish voters to a coalition drives other portions of the coalition away. More important, party leaders have not perceived Jewish voters as divisive. Both parties make appeals to Jewish voters and they do so without fearing the loss of key coalition members or the median voter. With the survival of Israel being one the primary political interest of Jewish voters, the opposition party can appeal for their support without disrupting its coalition. President Harry Truman's comment to State Department experts who were lobbying for a softer stance toward Middle Eastern Arab nations is indicative: "I have to answer to hundreds of thousands who are anxious for the success of Zionism; I do not have hundreds of thousands of Arabs among my constituents."[17]

Mexican Americans are an interesting group with regard to electoral capture. In a number of ways, their interests and voting behavior resemble those of African Americans, as they have low voting rates and high (although not equivalent) rates of support for Democratic candidates. And at times, some Republicans have attacked them on issues of illegal immigration, bilingual education, and welfare violations; more often, this has not been the case. Republicans have pursued the Mexican American vote, in part because of the group's concentrations in important electoral college states like California and Texas, and in part because they are not convinced that the Mexican American vote is loyal to the Democrats.[18] But perhaps most important, there are generally few signs that Republican leaders perceive the Mexican American vote to be divisive for larger party building, particularly at the national level.[19]

Rights, and Taxes on American Politics (New York: W. W. Norton, 1991); and John David Skrentny, The Logic of Affirmative Action (Chicago: University of Chicago Press, 1996), chap. 8.

[17] Quoted in Hansen, Gaining Access, 225.

[18] Although voting surveys do not support such an impression. Even in the 1984 election blowout by Ronald Reagan, voters of Mexican descent stayed largely grounded in the Democratic party. See Luis Ricardo Fraga, "Prototype from the Midwest: Latinos in Illinois"; and Henry Flores and Robert Brischetto, "Texas Mexicans and the 1988 Election," in Rodolfo O. de la Garza and Louis DeSipio, eds., Rhetoric to Reality: Latino Politics in the 1988 Elections (Boulder, Colo.: Westview Press, 1992); and Richard Santillan and Frederico A. Subervi-Velez, "Latino Participation in Republican Party Politics in California," in Byran O. Jackson and Michael B. Preston, eds., Racial and Ethnic Politics in California (Berkeley, Calif.: IGS Press, 1991).

[19] For an examination of the Nixon administration's pursuit of the Mexican American vote, see Paul Frymer and John David Skrentny, "Coalition-Building and the Politics of Electoral Capture during the Nixon Administration: African-Americans, Labor, Latinos," Studies in American Political Development (Spring 1998). More generally, see Santillan and Subervi-Velez, "Latino Participation"; and Federico A. Subervi-Velez, "Republican

Two groups in the 1990s have received national attention because of the efforts of their party leaders to actively distance themselves from the groups' interests. Gay and lesbian voters in the Democratic party represent both a stigmatized group for many other important voting blocs and are perceived by party leaders as potentially disruptive to efforts to build majoritarian coalitions. The Christian Right, while in many ways dominating certain aspects of the Republican party's policy agenda of the 1980s and early 1990s, has recently borne the brunt of similar behavior by its party leadership. Republican leaders fear losing significant numbers of economically moderate and conservative women voters over the issue of abortion. I will discuss each group in this chapter. As the chapter epigraphs reveal, attacks on both groups provide opportunities for party candidates to appeal to larger audiences. Nonetheless, there are important differences that make comparisons between the position of these groups with that of African Americans in the party system difficult. After this discussion, I will conclude the book with some possible suggestions to ameliorate the captured status of not only African Americans, but of gays and lesbians, evangelicals, and any other group that might find itself in a position of being marginalized by national party competition.

GAY AND LESBIAN VOTERS IN THE DEMOCRATIC PARTY

It is difficult to determine the degree to which gay and lesbian voters are captured within the Democratic party because they are a newly emerging political group. It is also unclear whether they will remain a united and coherent political group. Moreover, both parties are uncertain about the long-term disruptive potential of gay and lesbian voters. As I have argued, there is always a period of political "learning" by party leaders about the disruptive potential of new political groups. Party leaders may welcome a group with open arms, only to realize shortly afterward that they made a mistake. To date, there is a significant

---

and Democratic Mass Communication Strategies: Targeting the Latino Vote," in Rodolfo O. de la Garza and Louis DeSipio, eds., *From Rhetoric to Reality: Latino Politics in the 1988 Elections* (Boulder, Colo.: Westview, 1992). California's 1998 state elections are also indicative of this dynamic. Just a few years after anti–affirmative action and anti-immigrant propositions mobilized the state's Latino population to vote Democratic, the state's Republican leaders were actively trying to make amends. Perhaps most notable was Republican gubernatorial candidate Dan Lundgren's appearance at a Spanish speaking debate where he condemned a state proposition to end California's bilingual education program.

amount of controversy over whether courting the gay and lesbian vote will disrupt a winning national party coalition.

Gay rights came onto the national scene with the Stonewall Inn riots in New York City during the summer of 1969.[20] National party campaigns, however, would not discuss gay rights until the 1990s. In the early 1980s, in fact, gay issues were only just beginning to be discussed, generally in the Democratic party primary campaigns and in local congressional races. During the 1980 presidential primaries, Democratic party candidates Jerry Brown and Ted Kennedy attended gay fund-raising events in California. In 1984, Jesse Jackson, in a nationally televised speech at the Democratic Convention, made perhaps the first public reference in history to the existence of homosexuals as a political group in the United States. While gay and lesbian activists were forming both local and national political organizations and mobilizing voters across the country, their issues nonetheless remained largely absent from the agenda of either national party.

By 1988, the "gay vote" was beginning to enter public discussion and was considered largely up for grabs between the two major parties. Despite being unattached to either party, gay and lesbian political leaders were ambivalent about both parties' candidates because neither side made more than quiet or subtle appeals. The leadership of both party campaigns perceived that they would lose votes with a prominent appeal. Democratic candidate Michael Dukakis feared being linked to another "special interest" group: as his campaign director, Susan Estrich, would later comment, "The Republicans were painting us as liberal, so we stayed away from causes like gay rights that played into that."[21] Republican candidate George Bush wanted to avoid angering the Christian Right, a group with increasing influence in his party, especially given his tense relationship with another Republican party presidential challenger, Pat Robertson—a candidate who was the first choice of many Christian Right voters.

Similar to African American voters in the Democratic party, gay and lesbian voters have a number of significant strategic factors potentially working in their favor. As a politically relevant group, they are predominantly located in crucial electoral college states such as California, Florida, Illinois, New York, and Texas. In California alone, gay and lesbian voters probably comprised 10 percent of the state's electorate in 1992.

[20] For a history of the Stonewall riots, see Toby Marotta, *The Politics of Homosexuality* (Boston: Houghton Mifflin, 1981), chap. 4.

[21] Quoted in Jeffrey Schmalz, "Gay Politics Goes Mainstream," *New York Times* (October 11, 1992), sec. 6, p.18.

Party leaders in California, which has fifty-four electoral college votes and a history of close party competition, have recognized that these unaffiliated voters could potentially provide the electoral margin. Nationally, gay and lesbian voters are estimated at 17 million, a number that is roughly equivalent to the number of African Americans and much higher than the growing number of Latino voters. Perhaps equally if not more important in the modern era of enormous campaign spending, gay and lesbian political groups spend money in campaigns. In 1992, for instance, gay rights organizations gave an estimated $3.5 million to Bill Clinton's presidential campaign.

In 1992, activists mobilized gay communities and politicized gay issues in an unprecedented attempt to influence a presidential campaign. In part, this was due to the vocal homophobia of Republican presidential candidate Pat Buchanan. Deriding the Democrats as a "pro-lesbian" and "pro-gay" party, Buchanan's speeches during his run for the Republican nomination politicized gay issues for the first time in a national election. Republican Vice President Dan Quayle added to this politicization by emphasizing the difference between the parties' "basic values" and terming the Clinton-Gore team "pretty boys": "We do not recognize the moral equivalence [of homosexual and heterosexual marriages]. And I'm sure the gay rights activists will not allow Bill Clinton to say that there isn't moral equivalence."[22]

Equally important to mobilizing the gay and lesbian vote was that Clinton also placed their issues on the national agenda, announcing at a speech to gay political leaders relatively early in the 1992 campaign that "I have a vision and you are part of it." In actively reaching out for their votes, Clinton represented the first major-party presidential candidate in history to speak openly about gay rights and to court gay votes. Among his pledges during the presidential campaign, Clinton promised to appoint gays and lesbians to prominent administration positions, to significantly increase the amount of federal funding targeted for AIDS research and awareness programs, and to lift the ban on gays serving in the armed services. Clinton spent considerably more time discussing gay political issues than African American political issues in his coauthored book with vice presidential candidate Al Gore, *Putting People First*. At the party convention, while Jesse Jackson found his speech relegated to a limited television audience, two prime-time speeches were devoted to the subject of AIDS. In one of them, political activist Bob Hattoy stated, "I am a gay man with AIDS. If there is any honor in having this disease, it is the honor of being part of the gay and lesbian community in America."

[22] Quoted ibid.

With the Democratic party's encouragement, gay political groups and community activists enthusiastically mobilized support for the Democratic presidential candidate. Although there was some discussion about the potential problems gay issues might pose for the party's electoral coalition, it was not prominent.[23] Gay activists were evident as members of the campaign staff, and Clinton, although not centering his campaign on gay and lesbian issues, at no point during the campaign attempted to distance himself from their issues. Much of this was for good reason. While Republicans attacked Clinton and the Democrats as the party of gays and lesbians, most public opinion polls showed that key groups of national voters were not buying it. As Republican consultant Kevin Phillips commented, "There was a thought that this would be the new Willy Horton. But the [Bush] Administration overdid it. The gay-bashing turned people off. It's become a minus for the Republicans."[24]

Once in office, however, Clinton perceived more difficulty in advocating gay and lesbian issues. The president first recognized the potential divisiveness of promoting their cause shortly after his election, when he made public his intent to issue an executive order allowing gay and lesbians to serve openly in the military. This was a primary campaign promise that Clinton made to his supporters, and the fact that he initiated his presidency with this cause reflected not only his gratitude for the support of gay and lesbian voters in the 1992 campaign, but his lack of awareness of the potential intensity of the opposition. Phillips commented at the time that the divisiveness of the issue took Clinton by surprise: "It was not a big issue in the fall, almost a non-issue. I suspect Clinton didn't think there was much opprobrium attached to this."[25]

With proponents of the military's ban extremely well organized and entrenched in government bureaucracies, Clinton and Democratic mem-

---

[23] David Mixner mentions some concern within the Clinton campaign from southern members who felt that "the gay and lesbian community might not be able to deliver enough votes in the large industrial states to justify taking the risk of backlash in the South." *Stranger among Friends* (New York: Bantam, 1996), 219. For an overview of the gay and lesbian movement and national electoral politics since the early 1970s, see Urvashi Vaid, *Virtual Equality: The Mainstreaming of Gay and Lesbian Liberation* (New York: Anchor Books, 1995), chap. 4.

[24] Quoted in Schmalz, "Gay Politics Goes Mainstream."

[25] Quoted in "New President Faces Gay-Soldiers Conflict," *Congressional Quarterly Almanac*, (Washington, D.C.: Congressional Quarterly Press 1993), 455. Even meetings between President Bush and gay leaders were criticized by Republicans. After a meeting between gay leaders and Bush campaign chairman Robert Mosbacher, eight congressional Republicans (including Newt Gingrich) wrote a letter to the president denouncing the meeting as "a slap in the face to every voter who affirms the traditional family. . . . Offending 98 percent of your constituency to placate 2 percent is unwise. Not only that, it is politically unfounded." Quoted in Vaid, *Virtual Equality*, 124.

bers of Congress were soon besieged with opposing communications. Public opinion polls were generally mixed to negative on the issue, slightly although not dramatically different from results of the public opinion polls before the election, which Clinton had interpreted as favorable to gay issues. There was in particular, however, noticeably strong opposition to lifting the ban from a crucial group of moderate swing voters who had supported third-party candidate Ross Perot in 1992.[26] Clinton had won only 43 percent of the nation's vote in the 1992 election, and winning the support of these Perot voters for an expected two-way race in 1996 was deemed critical by his advisers.

Moreover, for a president who had won election as a "new Democrat"—someone not attached to the party's special interest groups like previous Democratic candidates—Clinton desperately wanted to place himself back in the electoral middle. A run of bad publicity for the president had led him to feel that his administration was "reeling, we were just reeling. . . . What does the President stand for. Is he a New Democrat? It was gays, Zoe, and Kimba" (both failed nomination efforts) that were dominating the public agenda. Having run as a candidate who would stay situated with the nation's middle, the President felt he needed to distance himself from the special interest groups commonly associated with his party.[27] Democratic party pollster Stan Greenberg urged the president to align himself with "family" and "mainstream" values: "President Clinton needs to identify once again with the interests and values of middle America. . . . He must resist demands from activists and pressure groups that he embrace values or cultural policies that are at odds with the moral convictions of most Americans."[28] Journalist Thomas Edsall asked, "Was [Clinton] so tied to some of the marginal Democratic interest groups that gave him strong support during the campaign that he would not be able to work on behalf of the larger national interest?"[29]

As controversy surrounding the issue mounted, the president searched for a compromise position, and received help from Defense Secretary Les Aspin and the openly gay Massachusetts congressman, Barney Frank. Aspin recommended that the Pentagon should no longer ask mil-

---

[26] See Scott James, "A Theory of Presidential Commitment and Opportunism: Swing States, Pivotal Groups, and Civil Rights under Truman and Clinton" (paper presented at the American Political Science Association, Chicago, Ill. 1995), 29.

[27] Quoted in Elizabeth Drew, *On the Edge: The Clinton Presidency* (New York: Simon and Schuster, 1994), 127.

[28] Stanley B. Greenberg, *The Road to Realignment: The Democrats and Perot Voters* (Washington, D.C.: Democratic Leadership Council, 1993), 2–3.

[29] Thomas Byrne Edsall, "Clinton, So Far," *New York Review of Books* 40 (October 7, 1993).

itary officials about their sexual orientation, yet would retain the latitude to expel members based on sexual orientation as a sole criterion. Meanwhile, efforts to officially end the ban on gays in the military would be suspended for six months. Gay and lesbian organizations were ambivalent about this proposal, but generally went along with Aspin's compromise. They were less supportive a few months later, however, when the president made efforts to further distance himself from gay rights issues. On March 23, in a press conference, the president responded to a question asking whether he would support restrictions on gays and lesbians in the military with, "If you can discriminate against people in terms of whether they get into the service or not based on not what they are but what they say they are, then I would think you could make appropriate distinctions on duty assignments once they're in." Gay rights leaders were openly irate. Bob Hattoy told the *New York Times* that he "almost started crying when he heard Mr. Clinton's remarks."[30]

As Clinton continued to try to distance himself from the policy, Congressman Frank offered the rather infamous "don't ask, don't tell" policy proposal; gay military personnel would not be asked their preferences, but neither would they be allowed to engage in homosexual activity while in uniform. Frank's suggestion provided the president some of the legitimacy necessary to allow him to compromise. Demonstrations at the White House in late June led to the arrests of leading members of gay political organizations. As gay rights advocate and early member of the Clinton administration David Mixner remarked, "We were purposely misled in an effort to keep us quiet (about the compromise over gay rights in the military). White House political operatives determined that we, as a community, had nowhere else to go and that even our anger would work in favor of the president by showing the country that he could stand up to the queers."[31]

Gay issues more or less dropped from the spotlight of the political agenda until they were brought up again by the Republicans during the 1996 election year. In response to a Hawaii Supreme Court ruling that same sex marriages were constitutional, the Republican-controlled Congress passed with extensive Democratic support what has come to be known as the "Defense of Marriage Act." Clinton, while proclaiming ambivalence, announced immediately that he would sign the bill, prompting Mixner to call it "this year's Sister Soulja—a way to show he isn't beholden to gay people."[32] Despite the disgruntlement of the gay

---

[30] Quoted in Mixner, *Stranger among Friends*, 307.
[31] Quoted in "New President Faces Gay-Soldiers Conflict," 460.
[32] Quoted in Frank Rich, "An F.O.B.'s Lament," *New York Times* (July 10, 1996), A15.

community toward Clinton, their numbers in key electoral states, their propensity to spend money on presidential campaigns, and the absence of a long-standing historical tendency to vote for the Democratic party (in 1988 it was estimated that 40 percent of the gay and lesbian vote went to George Bush), the Republican party generally made no public appeals for their votes. In fact, Republican presidential candidate Bob Dole made headlines in 1995 when he refused to accept a donation of one thousand dollars from the Log Cabin Republicans, made up of approximately ten thousand gay and lesbian Republicans. Meanwhile, Republican representative Robert Dornan reiterated the hostility of many party members to homosexual interests: commenting on the possibility of Republicans reaching out to the gay vote, Dornan quipped, "We have a [congressional] representative on our side who is a homo."[33]

Faced with similar ambivalence from Democratic party leaders, gay political groups have been confronted with the frustration (at least in the short term) of being marginalized as a captured group. Urvashi Vaid, the former executive director of the National Gay and Lesbian Task Force, expressed such sentiments when responding to the failure of gay and lesbian political leaders to influence Clinton: "The gay movement has established a beachhead in Washington by mobilizing some wealthy people and delivering some votes. But unlike the gun lobby (or the tobacco industry or the health insurance industry or any other major Washington force), we follow a pathway to political power that leads us to the locked, steel gate of antisexual cultural attitudes about homosexuality. The gay movement's use of politics of access cannot overcome the stigma of homosexual behavior." David Mixner responded with similar frustration: "The White House's political calculations are correct" since gay voters "have no place else to go."[34] Recognition of the importance accorded to electoral incentives has left the party's gay leadership divided — divided in a similar way to the African American political leaders during the 1980s. An expected protest in San Francisco by gay activists shortly after Clinton's signing of the "Defense of Marriage" Bill never materialized because gay leaders divided over the potential ramifications it would have for their preferred presidential candidate against Bob Dole. In a speech to gay voters, Brian Bond, the gay liaison at the Democratic National Committee, summed up the situation with understandable ambivalence: "I'm not going to sit here and patronize you on marriage. Quite frankly, it sucks. We are not going to get everything we want, but (Clinton) will listen to us." David Mixner

---

[33] Quoted in Jill Lawrence, "House Mates," *Washington Post* (June 2, 1996), W17.
[34] Vaid, *Virtual Equality*, 217; Rich, "F.O.B.'s Lament."

proclaimed at the same rally, "I'll vote for Clinton, yes. But I'll be damned if I'll give him the power to take away any of my freedom."[35]

THE CHRISTIAN RIGHT AND THE REPUBLICAN PARTY

The emergence of a conservative wing of the Republican party inspired primarily by fundamentalist Christian values and abortion politics is also quite new to national electoral politics. Abortion entered the political sphere a partisan issue only in the early 1970s,[36] and as late as the 1980 presidential election, evangelical Christians gave large numbers of their votes — even majorities in many states — to Jimmy Carter and Democratic congressional candidates.[37] Christian Right organizations began in 1980 to mobilize support behind Republicans at the congressional level, and their leaders took credit for the defeat of twenty-three congressional liberals, including well-known Democrats such as George McGovern, Frank Church, and Birch Bayh.[38] By 1984, it is estimated that more than 80 percent of fundamentalist Christians were voting for Ronald Reagan. Reagan and the Republican leadership were thrilled with the newfound support. Concentrated largely in the South, the Christian Right's exodus from the Democratic party in the region hastened a long-awaited partisan realignment. Reagan was able to appeal to evangelical voters with an agenda focused largely on economics and social policies that dealt much more directly with family issues than with religious issues. As a result, any possible divisiveness related to the Christian Right's religious agenda went, by and large, unnoticed by the party leadership.

Republican leaders first began to perceive that the Christian Right could be a potentially divisive force during the party's primary campaign in 1988. As evangelicals mobilized in huge proportions at the state and local level, a number of mainstream party members were either defeated or seriously challenged in Republican primaries where voter turnout is historically low. The fervor of the Religious Right over ideological purity tests within the party led national party candidates

[35] Both Bond and Mixner are quoted in Sharon Waxman, "Out in Hollywood, but Not for Clinton: Position on Gay Marriage Losses Him Support," *Washington Post* (June 12, 1996), C1.

[36] See Kristin Luker, *Abortion and the Politics of Motherhood* (Berkeley: University of California Press, 1984).

[37] For an excellent account of the Christian Right's emergence in the Republican party, see Duane Murray Oldfield, *The Right and the Righteous: The Christian Right Confronts the Republican Party* (Lanham, Md.: Rowman and Littlefield, 1996).

[38] See Steve Bruce, *The Rise and Fall of the New Christian Right: Conservative Protestant Politics in America, 1978–1988* (Oxford: Clarendon Press, 1988), chap. 5.

such as George Bush to speak out in opposition: "I raise this as a friend who believes deeply in your involvement. . . . A small minority now want control. There are those who would seek to impose their will and dictate their interpretation of morality on the rest of society."[39] One Texas Republican leader accused the Christian Right as having "unwavering ideas. They won't accept you if you have one little doubt about anything." Another warned that "if the Christian Right becomes a major portion of the Republican voting bloc, then it has the potential to destroy it. We would lose our centrist base."[40] "When you get a three-martini Episcopalian in a room with a teetotaling Baptist . . . you got a problem. One is telling dirty jokes and the other is there in prayer. It is like mixing oil and water."[41]

Pat Robertson's bid for the Republican party presidential nomination was similarly perceived as divisive within party circles. The eventual Republican party nominee, George Bush, continually tried to distance himself from Robertson and in the process was accused by Robertson supporters of locking them out of delegate elections. Robertson and Bush had a number of bruising fights over delegate selection in states such as South Carolina, Michigan, and Iowa. A political consultant for Robertson argued that the "Republican establishment leaders want us to sleep with them on election night, but they won't respect us in the morning. . . . I'm becoming increasingly pessimistic that the integration of evangelicals into the party is going to have a happy ending. What happened in South Carolina, [including] the description of a Robertson meeting as a Nazi rally, is the worst sort of bigotry I've seen in a long time."[42]

Except for a couple of instances, the Democrats have refrained from attacking the Christian Right in order to appeal to moderate voters. On one occasion, Democratic leaders looking for new ways to reach out to moderate swing voters tried to publicly tie the Republicans to Pat Robertson. Following the lead of public opinion polls that showed 63 percent of Americans were unhappy with Robertson's increasing influence, Democrats attacked the candidate in media ads as one who would abolish public education, outlaw all abortions, and set quotas for "born again" Christians in government.[43] Yet, while the Democrats have re-

---

[39] Quoted in Phil Gailey, "Washington Talk: Political Notebook," *New York Times* (February 5, 1987), A24.

[40] Quoted in John B. Judis, "The Charge of the Light Brigade: Fundamentalists and Republicans in the post-Reagan Era," *New Republic* (September 29, 1986), 16.

[41] Quoted ibid.

[42] Quoted in James A. Barnes, "Looking for Credibility," *National Journal* (April 25, 1987), 986.

[43] See Paul Gailey, "Politics: Evangelism and a Fight with Peril to Both Sides," *New York Times* (March 17, 1986).

mained committed to abortion rights, they have remained cautious about attacking a group advocating issues that are popular with national majorities. The issues of the Religious Right are as unifying as they are divisive. Neither party's candidates, for instance, oppose appealing to this group of voters with broader Christian themes. Almost all Republican candidates, out of deference to the Religious Right, oppose abortion and support school prayer. Democratic president Bill Clinton has advocated a number of the Christian Right's concerns, from increased family control over the media to the promotion of Christian values in campaign speeches. Only on abortion has the president consistently drawn the line between his constituency and the Christian Right.

The Christian Right is further emboldened in national politics because they have come to form one of the largest blocs within the Republican party's electoral coalition. In the process they have emerged with a great deal of institutional power within the party organization. In part, this is simply a result of numbers and resources. In 1994, the year of the dramatic Republican takeovers in Congress, exit polls placed the percentage of the Christian Right within the Republican party's electoral coalition as high as 40 percent. As is the case with gay and lesbian voters, their numbers are concentrated in many key electoral states, most notably Florida and Texas, where their numbers provide for a majority of the party's state vote. As with gay rights activists, the Christian Right is an important financial contributor to both national and congressional campaigns. The numbers are even higher in many of the Republican primaries, given the low number of less intensely mobilized party voters. The Christian Right has become one of the most mobilized voting communities in the nation and has, so far, not been met by any real form of countermobilization.

Mobilized Christian voters have used these numbers and resources to take control of many local party organizations, particularly the party's southern state organizations. In these states, the Christian Right has been responsible for a large proportions of the delegates sent to the party's convention. In 1996, the Christian Right in both South Carolina and Texas won the majority of these states' delegates to the Republican convention, bypassing prominent Bob Dole supporters in the process. South Carolina governor Carroll Campbell, for instance, finished twelfth in the balloting to represent the state's Republicans at the national convention behind eleven unknown Christian Right activists. Texas governor Kay Bailey-Hutchinson barely held on as a pro-choice delegate in her state's selection process, a process again dominated by the Christian Right.

In 1996, this issue moved to the forefront of the Republican party nomination battle, with party nominee Bob Dole continually attempting to find a way to distance himself from the Christian Right. In June of that year, Dole promoted tolerance toward pro-choice Republicans. Party leaders widely praised the move. One party pollster commented, "Senator Dole instinctively knows that the party's position on abortion signals intolerance to many women, moderates, and suburbanites . . . the core of the swing group you need to win a general election."[44] But the Christian Right publicly resisted this effort: abortion is their primary issue, and their belief that abortion constitutes murder generates moral fervor, making compromise extremely difficult.

That the Christian Right is currently struggling with Republican party leaders for influence in the party does not in itself signify that their interests have been in any way "captured." Except on the issue of abortion, the Democratic party has not made it clear that they do not want the Christian Right's vote. Except for the Christian Right's moral fervor and apparent unwillingness to compromise on some crucial issues, their presence in the Republican party is not in any way clearly divisive for long-term coalition building. The degree of stigma attached to these voters is mild and does not pervade broader policy issues. The battle right now for the Republican party is simply over whether the Christian Right is willing to compromise with less impassioned Republicans to maintain their party's ability to form electoral majorities.

THE PROSPECT FOR REFORM

I have argued in this book that African-Americans have suffered from party competition quite consistently throughout U.S. history. What alternatives, then, do African Americans and their political leaders have for more effective representation? One is to change the electoral structure. Making comparisons to other countries is difficult since, as Kenneth Benoit and Kenneth Shepsle argue, "racial minorities in other systems are frequently defined by a multiplicity of cleavages, sometimes owing to an imperial or colonial heritage but also to migrations, war settlements, religious patterns, the socioeconomic legacies of modernization, or subnational tribal or clan alliances; matters that are further complicated in that many of these cleavages are cross-cutting."[45] None-

---

[44] Quoted in Thomas B. Edsall, "Souljah Episode Echoes in Dole's Move; Clinton Took on a Rapper; GOP Rival's Gambit on Abortion Is Riskier," *Washington Post* (June 13, 1996), A10.

[45] Kenneth Benoit and Kenneth A. Shepsle, "Electoral Systems and Minority Representation," in Paul E. Peterson, ed., *Classifying by Race* (Princeton: Princeton University Press, 1995), 67.

theless, it is notable that the United States does not have a political system that represents groups proportionate to their votes, even if their votes fall short of a majority.[46] Most countries with various forms of racial, ethnic, religious, gender, and class cleavages have electoral systems that allow for some form of proportional representation. They offer the minority group greater opportunities for political voice. In national governing systems such as Israel, Iceland, Germany, Belgium, Finland, and South Africa, minority groups that are both politically and ethnically based have achieved a degree of consistent representation that is not comparable to what is available in the United States.[47]

Changes to the electoral structure are not easy nor are they likely to occur at the national level any time in the near political future. While a number of U.S. cities have experimented with non-majoritarian-based electoral systems, nothing of its sort has been tried at the national level. In 1986, the Supreme Court ruled in *Thornburg v. Gingles* that congressional districts could be drawn in order to provide for a form of proportional representation in the House of Representatives. By drawing the lines of congressional districts so that African Americans are the majority voting population of the district, black members of the House are now roughly proportional to the black population. And as we saw in chapter 6, the increased numbers of African Americans in the House provided the Congressional Black Caucus with substantial leverage during the 103d Congress. Public reaction to majority-minority districts

---

[46] Sri Lanka is a more extreme example of this situation that has led to harmful consequences for the minority Tamil population, a group that comprises roughly 22 percent of the population. Both national parties are centered around the majority Sinhalese population and often compete with each other to be more anti-Tamil. See Marshall R. Singer, "Prospects for Conflict Management in the Sri Lankan Ethnic Conflict," in Joseph V. Montville, ed., *Conflict and Peacemaking in Multiethnic Societies* (Lexington, Mass.: Lexington Books, 1990).

[47] See Benoit and Shepsle, "Electoral Systems and Minority Representation"; Arend Lijphart, *Democracies: Patterns of Majoritarian and Consensus Government in Twenty-One Countries* (New Haven: Yale University Press, 1984); and Arend Lijphart, Ronald Rogowski, and R. Kent Weaver, "Separation of Powers and Cleavage Management," in R. Kent Weaver and Bert A. Rockman, eds., *Do Institutions Matter? Government Capabilities in the United States and Abroad* (Washington, D.C.: Brookings Institution, 1993). In fact, Stein Rokkan argues that proportional representation developed directly to deal with racial, ethnic, and religious cleavage. "It was no accident that the earliest moves toward proportional representation (PR) came in the ethnically most heterogeneous European countries. . . . In linguistically and religiously divided societies majority elections could clearly threaten the continued existence of the political system. The introduction of some element of minority representation came to be seen as an essential step in a territorial consolidation." Rokkan, *Citizens, Elections, Parties: Approaches to the Comparative Study of the Processes of Development* (Oslo: Universitetsforlaget, 1970), 157 (cited in Lijphart, Rogowski, and Weaver, "Separation of Powers and Cleavage Management").

has been largely negative, and in recent years the Supreme Court has expressed similar antagonisms. It is a reaction that is shared by Democratic party leaders who fear that the increase in African American majority districts means a decrease in the overall number of congressional districts with Democratic majorities.

The existence of majority-minority districts provides for a vaguely proportional form of representation for black voters, but it remains entrenched inside a dominant two-party system in the legislative process. As such, the national majority on various legislative matters is still centered around white voters, and majorities can be found without the need to appeal to congressional members representing majority black districts (see the previous chapter's discussion of the 1994 Crime Bill). A more extensive form of proportional representation would not only allow blacks representation according to their numbers, it would hopefully break down white voters into enough subsegments that racial division would no longer influence party competition. Since party competition would no longer be centered around a white median voter, the incentives for party leaders would be much more flexible toward various race and non-race-based appeals. Environmental, religious, labor, and other political issues that divide Americans, regardless of race, ought to emerge in political campaigns that will allow for small parties to prosper without having to worry about winning over "swing" voters.

Even the smallest of electoral reform have been heatedly opposed by most voters and by leaders of both parties who fear losing control over the electoral process. Those public figures, such as Lani Guinier, who suggest wider-scale electoral reforms have often been discredited in national political circles as extremists and opponents of democracy. Nonetheless, I believe that such reforms are necessary if African Americans are to be better represented in the political process. If this book can aid efforts toward this goal, all the better. While the majority-based party system continues to dominate the agenda of American politics, I hope to make clear the necessity for changes. Moreover, by bringing race to the center of our understandings of American politics and institutions, I hope to challenge some of the theories that for so long have influenced our conceptions of American political life.

Without such reforms, what opportunities exist for increasing African American representation? Some of the common possibilities offered have been discussed throughout this manuscript; for instance, the possibility of African Americans voting for the Republican party, or an independent party (perhaps a specifically black political party), the possibility of organizational reforms inside the Democratic party, and the reliance on minority-rights mechanisms in Congress. In the rest of this chapter, I want to discuss two alternatives: the possibility of a political party to change the incentive structure by shaping the preferences of the national median voter and the possibility of external force on the party and political system by mobilized groups.

Parties as a Shaper of Public Preferences

There is an assumption that the party takes individual preferences of American voters as given and merely aggregates them into umbrellalike coalitions. This assumption exists, at least in part, because American parties tend to act this way — they take the preferences of voters as they find them. Congressional scholars, for instance, have long commented on the tendency of House candidates to appeal to "home style" or to "position take" in a way that conforms to what the member perceives to be the preexisting value or norm of her/his constituency.[48] Ted Lowi claims that "candidates frame strategies and appeals around audience identification — down to the finer points of Protestant candidates eating indigestible blintzes. In appealing to whatever characteristics are perceived as even remotely salient to voters, candidates tend to restore and reaffirm the identification of voters with these very characteristics."[49] The increasing frequency by which modern-day party candidates follow political consultants only exacerbates this tendency. Politicians who follow the polls avoid taking positions unpopular with public opinion. An issue initially popular with the voters is publicly supported by politicians. As the public listens to the politicians, they are reassured that their viewpoints are legitimate. Initially ambivalent public viewpoints, then, are reinforced. In fact, with the advancement of direct mail technologies, politicians can target specific groups differently. Thus, as Marshall Ganz has pointed out, campaigns can appeal to Catholic home owners on the issue of family values while at the same time appealing to single Jewish women by being pro-choice.[50]

But just as many "new institutionalists" have shown that a weak American state does not mean that it is without influence, the existence of weak political parties does not necessarily imply that they are incon-

[48] See Richard F. Fenno, Jr., *Home Style: House Members in Their Districts* (Glenview, Ill.: Scott, Foresman, 1978); and David R. Mayhew, *Congress: The Electoral Connection* (New Haven: Yale University Press, 1974).

[49] Theodore J. Lowi, "Party, Policy, and Constitution in America," in William Nisbet Chambers and Walter Dean Burnham, eds., *American Party Systems* (New York: Oxford University Press, 1975), 257.

[50] Marshall Ganz, "Voters in the Crosshairs: How Technology and the Market Are Destroying Politics," *American Prospect* (July 1994), 106.

sequential or unimportant.[51] If parties do not change voter perceptions, at the very least they do perpetuate and reinforce those perceptions. Often, this acts to reinforce the confusion of already inchoate and ambivalent voters. Anthony Downs contends that rational parties, in their effort to maximize votes, purposely offer ambiguous messages in order to offend the least number of people. This ambiguity, however, renders the public unable to remain "rational," or perfectly informed. Kenneth Shepsle, meanwhile, argues that party candidates employ a "lottery" technique by taking contradictory and vague policy stands in an effort to gain support of the voters who are situated at and close to the electoral median.[52] Again this ambiguity leads to confused voters. As Benjamin Page claims, the inability of voters to have a firm understanding of issues or to locate candidates is caused just as much "by conflicting information, as well as by the lack of information" put forth by parties as it is by a lack of interest from the voters.[53]

Alan Ware has nicely depicted how Democratic party candidates' efforts to avoid discussion of racial issues — because of their fear of alienating the existing preferences of their voting coalition — lead to a great deal of public confusion. In Denver, Colorado, during intense public debate over the role of forced school busing during the early 1970s, the position of Democratic candidate Patricia Schroeder was not to influence or educate, but to deemphasize the issue. She began the campaign by attempting to play both sides of the issue. She claimed that "busing was a tool of racial integration" but that she did not approve of "forced massive cross town busing."[54] Then she attempted to defuse the issue, arguing that busing was being discussed too much by voters and politicians alike. The real issue, she claimed, was not busing but the quality of education in Denver. Her strategy, Ware claims, "was designed to obscure this area of mass conflict and to draw attention in the campaign to an issue with which it could be conflated — quality education." In doing this, she "did nothing more to ameliorate conflict at the mass level over the relationship of the minority group to the majority. The lines of conflict had not been redefined, but had been obscured." White

---

[51] See James G. March and Johan P. Olsen, "The New Institutionalism: Organizational Factors in Political Life," *American Political Science Review* 78 (1984): 734–49; and Stephen Skowronek, *Building a New American State: The Expansion of National Administrative Capacities, 1877–1920* (New York: Cambridge University Press, 1982). Also see Murray Edelman, *Politics as Symbolic Action* (New Haven: Yale University Press, 1971).

[52] Kenneth A. Shepsle, "The Strategy of Ambiguity: Uncertainty and Electoral Competition," *American Political Science Review* 66 (1972): 555–68.

[53] Benjamin I. Page, *Choices and Echoes in Presidential Elections: Rational Man and Electoral Democracy* (Chicago: University of Chicago Press, 1978), 179.

[54] Alan Ware, *The Logic of Party Democracy* (New York: St. Martin's Press, 1979), 148.

voters, meanwhile, were left "to adapt themselves to a program they didn't vote for but was being imposed on them. It was not explained to them why, in the interests of furthering other objectives, they had to reconcile themselves to a policy situation they feared." Colorado politicians such as Gary Hart followed Schroeder's lead, proclaiming opposition to busing but at the same time arguing that the law should be obeyed until an alternative was found. Only two years after the busing debate, the Democratic party platform in Denver ignored the issue altogether, stating merely that it was committed to quality education.[55]

Recent scholarship has found that parties can do more than confuse and blur debate. James Carmines and Edward Stimson offer compelling evidence that when political parties changed their public positions on African American concerns, it led to changes in the preferences of party supporters.[56] John Zaller has found that party leaders and a unanimous media elite had a similar impact on the public in foreign affairs. Party leaders and other political elites offered cues to voters that shaped their policy preferences on the Vietnam War.[57] Elizabeth Gerber and John Jackson confirm the results of both studies and find that "voters take cues from the electoral participants as they develop their preferences. This means that voters perceive party positions and hear the debate surrounding the adoption of those positions and alter their own political attitudes in response."[58]

Providing evidence to demonstrate that party leaders play a direct role in opinion formation is exceedingly difficult. Unlike some nations where the parties dominate the public and, to a large degree, the private lives of voters,[59] American parties are just one of a series of political actors seeking to influence public opinion. Unlike some European parties, American parties do not control the media, schools, churches, or social groups. Providing evidence of the role of party leaders with regard to race is even more difficult since in the post–civil rights era there are so few examples of such leaders actively and publicly supporting unpopular racial issues. Neither the Democratic party or the Republican party has pushed African American concerns enough to test its influence, despite numerous openings to do so.

---

[55] Ibid., 150–51.

[56] Edward C. Carmines and James A. Stimson, *Issue Evolution: Race and the Transformation of American Politics* (Princeton: Princeton University Press, 1989), chap. 5.

[57] John Zaller, "Information, Values, and Opinion" *American Political Science Review* 85 (1991): 1215–38.

[58] Elisabeth R. Gerber and John E. Jackson, "Endogenous Preferences and the Study of Institutions," *American Political Science Review* 87 (1993): 639.

[59] See Joseph J. Houska, *Influencing Mass Political Behavior* (Berkeley: Institute of International Studies, University of California, 1985).

I want to offer, though, one interesting example of where the parties unwillingly shaped the debate over a racial matter. In the process, the Democratic party perhaps missed an opportunity to shape preferences further, and in a direction that would have been beneficial to significant elements of their constituency. The missed opportunity by the party was the 1994 headline-making struggle over California initiative Proposition 187. The proposition, passed by a large majority of the state's voters, was designed to cut back the number of illegal immigrants who enter the state by preventing such immigrants from using state resources and welfare programs. Economic woes and xenophobia on the part of white voters were widely accepted as the chief contributors to the measure's popularity at the ballot booth. From its initial placement on the ballot, the issue was exceedingly popular with state voters — those identifying as Republicans and Democrats, as whites, and as members of other minority groups. It is not surprising then that neither party initially opposed the measure.

By May 29, the *Los Angeles Times* found that 59 percent of a sample of registered California voters supported the proposition. Between the end of May and the beginning of October of 1994, only one prominent politician in the state of either party came out against the measure, State Assembly Speaker and Democrat Willy Brown. Governor Pete Wilson had staked much of his campaign for reelection on the passage of the initiative and, in the process, made visible proclamations on its behalf. Democratic politicians often did their best to outdo Wilson, making bold and tough pronouncements while standing next to the state's border with Mexico. By the end of September, 62 percent of those polled by the *Los Angeles Times* supported the measure, while only 29 percent opposed it.[60] Voters claiming identification with the Democratic party, meanwhile, were also strongly in favor of the bill, with 55 percent in support and only 35 percent opposed.

In mid-September, just six weeks before the election, the Democratic candidate for governor, Kathleen Brown, publicly came out against the proposition for the first time. The content of her opposition to 187, however, focused less on why the proposition was bad than on Governor Wilson's hypocrisy on the matter. Wilson, she claimed, "cut a hole in the fence to allow millions of illegal immigrants in, and now he wants to patch that hole because that's what the polls tell him to do." A few weeks later, she argued that Wilson has "got fingerprints all over the illegal immigration problem. As a Senator, he opened the floodgates to 1.3 million illegal immigrants."[61]

---

[60] *Los Angeles Times* Poll, September 13, 1994.
[61] Daniel M. Weintraub and Bill Stall, "Wilson Would Expel Illegal Immigrants from

In late October, other politicians also publicly voiced opposition to 187. On October 16, seventy thousand protesters and local Democratic party leaders marched through the streets of downtown Los Angeles. Two days later, two nationally prominent Republicans, Jack Kemp and William Bennett, came out against the measure, and were soon followed by members of the Clinton administration. Dianne Feinstein, the Democratic candidate for Senate in the state, as well as President Bill Clinton, also proclaimed their opposition shortly after Feinstein's opponent came out in favor. Feinstein made a well-publicized statement in front of the Mexican border promoting increased prevention of illegal immigration. With just two weeks to go before the November election, grass-roots organizations further stepped up mobilization efforts against the proposition, regularly making the nightly news and front pages of the state's major newspapers. In response, public opinion on the matter changed dramatically. A 26-point gap in favor of the proposition on October 15 turned to only a 10-point advantage on November 1. By election day, most state pollsters and news organizations were labeling the battle a near dead heat.

Proposition 187 ultimately won decisively on election day, and some would argue that the change in the polls was a function more of respondents lying to the pollster than to their actually changing their opinions. Not wanting to appear racist to the pollster, some voters may have refused to vocalize their support of the measure. Behind the curtain of the voting booth, their opinions no longer had to be concealed. There is no doubt some truth to this. Nonetheless, three significant points still stand out from this story. First, a strong majority of Democratic voters (64 percent) ended up voting against the measure. Just two weeks prior to election day, Democratic identifiers had supported the proposition by a 52 to 40 margin. Second, a similarly popular issue, the "three strikes and you're out" crime initiative (Propositon 184) passed with even higher proportions of public support. Interestingly enough, Proposition 184 had met with widespread public ambivalence in a *Los Angeles Times* poll taken in April of 1994. While 65 percent of the respondents favored the proposition, fewer than half of the respondents maintained their support if it meant a tax increase to fund new prisons. Fewer than a quarter of the respondents favored the proposition if it meant cuts in the state's higher education budget. Yet from the time of that poll through election day, no prominent state or national politician of either

---

Schools; Politics: Saying State Can't Afford to Educate Them, He Clarifies Stand on Prop. 187. Brown Charges Hypocrisy," *Los Angeles Times* (September 16, 1994), A1; "Brown, Wilson Clash on Crime, Immigration, Taxes; Debate: Challenger Discloses Daughter's Rape in Forceful Answer to Governor's Charge that She's Soft on Crime" (October 16, 1994), A1.

party came out publicly against Propositon 184 and at no time did public approval over the proposition fluctuate.

Third, unlike the anti–Vietnam War movement and the civil rights movement, the change in voter preferences on Proposition 187 occurred without the supportive dynamics of a larger social movement. Notwithstanding the late-breaking grass-roots effort, public pronouncements against 187 by party elites occurred largely in an environment where little reinforcing influences existed, save other elite criticisms of the initiative. *Something* must have been responsible for the dramatic shift in voter policy preferences. Party leaders were not only one candidate for stimulating this abrupt shift — they appear in this instance to have been the only viable candidate. Within the span of a mere two weeks, party leaders provoked a reexamination of policy preferences on an issue of extreme intensity and popularity, simply by voicing public antipathy to the initiative.

External Pressure

As long as racism remains an important facet of American politics, only agencies that challenge popular opinion can break down existing hierarchies. Electoral incentives in the United States have generally militated against parties doing so. However, a small but significant and growing part of the literature has realized that preference changes in the electorate are not simply a theoretical fantasy of ideological extremists bent on changing reality into their own skewed perceptions of the world. Such changes in policy preferences stimulated through parties have occurred in our political history and can be facilitated and encouraged by party actions.

Examples such as the one just discussed, however, ought to make potential interest group leaders wary of relying on the party for mobilizing public opinion. Party leaders are generally unwilling to take chances by promoting the interests of a group they perceive to be at odds with broader coalition-building. Alternative institutions that attempt to shape public opinion are also problematic. The media, for instance, are a powerful source for opinion formation, but they are not democratic and remain unaccountable to any specific interest or group of voters. Instead, they follow their own "rules," which can help movements reach their political agenda but just as often redefine it in ways detrimental to the group's aims.[62] The Supreme Court is also a powerful source, as its actions often inject issues into the national agenda and

---

[62] See Todd Gitlin, *The Whole World Is Watching: Mass Media in the Making and Unmaking of the New Left* (Berkeley: University of California Press, 1980); and Thomas E. Patterson, *Out of Order* (New York: Vintage, 1993).

help shape public preferences on otherwise latent issues. Yet like the media, the Court is not directly accountable to blacks or any other political group, and as such, it inconsistently furthers black representation. The Court's changing rulings on racial gerrymandering, affirmative action, and busing over the last decades provide just a few problematic examples of this.

The moments in which African Americans have most greatly benefited from electoral politics have been when outside political movements have been active and disruptive. In the 1850s, the abolitionist movement not only placed a great deal of pressure on political leaders for immediate results, it also mobilized public opinion by exposing the horrors of slavery and demanding its end. In the 1950s and 1960s, civil rights leaders had a similar degree of success. They placed a great deal of pressure on party leaders and successfully mobilized many northern and southern whites to oppose the continuation of legal discrimination.

As we know, party leaders respond to what they perceive as strategic advantages and opportunities. On issues such as race, the general perception of party leaders is that actively promoting African American interests is not an optimal electoral strategy. Interest groups, then, have little choice but to promote their issues themselves. Successful movements directed at racial hierarchies — whether they are by abolitionists, civil rights advocates, or anti-apartheid protesters — provide an effective way for civil rights supporters to mobilize public support and change the perceptions of national party leaders. Unfortunately, efforts to promote effective social movements are hurt by a number of structural disadvantages. For a group to persuade public opinion requires a great deal of strategy and discipline. The civil rights movement, for instance, captivated public support through disciplined organizations that effectively utilized nonviolent protest. In a number of excellent studies, however, scholars have shown the various problems that are virtually inherent to movement politics. As is common with any "collective goods," movements face problems with free riders. The fact that many supporters of movements opt not to participate or contribute financial resources makes it necessary for movements to rely on volunteer political activists. The reliance on activists, in turn, makes it difficult for movements to maintain cohesion and discipline in their organization, to effectively create and implement stategy, and to maintain control over their outgoing message.[63] Regardless, when party leaders avoid taking

[63] See Gitlin, *Whole World Is Watching*; Frances Fox Piven and Richard Cloward, *Poor People's Movements: Why They Succeed, How They Fail* (New York: Vintage, 1977); Jane Mansbridge, *Why We Lost the Era* (Chicago: University of Chicago Press, 1986); Clayborne Carson, *In Struggle: SNCC and the Black Awakening of the 1960s* (Cambridge: Harvard University Press, 1981); Doug McAdam, *Political Process and the Devel-*

on a group's issues for fear that it will hinder their electoral success, interest group leaders have little choice but to promote the issues themselves. Until the electoral stucture is changed, movement politics remains the most vital option for African American representation.

CONCLUSION

The brief discussion of the difficulty of social movements in maintaining access and representation leads us back to the potential advantages and possibilities of the political party. For better or worse, parties can provide the long-term organization and coordination, not to mention financial resources, that are so often lacking in movement politics. What is crucial, then, is to change the rules by which party leaders function. E. E. Schattschneider, whom I have cited throughout this manuscript as one of the foremost proponents of the competitive two-party system, was also very conscious of the impact that rules can have for group representation. He promoted the political party because he believed that black Americans and other disadvantaged groups could use their numbers to overcome the financial resources and insider status of the nation's elite. Writing at a time of optimism regarding the possibility of eliminating racist thought and behavior, Schattschneider had good reason to promote the two-party system as the best way to continue a democratic society.

At the end of the twentieth century, it is clear that racism and racial inequality will not disappear any time soon. The political party offers great potential in breaking down racial hierarchies and changing the way Americans think about race. However, the rules party leaders follow simply provide too much legitimacy for actions that reinforce racial prejudice and inequality instead of opposing it. These rules are not simply biased by consequence against African American interests; they were in many ways designed with the intent of marginalizing their interests. While our political rules will always disadvantage some groups in comparison to others, we must eliminate those rules based on long histories of government-enforced discrimination and prejudice. This history necessitates responsibility on the part of national leaders to behave in exceptional ways, especially if it means rooting out continuing vestiges of institutional and public racism.

---

opment of Black Insurgency, 1930–1970 (Chicago: University of Chicago Press, 1982); Mancur Olson, The Logic of Collective Action: Public Goods and the Theory of Groups (Cambridge: Harvard University Press, 1965); and Aldon D. Morris, The Origins of the Civil Rights Movement: Black Communities Organizing for Change (New York: Free Press, 1984).

Index

abolitionists, 35, 38, 49; in New York, 38
abortion rights, 9, 149, 157, 165, 193–96; and Hyde Amendment, 157
Adams, John Quincy, 37
affirmative action, 87, 89–90, 118, 144, 149, 157–58, 160, 162, 164; *Bakke* decision, 157; Civil Rights Act of 1991, 171; Mikulski Commission, 107; Philadelphia Plan, 103; Public Works Employment Act, 168;
AFL-CIO, 151, 154
Africa: Algeria, 150; Angola, 157, 159; and Congressional Black Caucus, 155, 157–65; Namibia, 155; Nigeria, 150, 156; reaction to civil rights movement, 97; Rhodesia, 155–57; Rwanda, 150; Somalia, 150, 160–61; South Africa, 155–60, 162, 166, 170, 178; Uganda, 157; Zaire, 150, 160; Zimbabwe, 158
African Americans: disenfranchisement, 15, 60–52, 72n, 79, 81; political interests (defined), 145–49; political leaders, 4, 23–24, 26, 45, 47, 63, 74, 78, 106–7, 110–11, 119, 192; public opinion, 147–48; representation, 5, 12, 15, 17, 19–20, 44–45; urban politics, 23, 26; (*see also* Jesse Jackson; and Congressional Black Caucus); voting rights, 49n, 56–65, 75–76, 79, 99, 144
Agricultural Adjustment Administration, 94
Aid to Dependent Children (ADC), 94
AIDS, 160, 165, 188
Alabama test, 38
Aldrich, John, 37–38
American Independent Party, 101
American Political Science Association, 16n
Ames, Adelbert, 67–69
apartheid, 144, 170, 178. *See also* Africa; South Africa.
Arafat, Yasir, 111
Arthur, Chester, 65, 73–74
Asia: reaction to civil rights movement, 97
Ashworth, John, 39n

Aspin, Les, 159, 173, 190–91
Atkins, James, 74
Atwater, Lee, 117

Bachrach, Peter, 12n
Baer, Denise, 17n
Bailey-Hutchinson, Kay, 195
"balance rule," 36
Baratz, Morton, 12n
Barnburners, 39
Barnett, Marguerite, 148n
Barry, Marion, 110
Bayh, Birch, 193
Begala, Paul, 181
Bell, Griffin, 157, 168
Bellmon, Henry, 102
Benoit, Kenneth, 18n, 196
Bennett, William, 203
Biden, Joseph, 169
"Black Bill of Rights," 155, 165
Black Democratic Caucus, 107
Black, Earl, 32n, 99
Black, Merle, 32n, 99
Blaine, James, 72–73, 75, 77, 80
Bobo, Lawrence, 25n
Bond, Brian, 192
Bork, Robert, 159
Bositis, David, 17n, 177
Boutwell, George, 59
Brennan, P. J., 156
Brooke, Edward, 169
Brown, Jerry, 187
Brown, Kathleen, 202
Brown, Pat, 100
Brown, Ron, 3–4, 118–19
Brown, William Garrott, 84
Brown, Willie, 107, 202
Browning, Rufus, 23n
Buchanan, Pat, 188
budget resolutions: Congressional Black Caucus and, 157–60, 162, 165, 171, 175
Bullock, Charles, 177n
Bullock, Governor, 71
Burnham, Walter Dean, 15n, 16n

PRINCETON STUDIES IN AMERICAN POLITICS:
HISTORICAL, INTERNATIONAL, AND
COMPARATIVE PERSPECTIVES

*Labor Visions and State Power: The Origins of Business Unionism
in the United States* by Victoria C. Hattam

The Lincoln Persuasion: Remaking American Liberalism
by J. David Greenstone

*Politics and Industrialization: Early Railroads in the United States
and Prussia* by Colleen A. Dunlavy

Political Parties and the State: The American Historical Experience
by Martin Shefter

*Prisoners of Myth: The Leadership of the Tennessee Valley
Authority, 1933–1990* by Erwin C. Hargrove

*Bound by Our Constitution: Women, Workers, and the Minimum
Wage* by Vivien Hart

*Experts and Politicians: Reform Challenges to Machine Politics in
New York, Cleveland, and Chicago* by Kenneth Finegold

*Social Policy in the United States: Future Possibilities in Historical
Perspective* by Theda Skocpol

Political Organizations by James Q. Wilson

*Facing Up to the American Dream: Race, Class, and the Soul of the
Nation* by Jennifer L. Hochschild

Classifying by Race edited by Paul E. Peterson

From the Outside In: World War II and the American State
by Bartholomew H. Sparrow

*Kindred Strangers: The Uneasy Relationship between Politics and
Business in America* by David Vogel

*Why Movements Succeed or Fail: Opportunity, Culture, and the
Struggle for Woman Suffrage* by Lee Ann Banaszak

*The Power of Separation: American Constitutionalism and the
Myth of the Legislative Veto* by Jessica Korn

Party Decline in America: Policy, Politics, and the Fiscal State
by John J. Coleman